The Sin Cloud

Jonathan Walton

Copyright © 2014 jonathan walton

All rights reserved.

ISBN: 0989805719
ISBN-13: 978-0-9898057-1-1

ACKNOWLEDGMENTS

I would like to thank my good friend, Philip Spence, for all the hard work and commitment he has shown in helping me through the process of writing and publication. When I have been impatient and thought about quitting, you've always encouraged me to keep trying. We've come up with a lot of crazy ideas late at night that haven't translated to paper, but they were fun anyway. Maybe one day we'll get to them. Thanks for all you have done and continue to do to help build a dream. Words cannot say how much you are truly appreciated.

Thanks to Jen Pavlu for another awesome cover design. Thanks also to Jared Pavlu, Ricki Pavlu, and Rebekah Leblue for the hard work and commitment to editing the manuscript. I could not do this without your help.

PROLOGUE

Darius rounded the corner in a full sprint and excitedly stopped near Hayden, who was sitting near the eastern most wall. As usual, he was alone, staring into the distance. They all wondered why he did it.

The same time everyday.

Same place.

Same faraway stare.

Almost reminiscent, but not quite recollecting. Deep intuitive searching, but never able to conjure up the memories. If only they could have read his thoughts. He was more bitter than before. His animosity toward God was burning brighter than ever. He had mentioned those feelings to the Timekeeper, but those days seemed so long ago. He had progressed in his attitude toward this God he vaguely remembered. He used to hate Him, but now, he barely even believed that such a God could even exist.

Because of the sullenness of his expression, they'd chosen

to never interrupt him, until today. Darius reached him out of breath.

"Sir Hayden, you're being summoned by the ruler of the city. He wishes to speak with you at once."

Hayden continued to gaze ahead, his features unchanged.

"I'm sorry, Sir Hayden. I told him you wouldn't like to be interrupted, but he said it's important and you'd want to hear it immediately."

No response.

"Sir, please. I don't know what to tell him."

No answer.

Darius worriedly touched Hayden's shoulders and shook him. "Sir Hayden, are you okay?"

Hayden's hypnotic trance was broken. "Darius, what's wrong? You know I don't like to be bothered here."

"I apologize, sir, but you must come with me at once. The high counsel is calling for you. The man himself wants to see you."

"Why?"

"I don't know. Maybe to see for themselves the giant who has caused so many problems among the Babylonians. Perhaps they want to look upon the man who has garnered so much attention from the Captain of the King's command, to see the feared warrior who shoots lightning bolts from his eyes and topples legions with his tenacity," he said with a laugh.

Hayden wasn't amused, "Those days are over, Darius. Abaddon Dearth must have bigger things to worry about now. It's been weeks."

Darius shook his head. "He's not the kind of man to let things go. Not him. He'll be coming until one of you are dead and probably murder the rest of us just for spite."

"Well, as long as we're here, we're safe. We could make out just fine here for a while."

"I dunno," Darius disheartenly answered. "Maybe if I can send for my family, perhaps I'd be okay. It's been weeks since I held my wife and children. Do you know how hard that is on a man?"

Something within Hayden instinctively cried out that he knew exactly what Darius was feeling, but where had that thought come from? There was no way he could know. He wasn't a father. He had no wife for that matter. Why had he suddenly felt the strange detachment Darius described?

He calmly cleared his head. "No, and you're right, Darius. You should take some time to be with your family. I'll have Amarsin send word to Marcus to have them escorted here at once. You've earned it."

Hayden stood and walked back toward the inner city. "Let's go see what they want. Hopefully they've granted you permanency. We could work on your family once they arrive, but that would be primarily procedural once yours gets done."

Darius smiled. "I appreciate all you've done for me. You've truly proven a brother."

. . .

Hayden stepped before the counsel with Darius at his side. Two guards stepped forward as they entered, their swords falling to form an impenetrable wall. The man in the center of the council stood. He wore a golden crown on his head, and a white silk robe over his body. A golden sash hung loosely around his waist.

He motioned his hand forward in a welcoming wave. "We wish to speak to you alone, Sir Hayden, of supposed Babylonian heritage. We have no need to speak to your servant."

Hayden scoffed. "He's no servant, Your Honor. He's my brother. One would do well to note the difference."

"And what's the difference, so I might make further note of it in the future?"

Hayden detected the arrogance in the man's tone but decided to humor him anyway.

"Well, Your Honor, he walks beside me and not behind me, speaks to me whenever he pleases, has sacrificed much to be on my journey, and-"

"He's sacrificed much for you. That can be said for most slaves. They all sacrifice for those they serve. It's why we have them," he said with a laugh.

Hayden paused to allow the room's laughter to cease. He took a deep breath to stifle the anger rising inside. The greatest intolerance he had in life was toward ignorance, and this was it in its purest form.

"Yes, that's true. But I've also sacrificed for him, and would again many times over. Therein lies the difference, Your Honor, between slavery and family. This man is family to me."

The spokesman agitatedly nodded. "Well, Sir Hayden, he's no family to us, as he's only been granted temporary protection, not permanence. Therefore, he's still under our jurisdiction. We wish to speak with only you."

"Anything you can say to me, you can say in front of him," Hayden indignantly proposed.

The man was growing agitated, and motioned for the guards to escort Darius away.

"Don't bother arguing with me, Sir Hayden. We have our ways here. He's protected because it's the law, but we don't have to like it. Likewise, you don't have to like our views, but you do have to tolerate them... Toleration, now there's a strong concept. The world would be a better place if we'd all just learn to be a bit more understanding."

Hayden smiled, almost arrogantly. "There's a fine line between toleration and compromise, Your Honor. I have no problem tolerating the opinions of others. However, I won't surrender my integrity or convictions on the altar of someone else's pretenses. Ultimately, I must live with the choices I've made; and I'd rather die than compromise myself."

The man in the white robe stepped down the first step and sat down. He made sure that Darius had been removed.

"You speak as a man who has nothing to lose." He briefly paused before moving on. "And we have a problem, Sir Hayden. One we think you can help us with."

"What's the dilemma?"

The judge flashed an expression of fear. "Abaddon Dearth is dead. He was found near his childhood home just days after our battle outside the Fortress. It was obvious that he'd been ambushed. The King of Babylon is demanding that someone show for an official inquiry into Abaddon's death."

"And you want me to be that voice?" Hayden incredulously asked. "You expect me to leave the safety of the city and return to Babylon where I was on trial just a few weeks ago? The king's man has been murdered, and you want me to appear before him on the city's behalf? Why?"

"No, Sir Hayden. I'm afraid you misunderstand my request. We don't want you to appear before the magistrates of Babylon. We want you to convince Amarsin Shamash that he needs to. We need him to leave the city and speak for us."

Hayden was appalled. "Why? If he does that, those loyal to Captain Dearth would seek him out. He'd be killed before he met with the king."

"Perhaps, but at least the king's quest for justice would be realized. We'd both benefit from this. The king would forget about you… and us."

Hayden was wroth. "I won't betray a friend to save myself. I certainly wouldn't entertain the thought to save you."

"Sir Hayden, it could come down to one life verses thousands," he said, almost pleading. "You'd let the future of our city be jeopardized for refusing to sacrifice one man?"

"It's not my position to make such a choice. I'm not god or king."

"Well, then perhaps you'll do it because the only person the king would listen to from your group is a delegation made up of Amarsin Shamash and his grandfather, Marcus."

"Ah," Hayden replied, the Court's intentions becoming clear. "You want to use Babylonian authority against the king. If the king respects the representative of the city, you think you'll be spared."

"Sir Hayden, we did nothing wrong. The only reason we must worry about defending ourselves is because the blood of an elitist Babylonian was spilled outside the gates of this grand city because of the antics of your group. If you hadn't barged into my city, none of this would have occurred. You owe us this much. Please, just grant us an opportunity for peace."

Hayden seemed disappointed. "Have you forgotten that this city was created to serve people in trouble? It's your duty. When the strong stop protecting the weak, humanity is in trouble. Sometimes helping people has a price. It can jeopardize one's pretty little notions about peace. But you must remain willing to pay that price, or this city has already become like every other city in the world. Are you so willing to sacrifice what has set you apart?"

"What's set us apart has been our leniency toward others concerning their mistakes. We boldly blink at the transgressions of people's pasts and allow them the opportunity to begin again without scrutiny."

"A noble gesture indeed, but forgiveness doesn't give you the right to hold the guilty hostage. True forgiveness means the atrocities of the past have been permanently removed. There's no longer anything to be lenient about. Everyone in the city stands on equal footing, because all men are free from the weight of their past."

"But we must still-"

"There is no but, Your Honor. You either forgive or you don't. It's that simple. In this case, it appears that you've been most unforgiving. You've only granted one of us permanent citizenship, and you're now asking him to sacrifice himself on the altar of obligation. I find no honor in this."

The leader turned without saying a word and walked back up the step toward the council members. They spoke for several seconds, leaving Hayden out of their conversation. He could see the tenseness with which they talked. There was urgency in the members' faces. He knew that look all too well. They were apprehensive.

He calmly approached the platform and climbed the few steps upward toward their small group. One of them motioned to the leader as he drew near. The leader whirled around and found Hayden standing face to face with him.

"I'm afraid you have us at a disadvantage, Sir Hayden. The veracity of your words has been razor sharp. You've opened our eyes to the error of our own logic. We mustn't use our goodness to manipulate people into our desires. True forgiveness means presenting each man with the opportunity to choose his own fate, even if his choice isn't the one we'd make for him... At times, he may even choose to bite the hand that feeds him or hurt the ones who've given him new life. Our duty, as the officers of this city, is to uphold our integrity regardless of the feelings and actions of those around us. We understand that now. Sorry to have inconvenienced you, Sir Hayden, and thank you for helping us see the light again."

Hayden politely smiled. "Grace is always given to those who equally bestow it... Besides, I may have an alternative solution."

"Good, because we weren't done with you yet either."

"You first then?"

"No, sir. It can wait. Please share your idea."

Hayden moved right in, "If the King of Babylon wishes to speak with Amarsin, you could welcome him with open arms. Present him with the niceties of your city. Let him witness first hand your hospitality and learn how many guilty Babylonians have benefited from your existence. It could be an eye-opener, as well as a safe place for Amarsin to lead this delegation."

The judge smiled. "A wise suggestion indeed. This committee shall ponder it and probably put it into practice if the king would be willing... and Sir Amarsin."

Hayden winked in their direction. "I think he could be thus persuaded... Now, what of the other business you have with me?"

The leader showed concern. "We're extremely worried about your man... Darius. It's why we didn't want him in here. He-"

"I assure you, that man is honorable. I'd lay my life on the line to vouch for his credentials."

"It's not that we're concerned about him. We're concerned for him."

Hayden was confused. "I'm afraid I don't understand."

"He's an Aksumite, is he not? That's what he reported on the papers he filed requesting permanency. I assume those reports are accurate."

"Yes. He's from Aksum."

"Well, we do our due diligence before granting anyone permanent residence... What he didn't report is that he's Aksumite royalty. Were you also aware of that?"

Hayden's lips pursed at the corners. "Yes. I'm aware, but that shouldn't be a problem. If anything, it further proves his honor. He doesn't gloat in the fact that he's the son of a king."

"His honors not in question, Sir Hayden. We just thought you should know, Darius of Aksum, son of King Adollion of

Aksum, is in trouble."

"What? Why?"

"His family is under attack. His country is in shambles. Many of his siblings have already been killed or captured."

"By whom?"

"There's been an uprising from within the Ethiopian province. Most of these uprisings are quickly dealt with, but someone influential is funding the coup. We aren't aware whom. Some say the Romans. Some say the Jews. We aren't sure if it's either."

"Why are you telling me this?"

"Respect, sir."

"Respect?"

"Yes, sir. You've come here and combated the great Babylon with higher principles than we've ever witnessed. King Adollion was known as a fair man among the world's noble alliance. Because it's only Aksum where the war spreads, many of the allies pretend not to notice… We don't have much to offer, but we can at least make you aware."

"Was?"

"Excuse me?"

"You said the king was known. Has something happened to King Adollion?"

"I'm afraid so… He's been murdered. The last remaining

factions are trying to raise support to keep the fight alive. This civil war will be over within months if no new hope is given."

"A civil war? Someone from the inside is fighting to destroy the Aksumite Kingdom?"

"Yes, sir. It's bad, sir."

"Who is it?"

"It's Prince Demsas, Darius' younger brother. He's leading the rebellion from inside. No one has been able to trace the external sources yet."

Hayden was stunned. "Are you certain?"

"Yes. The fact that someone powerful is funding this means the rebel leader is someone influential in the Aksumite culture. King Adollion was always well protected. His guard was one of the best in the business. No one could have gotten close to him. We knew it had to either be one of the elite guardsmen or someone close enough to the king to be granted private access. The king's own guardsmen have indicated that Demsas has blood on his hands."

"And why make Darius aware now? What's in it for you?"

"Nothing at all, but having men like King Adollion made the world a better place. Besides, Darius is in danger whether he stays here or goes there. Demsas has hired assassins to hunt his brother down."

"Why would he do that? Why not just let his brother find out about this months later, when he's ruler and there's nothing Darius can do?"

    The leader shook his head. "Because, Sir Hayden, Darius is the rightful heir to the Aksumite throne. If he ever returns to Aksum, he'll be the ruler by Aksumite law. You must protect your friend, Sir Hayden, and we're afraid that the only way to do so is to escort him across the great watery divide so he can present himself as the new Aksumite King. If he's as honorable as you believe, then he's exactly what Aksum needs."

1

The ship tossed on the boisterous waves. Lightning flashed across the blackened sky. Thunder echoed loudly, thumping the small vessel with powerful velocity.

It had been two months since Hayden had talked to the council at the Fortress. He'd made Darius aware of the news as soon as they'd left the council hall. Darius had taken it hard, as any one would. He'd immediately made plans to board a vessel headed across the sea. He'd been surprised when the one ticket he'd purchased had turned to five. Amarsin had agreed to stay and help forge peace between the Babylonians and the Fortress. M'ya, Leib, Hunzuu, and Hayden had readily chosen to make the journey to Aksum.

They'd sailed across the ocean until they'd reached the horn of Africa. From there, they'd sailed around its southernmost point and continued around the coastline into the Indian Ocean, finally arriving at the Red Sea through a small straight connecting the two larger bodies of water. Aksum was situated halfway up the western coast of the Red Sea, and was the capitol city of the Aksumite Empire.

Darius had taken every precaution to make sure his whereabouts were concealed. He had no intention of having this small vessel overran by pirates who'd been paid to collect his head. As far as he was aware, no one knew they were coming.

Thus far, they'd had a pleasant voyage. It had been long, but most voyages were when traveling across the world. His group and the sailors had developed a camaraderie that was rare between ship crew and travelers. Surprisingly, the fact that M'ya was female hadn't caused any problems. The ship's crew had been nothing but respectful toward her. They were a rough lot, but they scaled their dark sides back whenever she was on deck.

The ship's captain had taught them well. He was an honorable leader who demanded at least some attempt at virtue from his men. He paid them well, and they respected him for it. There are few things in life that can drive a wedge between a leader and those who feel valued by him.

Tonight was the first trouble they'd encountered, and they were only five miles from port. It was early morning, probably four o'clock. The captain had estimated their arrival at no later than six or seven, depending on the weather.

Darius approached Hayden, who was sitting in the middle of the deck, his clothes drenched from the heavy downpour.

As he drew near, Hayden looked up, seemingly realizing for the first time the ridiculousness of his waterlogged appearance.

Darius softly asked, "You don't want to join us inside?"

Hayden listened intently and heard the joyous music and singing from inside the cabins. He slightly smiled but calmly shook his head.

"I don't think so. Not tonight."

"Sir, what's wrong? You haven't been yourself lately."

"Don't rightly know, Darius. Mind is just racing I guess. I keep seeing images... Images that don't make sense. Broken fragments, like diluted memories. The woman. The kids. I see them over and over again in my mind. Over and over."

"All the time?"

"No. It's only happened a few times. Only twice since we left the Fortress, but it haunts me. When I'm not having the dreams, I'm thinking about them. Reflecting. Trying everything to remember, but nothing comes."

"I'm sorry. Perhaps something will happen here to help you remember. Or forget. Whichever would be best."

M'ya exited the cabin and nervously moved toward them. "How can everyone be so calm in such a storm? It feels as though the vessel is tilted sideways in the water. I keep expecting us to be overwhelmed. I'm a decent swimmer, but I'd have no chance of surviving in these waves."

Darius laughed. "My people are born on the water, M'ya. I was raised on the coast. We're mariners by trade, and are trained in smaller vessels than this."

She looked up at the mast, which was being violently whipped in every direction, and then fearfully moved closer to Hayden and sat down. "How do we stay on course?"

"Because the captain knows what he's doing. You're safe in the midst of any storm when that is true."

She pointed to the darkness engulfing them. "You can't see anything because of the rain and darkness. How do we know we're on the right course?"

"We know because we've put our faith in the captain of this vessel."

She nervously shook her head. "And how can we be sure he knows where he's going?"

"We trust him, because he's been this way before. When the unexpected comes, M'ya, you have to relax and know you're in good hands. You can rest easy, because the one in control of the vessel has been here before. He'll keep you safe, as long as you remain in the boat."

She looked at the waves threateningly rocking as far as she could see. "I don't know. I can't rest easy in this. No one could survive out there."

"Yet, as dangerous as the storm toils, we're at perfect peace here… M'ya, this vessel was built for this."

"What do you mean?"

"The water you're worried about is what gives this vessel buoyancy. The wind whipping against the mast is the very element that propels us toward our destiny. The very uncertainties you feel could destroy us are what the builder of this vessel designed to carry us where we could not otherwise go."

She smiled, fidgeting with the ends of her long hair. "I get that, Darius, but while the sea is raging, some people sleep, and others uneasily wait for it to stop."

Darius stood. "Well, I shall leave you two alone to worry. Tomorrow is going to be a long day. I'll rest while I'm able, for once we hit land, I'll need my every instinct to stay alive. I'd advise you to do the same. Sleep while you have the time."

Hayden shook his head. "When have you known me to sleep, Prince of Aksum? I'll leave the sleeping to the dead."

As he walked off, Darius yelled over his shoulder. "Learn to rest easy, Sir Hayden. Or you just might soon be joining them."

. . .

Hayden inched closer to M'ya. She tensely grinned up at him.

"He's right you know. We should try to sleep while we're able," she said, as she gently rested her head on his shoulder.

He knew they were right, but he was afraid to close his eyes. They didn't come often, but when they did, the images were terrifying. The kids dying. The bloody woman hanging upside down. The fragmented and flying glass. The empty feeling. The sickening but unexplainable guilt. It was all too much. He preferred the feelings of tiredness to the terror of unknown dreams.

She interrupted his thoughts by touching his hand. "At least come in from the rain. The men are putting the music away. You should get into some dry clothes. We can't have you getting sick the moment we arrive. We need as little attention drawn to us as possible."

Hayden smirked, "We have an irresistible master thief, an educated elf, an ancient warrior, a paranoid stranger, and the Prince of the Aksumite Empire in our group; we shouldn't stick out at all.

2

Demsas piously sat on the remains of what used to be his father's throne. He wore his father's crown and scarlet linen robe. The royal scepter was seated next to him, easily within arm's length. One of his followers quietly approached him, causing him to barely lift his head. The man uncomfortably bowed.

"Your highness, they've arrived. They're unaware they've been recognized. He's trying to keep a low profile, but it's going to be hard with the company he's chosen to keep. They're highly visible."

"My brother never had much between the ears. It's why I'm here, sitting on this throne, and he'll be dead within the week... Did you pay them yet?"

"Yes, Your Highness. Five of them, and with completely different specialties. There's no way they can all fail."

Demsas devilishly grinned, "Not if they're as good as advertised... Are they aware of each other's presence?"

"Yes. They've all been given an advance. Only the one who finishes the job will collect the second payment. They're all knowledgeable of that fact."

"Good... Good... Who are they?"

"Long list, sir. You sure you want to go through the boredom of the details?"

"I asked, didn't I, Aizan? Don't ever second guess me again, or I'll have your tongue removed and your eyes gouged."

"I'm sorry," he hesitantly stated. "We go way back. It's just hard to forgot our history sometimes."

"Well, forget it you shall, or you'll not be alive much longer."

He coldly stared into the eyes of one he was once close to. "Our friendship ended the moment I became king. Our past no longer matters. You're to serve me, and serve me well, or I shall find someone else who can. There's no time for pleasantries when running an empire. Surely you understand."

"Yes, sir," the servant bashfully agreed.

"Good, because it wouldn't matter if you didn't. Your feelings are no longer a concern of mine. I can't be an effective leader if I'm to worry about the feelings and whims of those who feel they've been close to me."

The servant hung his head, obviously hurt by Demsas' explanation. "I'll remove my personal feelings and attitudes from the equation. You shall be able to rule as you wish."

Demsas glared at him, trying to discern if he was acting facetiously or with genuine respect. Finally, he replied, "Good. I'd hate to lose the last person I used to know. I have high hopes for you one day, if you serve me well."

"Thank you, Your Graciousness."

Demsas held up his golden chalice and gulped down the remainder of the wine. After he finished the last swallow, he slammed the chalice down hard enough to splinter another piece of the degraded throne.

"So, tell me who are the lucky ones to please me by killing their king's enemy."

"Well, as I said, the list is long, but I anticipated your request, so I had them come here today. They are just outside, sir… Would you have me bring them in one at a time or all together?"

"Bring the teams in one at a time. Give me a chance to get to know them."

The man motioned toward the guards at the doorway. One of them stepped into the hall and came back a moment later with two men at his side. They were of average height, but their muscles bulged from obvious training or hard physical labor. Demsas guessed from their scars that they were fighters. Each wore a lightweight breastplate and carried a small shield strapped to their back. A large sword hung at their sides, and several small daggers were strapped along their hardened bodies.

The servant stood before them. "These men are brothers, retired gladiators from Rome. They continue living off the skills they learned there. Their record is spotless, both in and out of the arena."

The king drunkenly clapped his hands in joyous celebration. "A wondrous choice. I couldn't have done better. Impressive specimens. And you've brought the glory of the arenas to Aksum. Perhaps once they've removed my brother's head, they'll headline a fight forging Aksumite bravery and Roman pride."

He clapped his hands again. "Well done. Well done."

The servant motioned the two men away, and they turned and confidently sauntered from the room. As they exited, the guard followed them out and returned moments later with someone of obvious Ethiopian descent. His dark features were common to the area. He'd definitely not stand out in a crowd. Compared to the men who had just left, this man appeared nothing more than an average black man in the Aksum Empire.

The king bellowed, "Is this a joke? You bring such a plebe now after stimulating me with such physical specimens before. This is a grand disappointment."

He paused, before sloppily waving his arm at the three guards stationed around his throne. "Kill this man at once, and have his bloody corpse removed from my presence immediately."

The first guard moved toward the smaller man without hesitation.

"Wait," the servant screamed.

It was too late. The guard attempted to draw his sword as he quickly advanced on the seemingly helpless man. However, before his sword cleared the scabbard, the small man was on top of him. The guard rocked backward, clutching his throat. He was dead within seconds, the small man holding to a small curved dagger that had materialized from nowhere.

The second guard wildly swung his sword outward. The small man easily ducked underneath and stepped into him, knocking him backward. The dagger easily found the soft place in the guard's armor, forcing him to his knees. After attempting to stand three times, he hit the earth face first, his final breath being pushed from his body by the hard impact of the throne room floor.

The third guard stopped his rush and warily circled the man.

The king laughed, surprised by the small black man's agility. "Stop it. I must save one of the guards for my own protection."

The man condescendingly glanced at him, "Perhaps your guards should be better trained."

The king judiciously examined the small man before him. "You've proven yourself a viper among the reeds. You strike with the passion of a serpent; only your venom is more deadly. What are you?"

The man didn't reply, this time continuing to stare into the eyes of the king. Aizan finally interrupted.

"He's a Mamluk, Your Highness."

The king scoffed, "A common slave, too bad for him."

The man's face contorted, demonstrating his obvious displeasure. The king laughed again.

"You don't like me? What a pity. I could have liked you. It's too bad you're so ordinary."

His anger was obvious. "I'm no commoner."

"Oh, but you are. A slave no less."

"I'm not a commoner. Of the twenty-five thousand slaves taken from this Empire every year, only a few are hand selected for the Mamluk. I once was a slave, but now-"

"You're still a slave… And you'd do well to not forget it… You may have been trained to kill, but your heart's still damaged by the flawed blood coursing through your veins. Being blessed with the art of the assassin doesn't preclude you from your inferior roots."

The man held his tongue. The king calmed after a few moments and glanced at him again.

"You've learned your art well. So, slave or not, complete the task and you shall be highly rewarded. Fail me, and I'll have you returned to the fields or mines from whence you came. Remove yourself from my presence."

The man stormed out of the room without glancing back. Another man entered wearing the ornamental coat of arms of a highly decorated Roman soldier.

"Your Highness, this man was a Salararius for many years. He was noticed by the powers that be and was the first of his kind to be converted to the Praetorians. He got in trouble because of his affections toward one of his charge's wives. They were caught together. She was beheaded, and he would've been had they found him. That was several years ago, and he's made a lucrative living as a contract killer ever since."

The king was impressed. "So, after serving as a mercenary to the Roman army, he was converted to a personal body guard to one of the Roman elitist. Only the best men are reserved for such a fate."

He smirked, "All that prestige and power with no self-control. What a pity. He could still be reveling in the riches of Rome. Now, he stands a hired killer in the war torn districts of Aksum."

Aizan appeared concerned. "Sir, we're honored to have such a man in our hire. Are we not?"

The King held his head high. "We are most certainly… Now, shall we continue this parade of gallant men, or are we finished with the pageantry?"

The servant motioned for the man to leave. The decorated officer gracefully moved toward the exit, his long red sash flowing behind him. The servant appeared nervous.

"Prepare for the next one, sir," he said, as he anxiously stared toward the empty doorway.

"What could be more grand that what I've already seen?" Demsas muttered in broken syllables.

She elegantly moved toward him. Her long black hair hanged down her back, ending right above her waist. She was petite but incredibly toned and exceptionally stunning. Her eyes were piercing blue and flawlessly cat-shaped. She demanded the attention of every man in the room. Her distinct features were imaginatively concealed behind her rustic attire. Her walk was mesmerizing.

The King gawked at her like an adolescent boy, unable to peel his eyes away. He motioned for the one guard still with him.

"Away with you. Go and bring me another chalice. I want her to drink with me."

The servant quickly approached, "Your Highness, may I speak to you as your friend? Only this once?"

The king half turned and glared at him for a moment. Finally, his expression softened.

"Only this once, Aizan. Don't ever ask me again."

Aizan nodded. "Yes, sir, but you shouldn't drink with her, sir. Please."

"And why not? She's the most beautiful woman these eyes have ever beheld. She's a goddess and meant for the likes of a king. It's a magnificent thing I fit that description."

Aizan handed the king an amulet. "Please, put this on immediately. Don't let her see it."

The king looked down. "A kitab. Why would I need a kitab?"

"To ward off the evil, King Demsas."

"That's absurd. Someone that beautiful can't be evil. It wouldn't be right."

"Sir, she's a *bouda*, the epitome of evil."

"Ah, you've given me the medallion to ward off the stares of the evil eye." He laughed. "You can't tell me you're a believer of such things, Aizan. You should be more educated than that."

"Sir, we're all believers. Most of this empire has dealt with her kind. We've witnessed the effects of the *bouda* on our people. They've caused much damage and inflicted much pain. They dominate us by causing disease and famine. She terrifies me, but she's our last resort. She'll succeed if the others don't."

"Indeed she will, for how can a woman such as this fail?"

She courteously bowed before him. "Your Highness, I'm most grateful to be asked to be of service to you. I long to serve you, my King, any way that I can."

He looked toward Aizan and smiled. "You did well boy, bringing her to me. And she longs to serve me, any way I please." He emphasized the last part a little too much.

Aizan uncomfortably grinned. "Sir, I beg of you to be careful. You can't afford to be reckless."

The king looked at her, measuring her from head to toe. "She looks harmless enough to me. I think getting to know her should be most challenging... and amusing."

He moved toward her, the guard placing a full cup of wine in his hand as he walked her way. Her long hair hanged in front of her body on the right side. He started at cheek level, placing his hand in her hair and running it down toward the end. He then placed the cup of wine in her left hand.

"Drink with me."

She met his stare with one of her own, and he quickly looked away. Perhaps Aizan's tales had him more nervous than he wanted to admit. Clutching the kitab tightly in his hand, he relaxed for a second, and then dropped it into his pocket. She noticed his awkward movement and confidently smiled.

"I'm afraid you've asked me to do something I've sworn to never touch."

The king looked at his servant. "A *bouda* who doesn't drink. I've never heard the like, have you, Aizan?"

"No, sir."

She politely smiled. "I'm sorry if my sobriety offends you-"

He returned the smile without looking into her eyes. "I would never be offended at the likes of you. Never."

"I would that were true, sir, but most people find my kind severely offensive. I'm almost certain you will too, before the story of your life is concluded."

He chuckled from deep inside. "Are you truly *bouda*?"

"That's what they say, Your Highness."

"So you kill people with your stare?"

"I've been accused of such," she replied, with no remorse.

"And… are you truly possessed by demons? They truly afflict people who look too deeply into the windows of your soul?"

"That's my reputation, my King. I hope you don't find it displeasing."

He slightly nodded his head, verbally ignoring her statement. "And what of your family? What be their profession?

"My father was a potter."

"A potter. The *tebib*. You're truly bouda indeed, inherited the name and the curse rather honestly it appears. Potters have been highly associated with the bouda."

"It does appear that way."

"Was your father truly enlightened? He knew of deeper truths by supernatural design?"

"Definitely not. He was a simple man accused of heinous atrocities that he could never have undertaken. His heart was too kind."

"And yours?"

"No. I'm afraid there's no kindness left in me. He was treated so harshly by the people he loved that I've nothing left but resentment."

"What happened to him?"

She closed her eyes, obviously disgusted by the memories. He waited for a few seconds before prodding her again.

"What happened?"

She looked into his eyes, and he held her stare; spellbound by her hypnotic charm. Her nostrils flared, her fury evident.

"They gouged out his eyes with molten daggers. Then they tied my mother to him in the great sea. They ran her through with a spear and dropped them both a half-mile off the coast. If my father could swim with her weight on his shoulders, he could live. They made me watch from a nearby vessel... He tried his best. She did too, doing her part, fighting against the crashing waves until she was too weak to continue treading. Once she died, he couldn't fight her and the waves. Both of my parents sank to the Red Sea floor... And why, because he practiced a different trade, and the others were superstitious."

The king shook his head, pretending to be revolted. "It's foolish to persecute a man because his knowledge is different from the land's proprietors... And what became of you?"

"I was called a *mingi*, the cursed. They thought my very

breath was a testament to the dead, that I was somehow conjuring satanic forces. They would have killed me too, but a kindhearted ship captain took me under his tutelage. I owe him my life."

"Well, serve me *mingi,* and you'll have enough to repay your debts."

He pulled her close to him, holding her body against his. She coolly allowed herself to be held there. She could feel his heart beating against her chest. He looked into her eyes for a moment, and then felt a horrible dread. A choking feeling arose in his throat. He unlocked his gaze from hers and allowed her to pull away.

He responded, half irritated and half mesmerized. "Before this is over, I'll see your spell broken. You'll be mine."

She crossed her legs and slightly bowed, before calmly walking toward the door.

He watched her leave, longing after her. Even as he stared, he had the premonition that his lust could get him killed. He'd have to be more careful when dealing with her. He'd never been a believer, but something about her stirred his deepest doubts. If the stories were true, there was nothing more dangerous than the *bouda.*

3

Darius moved further into the tent. It was extremely large, divided into several rooms by fabric stretched from post to post, serving as thin walls. He'd been warned not to go to the meeting, but his instincts told him it was worth the risk. He'd waited until the others were asleep, crawled out of bed, and then made the three-mile jog into the city. Arriving just before daybreak, the morning sky was still black from the still night. The tent hadn't been hard to find. The symbol on the flap matched the one he'd seen carved in the sand as he'd exited the boat. Someone had known he was coming and had arranged this rendezvous. He'd read the minuscule hieroglyphics and quickly stamped them out with his foot. No one had seemed to notice.

There was a sudden movement behind the nearest curtain. Although he much preferred the bow, the close quarters made that impossible. He removed his dagger and inched forward.

"Who's there?" He quietly asked, keeping his voice low to hear anyone approaching.

The dancing flames cast an eerie, iridescent reflection off his face. The man smiled as he stepped from the shadows. His hands were empty, and he held them out in a non-threatening manner. Darius continued to extend his blade in front of him, as the man moved closer.

"Demsas?" Darius asked, surprised.

"Brother, my brother," Demsas answered, as he moved toward Darius.

Darius sheathed his knife, and the two brothers embraced. Tears streamed down Darius' face. He stood away from the embrace for a moment, and looked into his younger brother's eyes. After a couple of seconds, he moved closer into the embrace again, crying on his brother's shoulder.

Finally, he broke the warm hug. "Where are the others?"

Demsas held his head low, his voice barely audible. "There's none left. It's only you and me, my brother."

"Dead?"

"I'm afraid so. They've all been killed."

Darius fought to hold back the tears. "All ten of them?"

"We're all that's left of our father's seed, Darius. We're his only heirs, the only bearers of his regal heritage."

Darius fell to his knees. "Nooooooooooooo! Nooooooo! Noooooooooo!" he wailed.

Demsas knelt down, pulling Darius' head toward his shoulder again. "There's no shame in crying, my brother. Let the tears drown the sorrow of your heart."

"I wish I could have been here."

Demsas rubbed his hand on the back of his brother's hair. "Fate has seen fit to bring you back to us. Perhaps you're here for a reason now."

Darius wiped the tears from his eyes and gripped Demsas' hand. Demsas pulled him to his feet. Darius' pain was evident, but he seemed relieved.

"It's good to see you, Demsas, especially after the horrible things I've heard."

Demsas' expression didn't change. "What things, my brother?"

"I was told that you executed father and were having our siblings offered as sacrifices in the streets. Their souls were given as eternal rewards to the ancient gods for allowing you to rule in father's place… Where'd these stories come from, Demsas?"

"I don't know, my brother. I'm not sure who spread them, but one thing I can tell you for certain…"

He paused, coolly measuring Darius, who was eagerly listening. Demsas callously continued.

"I can tell you; the rumors are true."

Darius was stunned. "What?" He almost screamed the words.

"Yes, my brother." Demsas separated himself from Darius.

Darius drew his dagger and angrily held it in front of him.

Demsas chuckled, "You can put the knife away, my brother. I've no wish to harm you today."

"I don't understand. What have you done?"

"Preserved my future brother," Demsas answered matter-a-factly. "I've made sure the last has become first. The younger has moved ahead of his elder. The kingdom is mine now."

"The kingdom. You're worried about the kingdom. What of your family? They were of no consequence to you?"

Demsas seemed annoyed, "Why ask a question you already know the answer to? Why should I spend my entire life eating your leftovers? I possessed the influence, intellect, and courage. All I needed was the opportunity. But that could never come, could it brother. Because there were too many others standing in the way."

"Demsas." The tears fell again, rolling down Darius' cheeks. "We would have given you anything. Father would have made sure your inheritance was certain."

Demsas seemed genuinely offended. "Inheritance? You

think this is about inheritance. It's not about inheritance at all."

"Then what is it about?"

"It's about power. About respect."

"And you've earned it now? The people won't respect you. They loved our king."

Demsas lowered his voice, "If you can't have respect, then fear is the next best thing. I have the power. They may never love me the way they loved him, but they will learn to dread me."

"You're a sad man, Demsas. All you could have been is forever marred because you refused patience."

Demsas dismissed the notion with a wave of his hand. "Patience. Tis a wonderous virtue, so I've heard. But not one of my strong suites."

"Eventually, the kingdom would have been at least partially yours. Father would have given you a province."

"A province. No one respects the leader of a province. The throne, that's what I wanted."

"You could have had it another way." Darius sadly replied.

"No. This was the only way. I had you removed and taken to another land. It still wasn't enough. Father held out hope for you, Darius. If you would have returned while he was still alive, he wanted the kingdom to be yours."

"You? How?"

Demsas laughed. "It was easy. You weren't careful. I knew where you'd be. I knew who to pay and how much to pay them. Getting rid of you was the easiest thing I've ever done."

Darius staggered, before falling to his knees again. "How could you? My wife? My child? How could you have taken them from me? How could you have ever hated me so much?"

"I despised you. The favored son who could do no wrong... It's a pity, I took them from you once, and now I've taken them from you again... You've been away so long you don't even know yet, but they've all been killed, Darius, by one of my assassin's swords. You couldn't even hide from me in your new world."

Darius looked up, and Demsas shook his head in disgust. "Even now you prove your weakness. Stand up like a man."

Darius rose to his feet and sheathed his knife again. "Why did you summon me here, if not to have me killed?"

"I did it for father. My last tribute to a man who rarely acted as if I existed."

"For father?"

"Yes. I'm making my intentions known to you like I did the others. I'm going to have your head. You're the last piece to the puzzle, Darius. After you, there's none left to combat my claims."

"It doesn't have to end like this." Darius pleaded.

"Oh, but it does. After today, brother, if you ever see me again, have your sword in your hand."

"Demsas, please. I'm begging you."

"Watch your back. You're going to die soon. They're coming for you. You've been warned. Now, I shall unleash my wrath."

Demsas disappeared into the shadowy blackness, leaving Darius there to shed his tears.

4

Darius moved through the streets trying to remain calm. What had happened to Demsas? He'd never been troubled as a child. He'd been full of life. Funny even, always the center of attention. How had he turned into such a monster?

He walked near the dirt walls of the city, making sure no one could approach without his awareness. What had Demsas meant, turning them loose? Should he be afraid? Demsas had made sure everyone else in the family was already dead, so the answer to that question seemed rather obvious.

He carefully passed a small opening in the wall. As he moved past it, he heard a voice gently call from inside.

"Darius. Come in, quickly."

Darius drew his dagger. It seemed to be becoming a

permanent extension of his hand. Restoring order to his father's kingdom was going to be more difficult than he'd planned.

He entered the small opening, following a narrow hallway twenty yards before it opened into a large clearing. Another narrow hallway was across the room. He heard the gentle voice again, calling from somewhere down the new corridor. He quickly moved to follow.

Finally, he stepped into another clearing. A man stood in the room wearing a wood mask with various ornamental colors. It appeared as some sort of covering worn during a traditional, spiritual rite of passage ceremony. Darius eyed the man suspiciously. The man wouldn't return his gaze.

"My time is short, but I feel I owe it to your family. This is the only help you'll receive from me going forward. I'm now loyal to our new king. I took an oath to defend whoever is the appointed King of Aksum. I don't agree with what's happened, but I'm sworn to defend the position, not the man."

Darius nodded. "I respect your position-"

The man interrupted, "However, the previous king, your father, was always fair with me. I owe him this much."

Something about the stranger's voice was oddly familiar. He had the intonation of a young man but spoke as though he was acquainted with the prior king's family dynamics.

"How did you know him?" Darius curiously asked.

"The king? I served him. I know the new king well. I've known your family for a long time."

Darius squinted his eyes, trying to peer through the man's mask. He couldn't make out the features, but he recognized the warmth in the eyes.

"Aizan, is that you?"

The man slowly lifted his hand upward and removed the mask. Aizan stood before Darius. The two men embraced.

"Aizan, it's good to see you... How did it come to this?"

"Your brother has the darkness growing in his heart. I've seen it in his eyes. He's been done in by envy. Jealousy poisons his heart and corrupts his thoughts. He's given himself to the dark side, and there's no coming back once one has willingly relinquished their own soul."

"And what of you, Aizan? What are you still doing with him?"

"I carry the duty of a guardian, the same as my father and his father before him. We are protectors of the throne of Aksum, regardless of who sits on it."

"Hasn't the throne been defiled enough? At times, doesn't guarding the throne mean protecting it from the tyranny of madmen?"

"He wears the crown. He holds the scepter. Until someone else leads, I must uphold my sacred duty."

"Then why are you communicating with me now?"

"Because I only hope that one day the compassion and fairness of your father will return to the throne. I long to serve under those conditions again. I long to serve you."

"But you are Demsas' friend. How has your allegiance so quickly become misaligned to his purpose? Surely you know his desires concerning me."

"Because he serves only his own desires. That's not the purpose of a king. And yes. I'm well aware of his plans for you. That's why I'm here."

"What do you mean?" Darius worriedly asked.

Aizan ashamedly answered, "He had me hire professionals to make sure you're killed before his inaugural ceremony. There are those among us who heard you were alive. Since the king died, they've sworn allegiance to you. They're afraid to speak out, but a remnant remains who pray to the gods that you'll rise up to fight... Demsas wants to make sure you're removed from the picture before those residual factions are united by your arrival."

"What should I be watching for?"

"They are all dangerous." Aizan looked at Darius sympathetically. "I swear to you, I only did it because I'm sworn to do the king's bidding. I would never have taken such actions on my own. I believe in you, Darius. I always have. You are your father's son. You have his heart."

Darius looked him in the eyes. "I don't hold it against you, Aizan. If not you, he'd have gotten someone else to do it. In such case, I wouldn't have been warned... How will I know these men when I see them?"

"They're all skilled at making sure you don't see them, until its too late... I can tell you this: Two are gladiators from Rome; another served as a mercenary before being hired as a personal bodyguard to one of the Caesars; another was forced into slavery only to be taught the art of war. They're all dangerous, Darius, and they'll stop at nothing to make sure you're killed."

"There are only four of them. I won't make it easy."

"Actually, there are five. The fifth is the most deadly."

Darius shook his head. "The more the merrier, I guess."

"Not in this case, sir. She will kill anyone who gets in the way. There's no stopping her."

"No one is beyond being stopped, Aizan."

"Darius, she's a bouda."

Darius cringed at the mention of the name. "Are you certain?"

"Yes."

His concern was obvious, "I don't understand, Aizan. I know you had to hire professionals, but did you have to find the one assassin I can't escape? Are you sure you're hopeful I'll survive?"

"Most hopeful, sir. But I didn't go looking for her. She got word that Demsas was looking for an assassin to bring him the throne. She volunteered. She sought me out herself."

"There are a few who think the legends aren't true. How do you feel, Aizan? You've been in the Empire longer than I. I feared her kind as a child, but have known nothing of them as a man. The boyhood apprehension has lessened."

"I fear them more now then I did in adolescence, Darius. They were only stories then. Now, I've seen them for myself. They are real."

"What do they do?"

"They are evil. They stare with half-demonic and half-human indecency. It turns you inside. Many have been rendered sick and found dead because of their untimely stares."

"That can't be real."

"Look around. The amulets worn, the tunics bundled tightly around faces, the people who refuse to make eye contact. We live in fear of them."

Amulets?"

"Yes. They're said to ward off the evil from the stare."

"And the tunics?"

"If you feel you're approaching one, you pull it tight and don't give them your eyes. If they find an opening, they'll force out your soul."

Darius shuddered. "How can I defeat her then, if she's coming for me so passionately?"

"You don't. You can't."

"Someone must know a way."

Aizan thoughtfully considered before responding, "I've heard tales, but have never seen him."

"Who?"

"There's one in Dahlak who fights demons. He's been blinded by the light and shines his purity into every dark cranny he can find. Perhaps he would know a way."

"Dahlak, the gateway to hell. That island is forbidden."

"It could be your only way."

"And how will I know if I find this man among those on the island. It's full of witches, warlocks, and the possessed. How will I know him?"

"He won't be hard to find, Darius. Just look for the only Jew."

Darius' mouth fell open. "You can't be serious. A Jew, in Dahlak."

"He's there. He's survived there for over a year now. He's obviously got a higher power on his side. Find him. He could be your only salvation."

5

Dr. Poole stood over Hayden's bed. He'd been looking over the changes recorded in the chart and wasn't pleased with what he'd been reading. It had been two weeks since Hayden had unexpectedly shown signs of brain activity. That had not changed since. There had been no other flutters; the recordings had been stable.

However, he wasn't close to being out of the woods. There were still a lot of factors that demonstrated the depth of the coma. The trauma from the gunshot wound had caused severe damage to the cerebral cortex. The gray matter covering the outer layer of the brain had been highly disrupted. That sort of impact was almost impossible to fully recover from.

Hayden had been under close observation since the night he'd been rushed in to undergo hours of intensive surgery.

The nurses had measured his responsiveness to physical stimuli. Other tests indicated positive nystagmus under various test conditions. Several CT scans were taken. EEG readings demonstrated no complications from seizures, but they showed no marked improvement over the last couple of weeks either.

What concerned Dr. Poole most was that Hayden's breathing patterns had become more irregular and shallow over the last couple of days. Further testing had been recommended, and the doctor was now examining the results.

Someone spoke to him from the small chair in the corner. "How's it looking today, Dr. Poole? Any progress."

"I'm afraid not Mrs. Vice President. I'm afraid his condition has actually taken a turn for the worse."

"How so, doctor?"

"Well, as you know, comas are extremely complex. They can last only a few days or up to several weeks on average. It's true that some comas have lasted years, but those are extremely rare... He's already been here over a month."

"Yes." She replied, waiting for him to continue.

"Well, it appears that even if he comes out of the coma, he's probably headed for a vegetative state. The damage was just so great to his brain. I don't see him ever being able to communicate or walk again."

"But isn't it too soon to tell?"

"Yes," he reluctantly replied, "It's still early, but every day he doesn't wake up lessens the odds he'll come out of this."

"Well, Dr. Poole, all of this we knew yesterday. Why are you concerned that he's taken a turn for the worst today?"

Dr. Poole looked back to the charts before turning to her with a sullen expression slightly hidden behind his attempt at a poker face.

"I had x-rays ordered because of his irregularity in breathing... I'm afraid he's developed early symptoms of pneumonia. If he doesn't respond to what I'm trying to do for him, it's not going to be good."

"Is that common? I thought we'd be okay since you were caring for him around the clock."

"Sorry ma'am, but it's very common. One of the greatest dangers to someone lying down all the time is pneumonia. We're hoping to keep it controlled, because his body has no way of responding or fighting it off without our help."

"What could that lead to?"

Dr. Poole closed the file and sat down on an undersized chair across from her. "I'm afraid it could lead to his death. The pneumonia is secondary to the damage caused by the gunshot, but it could be what does him in."

"What's your best prognosis?"

"Realistically, I'd give him about ten days. Entering the faith equation, I believe he could fully recover. Somewhere between there lies the truth."

"My husband probably wouldn't agree, but I've learned to ere on the side of faith. You just keep caring for him, Dr. Poole. He's going to come out of this."

"Yes ma'am. I plan on it. I just want you to know where we stand."

"We're standing on the Rock aren't we, Dr. Poole? And, we both know what happens when we stand there."

"I do, and that's what it's going to take. We need God to finish what He started. We still need a miracle."

6

Torben Mayes stood in front of the door in the empty hallway. It had been a lot harder to find than he'd thought. The doctor hadn't made it easy. The next crisis was getting in. The doctor had failed to tell him of the safety precautions he'd taken in order to protect what he'd hidden.

Getting through the door was proving difficult. He hadn't always been on the right side of the law. As a teenager on the streets, he'd developed a great deal of street cred by learning the art of professional criminalization. Picking a lock was a piece of cake. He could have most doors unlocked within six seconds, and that was on his slow days.

This lock was different. He'd tried to pick it with the tools from his pick set, but had been unsuccessful. He didn't want to be noticed, so he had tried three times, and then decided he had to move on. He'd thought about it for a few minutes and decided to make a bump key. After a little while, he'd returned to find the bump key wouldn't work either. In desperation, he finally attempted to kick the door in.

The loud sound of his foot against the wood caused the neighbor to open her door and peer outside. Torben leaned against the wall like he wasn't aware anything had happened. She eyed him suspiciously, while he pretended not to see her. Finally, she closed the door. He heard the chain fall away, and then the door opened again. The woman quietly stepped into the hall, wearing a bathrobe. She was in her mid thirties. Her hair was still dripping wet and held over her head with a towel. Her glasses were fogged from the outside air, and she was struggling to see through them, bending her head and squinting to peer over the top. Despite her humorous demeanor, she was incredibly attractive.

"What are you doing there? I've never seen you around here before."

"No ma'am. You haven't," he said, figuring the best way to disarm suspicion was honesty. He didn't figure she'd heard that the doctor had finally succumbed to his cancer. He turned and took a slow step in her direction.

"Sorry to have startled you. The good doctor passed away a couple of days ago. I was at the hospital with him when it happened. He asked me to come by and check on something before others were able to scour his belongings."

"He was a strange man. What does he have in there that he doesn't want others to see?"

"I don't know. He just told me where to look. Said I

should remove it before others arrived."

"It could be something incriminating. He didn't always seem right. Like maybe he was in to something illegal. Don't you think we should just call the police?"

"No. No. I wouldn't do that just yet," he said, trying not to sound overly alarmed at her suggestions.

He calmly looked at her. "I gave my word to a dying man. I'd hate to not keep my promise. I'll take a look at it. If it's something the police need to know, I'll tell you. We can call them together."

"Who are you? How'd you know him?"

"I'm a police detective. I was investigating a case that he had slight ties to. He was helping me find the truth when he died. He told me to come here to New York and look in his apartment. He said no one knew about it, so I'm a little unsure why it's so hard to get in to."

"Well, do you have a key?" She sarcastically asked, placing a hand on her hip and slightly protruding the hip a little sassily.

He internally cringed. "No ma'am. He didn't have it with him. Quite honestly, he wasn't totally coherent most of the time… I could just be on a wild goose chase. I don't know. I just decided to give it a chance. It seemed urgent that I find what he wanted me to."

"And just how do I know you are who you say? You aren't the first person to come looking since yesterday."

Torben tensed. "Did they get inside?"

"No. They didn't. I listened to them. They fidgeted with the lock just like you. Had the same luck as you too."

He smiled. "How many were there?"

"There were two of them."

They haven't been back?"

"No. Haven't seen them, but I'm expecting them again. One of them had his cell out. He walked around in the hall talking. Stood close to my door. He wasn't very careful. He-"

"What was the other one doing?" He excitedly interrupted.

"I don't know. He was doing something by the door there. You can't really see from my apartment. I was focused on the one by the door anyway. He scared me. Walked right up and stood there for a couple of minutes. Just talking away."

"What was he saying?"

"He told someone that he wanted to break in the door."

"Whoever he was talking to must have told them not to, because when he got off the phone, he told the other man they were just going to come back in a few days. He said the boss thought someone would be coming with a key. They should just wait until the key arrived. Then no one would know they'd been there."

Torben turned back and walked toward the door,

examining it more closely. That's when he noticed it, a slight discoloration in the keyhole.

"What are you looking at?" the woman asked.

"Nothing. Just go back inside."

Truthfully, he didn't know what he was looking at. There was a slight metallic ridge that had been placed in the slot of the keyhole. He pulled a pair of specially crafted tweezers from his trade bag and tried to remove it. It slightly turned, but wouldn't come the rest of the way out. He examined it more closely.

He flinched when she touched his shoulder. "What's there? You must have found something. You're rather jumpy."

He pointed to the notch. "It's some sort of sensor. You were right. They've been waiting on my arrival. They've got to be close. I probably disturbed it the moment I hit it with the bump key. I've got to get out of here… Go back inside ma'am, and when they come, don't come out in the hall. I don't know what I'm looking into. He didn't tell me, but I've got a feeling it could be dangerous."

He quickly turned and took three steps down the hall.

"Sir," she called from behind him. "Can you prove you were really with him when he died?"

"I don't know how. He was in the hospital. Room 1711. I suppose you could call them. One of the nurses would probably remember me. I was there for a while."

"That will take too long. Tell me about him."

"Uh... He was dying of cancer, so I don't really know if he'd be as you remember. He'd shrunken to just the shell of what I imagine he had been. He-"

"How was he acting?"

"He was in and out of coherence. His mind was really playing tricks on him. He was-"

"Was he saying anything strange as he behaved irrationally?"

"He wasn't really irrational, more like he was just losing reality for a few moments. Then he'd become lucid again. He died only moments after he told me what I needed to know."

"But was he saying anything bizarre?"

"He kept saying that death was coming for him. He could feel it. Sort of freaked me out. Scares me even more that he was right."

"That's it? Nothing else?"

He shook his head, "Other than the information I needed, there was nothing else."

"Okay," she said, as she turned and abruptly moved away.

He thought hard for a moment, watching her walk away.

"Wait," he yelled, just as she was about to close her door. "Wait, please."

She closed the door anyway. He heard the chain latch again. A moment later, the door slightly opened. She nervously peered back, the chain stretched across her face.

"I remember something else… When he would slip into incoherence, he kept calling me someone else's name. He would say it over and over again. It was rather frustrating."

"Barry?"

He tried to remember. After a second he shook his head. "No ma'am. Close though. It was Larry. He would say, Larry-"

"Is that you?" she excitedly finished with him.

He inquisitively studied her, "Yes. How'd you know?"

She closed the door, and the chain once again unlatched, allowing her to open it. "Come inside."

He stepped into her apartment. She quickly closed the door behind them and locked the chain back in place. The apartment was relatively empty compared to what he would have thought for a young woman living alone. It was surprisingly absent of photographs or any other identifying features that made a place feel like home. It was void of personal touch.

"What's going on?" he asked her, alarmed at her sudden excited but concerned expression.

"He knew this was coming. He told me he was going to die soon, and they'd come looking for it. They couldn't as long as he was alive, because they were afraid if they moved on him, he'd reveal them."

"Who?"

"I dunno. He never told me. Said it was better I didn't know… I only know they terrified him. He tried to hide it, but it was obvious. He said they'd come for what he'd been collecting."

"Collecting?"

"Information. Don't ask. I don't know what about."

Sudden movement in the hall caught his attention. He slowly walked to the door and gazed through the peephole. There were three of them. Dressed in black and moving fluidly. He almost panicked, his heart pounding in his chest. He was unarmed, and they no doubt carried an arsenal.

It was obvious. They were professionals, a specialty team paid big money because they didn't know how to fail. He silently stepped away from the door and toward her. When close enough, he whispered.

"Quietly, look and see if those are the men you saw before. Don't make a sound. They're dangerous."

She tiptoed to the door and looked into the hallway. She turned around and nodded to him. He motioned her away from the door. He took her place and tried to watch. They moved to the door down the hall that he'd been trying to get in to earlier. Standing in front of the door, they were completely out of his line of vision. He leaned more closely and tried to listen.

They were fidgeting with the door. One of them cursed.

"The sensor's been moved. Whoever was here must have seen it and got away quickly. I told you we should have been more careful staking out the place."

Another one angrily replied. "Shut up. You know as well as I do that no one has ever seen the sensor before. It always works."

"But if we'd have been closer, we could've arrived before he left."

"Well, he couldn't have gone far. Let's go downstairs and ask to see the video footage. I'm sure the manager could be persuaded to allow us access to the security feed."

Torben shook his head and looked at the girl. "We're in trouble."

Looking through the peephole he watched as the three walked past the door. The elevator opened a few seconds and then dinged closed.

He suddenly leapt forward, "Quick. I've got to get you out of here. They're going to look at the surveillance tape and see that I came into your room. It will only take them minutes to discover I'm still in the building."

"Come here," she said, the fear written across her face. "There's something I need to show you first."

She brought him to the back room of her apartment. A door was locked against the back wall, like a hotel room door joining two suites. This is the only entrance to his apartment.

He had the windows barricaded off. He walled the front door off from the inside."

"What?" Torben said, his forehead wrinkling in confusion.

"He wasn't crazy, detective. He wasn't losing his mind. He did know he was dying, but he was never out of his right mind."

"I don't understand."

"It was a code… Look, he's been paying me to stay here the past few weeks. He said someone would come, and I should let them in his apartment. He said they'd know the code. If they didn't, I was to tell them nothing."

"A code?"

She grinned. "He was a bit creative… Larry, is that you."

Torben chuckled. "He should be put up for an Oscar. Sure had me fooled."

She motioned for him to come toward her, as she moved toward the door and unlatched it. He opened it, and she called to him as he stepped in.

"I'm going to get a head start going down the fire escape. Meet me at the bottom as quickly as you can."

He nodded and swiftly moved to the front part of Dr. Shultz's apartment. She hadn't been lying; the door had been completely walled off from the inside. There was a solid wood partition fortified with a solid metal plate that had been screwed directly across the doorframe.

He could feel the surge of adrenaline. He was running out of time. Scanning the room, he easily spotted what he was looking for, the painting at the back. It was obviously a forgery, but it didn't matter. He ran and quickly ripped it from the wall. Taped to the back was a large eight-and-a-half by eleven envelope, sealed and taped over the top. It was obvious that it hadn't been disturbed.

He hung the picture back up, just as the elevator lightly chimed in the hallway. He ran back down the hall and climbed out onto the fire escape, pulling the window closed, just as the door crashed in from the outside. He was already running down the fire escape as the three men entered the room.

He was almost to the last step when a car flew around the corner. It was black. Unmarked. And coming toward him threateningly fast. He hit the ground, running down the alley, praying he'd make it to the open street before being slammed into from behind. Unexpectedly, someone yelled at him.

"Get in, you fool! Get in!"

He turned to see the woman from upstairs. He made it to the passenger side just as the door opened. The sudden report of a gunshot broke the overwhelming silence he'd been surrounded by. The deafening report of a rifle caused him to dive into the passenger's seat, as the back glass shattered.

The woman pressed the gas and the car rocketed forward. Five more shots ricocheted off the car, as they turned the corner and merged into the heavy traffic. Three men stood at the top of the fire escape. One of them spoke into a headset protruding from an earpiece concealed inside his left ear canal.

"No, sir. He got away with the file. The door in the hallway was a fake entrance. The only way in was through the apartment next door. Genius plan."

There was a long pause, and then the man spoke again.

"No, sir, he's not lost in the wind. I was able to hit his car with a tracker while the others were shooting. He doesn't know we'll be tracking him. As long as we're within a twenty mile radius, we'll know his every move."

Another long pause.

"Yes, sir. I'll make sure that when we recover the documents no one will ever see him again. Just like the others."

7

Hayden aggressively moved toward Darius. He raised his hand, as if to strike him.

"Seriously, you could've been killed. If what you're saying is true, you don't need to go anywhere alone. We didn't come all the way here just to have you murdered in the streets."

Darius dismissed him with a wave. "I can take care of myself. I appreciate your concern, but if you think I'm going to put all of you in danger merely to protect myself from some hidden assassins, you're mistaken."

"That's what friends do, Darius. I'm not your friend only when you're trying to save me from powerful men. I'm also your friend when you're the one in trouble. You know that."

"Yes. I do. But if anything happened to any of you, I wouldn't be able to live with myself. I've already lost all my family because of this; I can't lose the only other people close to me. You must understand my position."

"I do. And you must understand ours. To abandon you because your enemy seems strong is worse than death. We're at your side, Darius. Like it or not. Life or death. We're here."

The others readily agreed. Darius reluctantly shook his head. "I understand, and I appreciate your friendship. I shall be more careful."

Hunzuu spoke from where he was sitting near the fire. "Five assassins. These guys aren't easy to avoid, Sir Hayden. They could strike at any moment, and you'd never know they were coming. They could be the bush you're about to walk past, the watery stream you're about to cross, the petite elderly woman you smile at as you go by, the storekeeper, the market peddler, the beggar on the street. The best of them know how to blend in. It's what makes them dangerous. They could be anyone or anything, at any time. We must always be watchful."

"And how do you know so much about assassins, Hunzuu?"

Hunzuu seemed remorseful, but also slightly proud. "Because in my day, I was one. I've since done my duty training more than a few. I know the type of men of which you speak, and they won't stop unless they're killed, or you are."

M'ya was concerned. "What are we going to do? What's our next move?"

Someone moved in the shadows outside of the campfire. A dark tenseness gripped the small group. Darius laced an arrow. Hayden drew his sword. Hunzuu drew the feared Sword of Tiber, which he'd held since Hayden had given it to him at the Fortress. Leib moved closer to them, clutching a small dagger in each hand. M'ya edged near Hayden.

Hayden boldly called into the darkness. "Who goes there?"

A jolly voice answered back, a little to joyous for the occasion. "It's your captain. I've come to discuss a new deal."

He slowly entered the camp's flickering light, as they warily avoided him. He noticed their evasion a few seconds slower than he should have, and a boisterous laugh exploded from his lungs.

"You sure are an overly cautious crew. I've heard the rumors, but I didn't expect things to have changed so rapidly. You know me. I'm no killer."

Hayden stepped forward first. "We apologize. We just aren't sure what to expect. It's not every day one discovers he's being hunted by the world's most elite assassins."

"Indeed it's not, a fact we should be most thankful for, I suppose."

Hayden smiled. "What brings you here?"

"A little birdie tells me that you're looking for someone to take you to the island of Dahlak. I don't know any who would venture there. That island is forbidden."

Hayden remained silent. Finally, the man continued, "Well, have you found any takers?"

"None yet. You volunteering?"

"I'm a desperate man, in need of desperate help. If the price is right, I'd sail you past the gates and into hell itself."

Hunzuu spoke from the shadows. "I like you, captain. Make sure your greed doesn't lead to an untimely death."

"Not greed, my friend. I'm afraid its need. My family has suddenly accrued an unreasonable amount of debt. If not paid soon, my sons and daughter will be taken from my wife and I. She can tolerate my long absences only because she has them near. If they're all taken, it would end her life."

Hunzuu nodded a silent understanding. "Necessity at times outweighs wisdom."

"Agreed," Hayden stated while turning toward Darius. "Any suggestions? You're the future king here."

Darius replaced the arrow in his quiver. "Captain, if you will be in my employ until this is over, my first order of business will be to repay whatever debt you owe, to whomever you owe it... Agreed?"

"And what if I serve your purpose here, and Demsas continues to reign?"

Hunzuu chuckled. "I like a man who at least examines the negative alternatives."

Darius didn't smile. "Then we'll all be dead, and you'll be

considered a traitor to the throne. Your debt will be the least of your worries."

The captain nodded. "Do you at least find our chances reasonable?"

Darius smiled now. "Most likely we'll all be dead within the week. You still sure you want to sail us to Dahlak?"

The captain thought for a second. "I'll most likely not receive a better offer elsewhere. Got to die sometime... I'll start assembling a crew first thing in the morning. Most of the men are looking for work. We should be ready to sail by evening, if that would be pleasing."

Darius shook his head. "Tomorrow evening would be fine. We'll be there."

The captain started to turn, when Hunzuu stopped him. "Captain, hire no one for this voyage that has not already sailed with you many times. Hire as light a crew as possible. Turn away all strangers, regardless of how much they offer to join your expedition. If I find out you've taken on other travelers, I'll kill you myself."

The captain smiled. "I hate to know how you'd act if you didn't like me, sir."

Hunzuu returned the grin. "Yes, you would, Captain. We can't be too careful. I'll not apologize. Be safe out there. Hire well, and we shall see you tomorrow evening."

The captain sullenly nodded and silently disappeared into the blackness.

8

    Amarsin stood before the high counsel that had called on him. The king had sent a delegation two days ahead of his arrival. The delegation consisted of hundreds of armed guards and ten of Babylon's elite judges. The guards perused the streets of the Fortress, ensuring that all proper safety measures were intact to protect their king upon his arrival. Although tension thickened the atmosphere, there had been no hostility between the king's men and the Fortress soldiers. Each side had been extremely careful not to break the rules of diplomatic courtesy.

    The highest-ranking member of the counsel motioned for him to sit down. He nervously took his seat, facing the ten. The head member pounded the table with a wooden mallet.

    "The trial has officially begun." He motioned for a man seated upfront with a large scroll. "Let the record state that we have before us Amarsin Shamash, Babylonian attorney in training, and grandson of revered Parliamentarian Marcus Shamash."

Amarsin apprehensively raised his hand. "I thought this delegation was present to open an official inquiry into the actions of Captain Abaddon Dearth. He was operating against the high command of Babylonian Parliament. It's also our understanding that he wasn't following the king's authority. He followed my party deep into unlabeled territories while still claiming Babylonian privilege. How has an open inquiry turned into a trial?"

The chairman laughed. "I'm afraid you're misinformed. This delegation was sent to obtain the preliminary facts in the case of Hayden Smith and Amarsin Shamash versus the people of Babylon. It appears your friends have abandoned you, and you alone are left to carry the weight of their guilt."

Amarsin masked his concern in aggressiveness. "Guilt? Am I thus doomed already? I've not been granted one sentence of defense yet, but it appears you've already decided my fate... Besides, you know the rules, as long as I'm in the Fortress, your delegation has no authority to harm me, regardless of your findings."

"If we find you guilty, we'll hang you from these very walls. Make no mistake; Babylon does not fear the likes of the lone army of this isolated city of protection. If we choose, we could have this place surrounded within the week. Our navy would be anchored immediately off the coast within two. This would be a city under siege. No one would be allowed in or out until we decided we were done. How long do you think your city would hide you then?"

Amarsin was angry. "You've made a mockery of Babylonian honor. You were allowed in solely on the basis of what amounts to nothing more than lies. Your intentions, while appearing peaceful, have been nothing more than concealed hostility. Like a serpent, you've slithered your way into this city to spread Babylonian corruption like venom."

"And like venom paralyzes, so do we. We've stationed over two hundred of the king's best-trained soldiers, already within the walls. We've devised a plan that would take only hours to incorporate, rendering this city completely vulnerable in two days. Do you really want to be the reason this city is toppled to the ground?"

"And what if I merely decide to leave so the city can be spared. Will I get the benefit of a trial in Babylon?"

"There are a hundred men dying for a chance to kill the one responsible for the murder of their hero. You wouldn't make it forty feet outside the walls."

"So, you've put me in checkmate."

"It appears that way. You've nowhere to go, no friends to help you fight, no means of escape, and no choice but to stay and defend what fragment of honor you have left. You must decide the fates of yourself and your so called friends."

Amarsin scowled. The man's smile increased.

"Tsk, tsk, tsk... Now there's an advantage to you being the one left here to face us."

"Of course. What would that great advantage be?" Amarsin mordantly asked.

"The Babylonian deferment."

"I'm unaware of that edict."

"I thought you would be. It's buried in the classic laws of our ancestors, but it's still available, as it has not yet been repealed."

Amarsin sat silently and stared at the man, whose fake smile continued to glow. He was obviously enjoying the moment.

"Aren't you at least a little interested, Mr. Shamash? This could be your salvation."

Amarsin shrugged. "I don't know. You wouldn't be making me aware of a solution unless it was going to be painfully expensive."

"Expensive indeed, Mr. Shamash. You could have your penalty deferred onto the other guilty party. You agree to testify against the other rebel, Sir Hayden Smith, and your atrocities will be fully pardoned. You'll be granted the right to leave the Fortress and return to the heart of Babylon. You'll even be given the rights and benefits you held prior to the misunderstandings. You-"

"And what will happen to him?"

"He's a traitor to Babylon, and responsible for killing one of our most noble leaders over the past few decades. Captain Dearth's absence is already severely felt among us. And it couldn't have come at a worse time."

Amarsin appeared uninterested, trying to hide his frustration and anxiety behind a mask of boredom. The spokesman wasn't unnoticing of his tactic.

"Pretend to be unconcerned all you'd like fat man, but everyone in this room knows that your heart wants to beat its way out of your oversized chest. You forget that we all saw your babbling antics in trying to save Sir Hayden in Babylon."

Amarsin's face grew fiery, not from embarrassment, but from rage. "That was, as you said, sir, months ago. I've faced the wrath of the gods, coolly stared the reaper eye to eye, and stood against pirates, thieves, and the best that Babylon had to offer since then. I've traveled the raging river south and survived it all. I'm not the same man I was... So, pardon me for not appearing overly worried that a man of your stature could afflict me to the point of trepidation. If I appear unmoved, it says nothing about my feelings concerning the preeminence of Babylon; it completely speaks of my lack of respect and complete disdain for the likes of you."

The man was irate. He grabbed the mallet and pounded the desk. "I sentence you to be executed at first light tomorrow. You shall be pelted with stones until your life spills out onto the sand of this city. Your body will be dumped into the raging river you survived and carried into the great gulf beyond. Your soul will wander the lost places of the earth because your family will never find you for proper burial. You'll be doomed to eternal darkness, because peace will escape you in the afterlife."

It was Amarsin's turn to smile. "If only you had that power. You're nothing but a common spokesman of a lowered counsel. You aren't even good enough to make the parliament. Go ahead. Kill me. Why wait? Take my life now... Only, we both know the king expects to see me in two days."

Amarsin thoughtfully looked at the other members of the appointed counsel. "Members of this committee, I implore you to answer. Who would you hold responsible for my death if directly asked by the king."

No one answered him, and he allowed the silence to linger. Once sure he held the floor, he continued.

"Furthermore, members of this committee, I highly request to have this spokesman reappointed to another case."

The man leapt to his feet. "That's absurd. You can't have me reappointed."

"I can, and I shall."

He looked to the members of the panel again. "I exercise my right to have him removed. It's painfully apparent that he's unable to be a fair mediator. I'm unsure what vendetta he has against me, but I've shown no quarrel towards him. Yet, he has unfairly convicted me without the benefit of a trial. As a Babylonian citizen and family of a distinctive Parliamentarian, I've every reason to expect the privileges afforded someone of my rank."

The spokesman violently shook his head. "Your mind games won't work on us, Mr. Shamash. You may have saved your life for today, because you're right about the king. He wants to speak to you himself. However, you're wrong about this board. We owe you nothing. You're rights have been revoked unless you agree to the terms that I've laid before you previously."

Amarsin hesitated. After a few seconds he calmly asked, "So you're saying that if I sell out my friends and agree to testify against them, they'll be convicted, but I'll be completely pardoned and released without question?"

"Yes… That's the gist of it."

"And what of the hundred men waiting to kill me the moment I step outside of this wall?"

"The king would grant you a personal mark. You'd be given immunity and wear his crest. No one will be able to harm you."

Amarsin shook his head in disgust. "You make an extremely sick offer, but I'm afraid I have no other choice but to consider it. I'll give you an answer before the king arrives."

"Don't be foolish, Amarsin. There's no other way out of this. You give us what we want, and you'll live. Refuse us, and you all die anyway."

"What should I do between now and the… uh… trial?"

"Nothing. The outcome has already been determined. For the people here at the Fortress, we'll put on the show of a balanced courtroom. However, your fate has already been sealed. Denounce the other traitors to the throne. Live another day, Amarsin. Is that not the Babylonian way? A man must be true to himself. Live to fight another day.

Amarsin left the meeting, his mind racing with possibilities. He'd always been an opportunist. He couldn't fight it. It was in his blood. Part of his DNA. He was a Shamash, and the family did whatever was required to get and stay on top. No matter what or who it cost. That was the way of things. It wasn't just the Babylonian way. It was the Shamash way.

With the help of Sir Hayden, he thought he had defeated that savage part of him. However, here it was again, his selfish nature rearing its ugly head. He lowered his face into his hands and ashamedly cried. Why was he struggling with this decision? They were his only true friends in this world. Could he so easily sacrifice them to save his own skin? He would like to think it wouldn't be possible, but somewhere inside he knew the truth, and he hated himself for it.

Live to fight another day.

9

Hunzuu boarded the ship first and warily looked around. The captain joined him a moment later.

"Welcome back aboard. I think you'll find our supplies sufficient."

"We should indeed. The journey is but a frog's leap across the water. We shouldn't need much."

"Ah, but comfortable you shall be the entire way."

Hunzuu sternly turned toward him. "It's not comfort I seek, captain. It's safety. If you cannot accurately guarantee the wellbeing of your future king, we have no wish of boarding your vessel."

"Sir, I know what's at stake and have vouched for each person on this ship myself. I've been most careful."

"How many crew members are there?"

"I have four of my personal crew, including my son and daughter. There are also ten other crewmembers including a night watchman and two slaves. I've checked and double-checked everyone's credentials. They're all good."

Hunzuu eyed him suspiciously. "Captain, if trouble starts at any time, I'm coming for you first. I'm not going to question where the problem originated. I'm just going to assume you're the culprit. You understand me?"

"Understood, but you have nothing to worry about."

"Then neither do you," Hunzuu replied, as he turned and motioned just south of the dock. Hayden saw his wave and moved toward Darius. He reached him in a couple of seconds and whistled across the way toward M'ya and Leib. He pointed toward the ship, and they immediately moved toward it. Hayden looked at Darius.

"Stay close to me."

He positioned his backhand on Darius' forearm and moved toward the ship, slowly but steadily. Darius stayed right with him, understanding they were trying to keep him protected.

M'ya and Leib made it to the platform first. Within a few seconds they'd both successfully boarded the vessel. Hayden pushed Darius forward and followed right behind him up the wooden steps. They all joined Hunzuu in the center of the main deck.

. . .

On the back deck, a slight rustle would have been heard had anyone been around to listen. One of the slaves had been dragged from his quarters and momentarily placed behind the large supply crates. The slave had been stripped of his servitor garments and then tossed from the deck to the water below. A metallic weight had been tied to his ankles to make sure his body wouldn't surface before the ship left the port.

The perpetrator carefully placed the slave's clothing over his own, and then made his way down the ships middle corridor. It had been too easy. The crew was small. Only one guard roamed the vessel. His target was just entering the vessel on the other side; so all eyes were on him. The main security faction would be focused on his movement, a slight miscalculation on their part. The most important position on the ship wasn't the location of the one being protected. That was a mistake. The most vital place on the vessel was the one left exposed. That's how he'd chosen his opening. Timing and circumstance, and they'd played right into his hand.

He'd chosen well. The man lying in the bottom of the ocean looked uncannily like him. Their hair was both shoulder length and braided. They were about the same build and height, complexions both equally dark, and facial features similar. If the assassin didn't know better, he would've thought the two of them were brothers. The only difference was that one of them was lying among the pearls in the depths of the port, and the other was walking toward a target that would make him wealthy for life.

He knew enough about being a ship slave to know that no

one in the crew would recognize a switch had been made. Slaves on small vessels weren't permanent. Each time a voyage was undertaken, the captain would visit the shipmaster's slave quarters to rent workers. Of course, the slave got nothing for his labor but a room and enough food to stay healthy and strong on the journey. He'd been in those shoes before being selected for his current profession, and it hadn't been pretty. He'd been in small, eight-by-eight cabins with ten people to share the floor. Those days had only made him angry, and hungry for more. The intense and deadly training he'd endured hadn't been a struggle for him. It had been a pleasure. Finally, he'd been given the opportunity to express his rage at the unfairness of life.

He knew he'd killed some who didn't deserve to die. He also murdered those who did deserve it but weren't ready for the afterlife. He'd been the reason more than a few had unpreparedly faced the gods in judgment. He'd sent his fair share to the underworld, and he didn't regret a single one of them.

Since he'd broken away from the training school, he'd been a hunted man. That had been years ago, and they'd never caught up with him. He'd finally started believing they'd just given up. That's why he'd migrated so far south, to escape their trackers. He'd evaded them well, and now his destiny was his own. He belonged to no man.

Since he'd been his own employer, he'd done better than anticipated. He'd quietly become one of the better contract killers in the most highly private circles. Many knew him simply as the Bubonic, in reference to the great plague that crippled the Roman Empire before it was rebuilt to greatness. Like the plague, his targets were dead within a week after he identified them. He was the Black Death.

All he had to do was avoid the other slave on board until he could get close to his target. He felt the small dagger in his belt, within a reflexive grasp's range. Like a viper's strike, he could have it out and in the kill zone before anyone knew he was around. He'd be making his exit before anyone recognized he'd been on board. Killing was all too easy for him. It was natural, like sleeping.

. . .

The anchor was lifted and the small vessel set sail for Dahlak. The captain approached Darius.

"Now that we're out to sea, sir, which one of the many islands of Dahlak are we headed for?"

"Have you heard of the Jew that dwells there?"

"I've heard the myths, but never seen him for myself. Always supposed those to be urban legends, although I guess it's possible a stranger could survive the evils of the islands."

Darius nodded. "And what have you heard of this man?"

The Captain thought for a moment. "He teaches about a god we know nothing of. A god that can't be seen, isn't honored by idols, and doesn't piously rule from his throne with lightning bolts ready to execute swift vengeance on those who disobey him. Supposedly, a god of wise judgment, tempered with mercy and compassion. A god who will one day come to save his people."

Darius was suddenly curious. "So, a Jewish god who will deliver the Jews from all who oppress them? He spreads the filth of a racist god among our people?"

"Not from what I've heard. Quite the contrary, actually. His God will take any convert by way of allowing them to become a proselyte... I'm afraid things have changed here over the last few years. This part of the world has been engrossed with strange darkness. Many false doctrines have made their way into our lands. Wars have ravaged homes across the eastern world. Crusades have been fought over which god rules supreme and which dogma will ultimately rule. Islam has spread into our ranks, but so far has been kept at bay. Its only known progress has been into the regions of Dahlak."

"So, Dahlak is war torn between Islam and the malevolent darkness of witches' covens? Satan's servants and Islam's disciples have mingled?"

"I'm afraid so. Our people are in danger of being overtaken by the false radiance of Allah or the fictitious angels of light. Both come as wolves in sheep's clothing, ready to swallow the sanctity of our gods in their wake."

"And what of the Jew?"

"The Jew is different. I've heard tales. He's dangerous, but only because there seems to be a higher power in what he believes."

"And what does he believe?"

"He believes in The One."

"The One?" Darius enthusiastically repeated.

"Yes, The One. Our gods are many, more than the stars. He claims to follow one God who alone possesses all the power of our gods. He claims that Islam is a disease polluting the world and that the God of Israel is the cure."

Darius was still struggling to grasp the concept. "One god who has all power. I would that were so. It would make teaching the little ones to pray much easier."

The captain laughed. "I gave up, like so many others. It seems they weren't listening anyway."

Darius smiled. "I hope to change that, sir. Restoring this proud nation will hopefully turn the favor of the gods back in our direction, perhaps restoring our faith in the gods of our birth. The Jew and the push of Islam will be removed from our shores, and the darkness of Dahlak will be forced back with them, forever ridding us of the dark one's fury."

"The Jew may not be so easy to remove. He's done strange things."

"Magic… Like the sorcerers?" Darius inquired.

"No. His magic has been different. He's worked against the powers of darkness, and although they've marked him with incantations for over a year, the troubled spirits have yet to harm him."

The captain seemed afraid, but Darius motioned for him to continue.

"I don't know why, but I've heard rumors from the

rumblings. The darkness of Dahlak is disturbed. It's never been threatened, not by any of the teachings that have soiled its shores. Most foreign apostles have been reduced to ruin or merely disappeared never to be heard from again. However, despite Dahlak's propensity for rejecting opposing theologies, the spirits are disturbed by talk of this one God. Whisperings in the darkest corners of Dahlak have indicated that for once, the obscurity that's ruled for generations may have discovered its greatest threat."

Darius was genuinely intrigued. "For generations we've sought a way to cleanse the dank oppression of evil from the islands. I'd welcome any god who could rid our shores of such wickedness."

"As would I, sir… As would I."

Darius thought back to answer the captain's question that had started their discussion. "Take us to the island where the man teaches about the one god."

Hayden was listening from the corner. He didn't say anything, but was curiously taking it all in. Here was the god talk again, and it stirred something within him. There was a burning inside, a yearning for something deeper that he couldn't quite explain. He felt it whenever someone mentioned the one god. He'd once felt an unthinkable dread and feeling of bitterness when that god was mentioned. Now, the rage had turned to hunger. He almost wanted to pursue an experience he knew could've never occurred. It was almost as if someone were calling him higher, pulling him deeper into a place he'd never been. He was reluctant, but curious to follow. Perhaps this man who spoke of the one god held answers he desperately needed.

M'ya moved close to him. It seemed she was always there, and he was keenly aware of it. However, despite her nearness, she wasn't a nuisance. He enjoyed having her around. She made him feel strong and important, somehow adding purpose to his life. Her strengths were evident even in her flaws. If ever he'd met someone who was perfect in her imperfections, it was M'ya.

She'd been nothing more than a common thief struggling to survive when he'd meet her, but she'd turned into so much more. Her inner radiance had been allowed to shine, brought out like a diamond from the rough. She'd become his friend, confidant, and one of wise intuition, with a kind heart and beautiful spirit.

He'd felt such an emptiness when she'd fallen from the raft and been swept away by the raging waters. They thought she'd been lost forever, and he hadn't been able to come to terms with that in his mind. He'd do anything to make sure she was protected. When Abaddon Dearth had placed the blade against her throat, he'd faced the greatest fear he'd ever known. Losing her.

He smiled at her. "Do you feel that?"

"What Hayden?" She tiredly asked.

"That chill. The hair on my neck is standing on end."

"I feel nothing. Perhaps it's the wind coming in off the water. It's been a little colder than normal… The men in the galley are afraid. They said it gets colder the closer we get to the islands. The fog is overwhelming. None of them have ever been to the large islands. They're afraid of what lives there."

"The inhabitants? They are mere mortals, as are we."

"Not the natives. They're afraid of what can't be seen," she said, a hint of dread in her voice.

"Come on, M'ya. Don't tell me you're a believer in such things."

"Believer or not, Hayden, I don't have to believe to know that they believe. I'm afraid because they are. These men are hardened. They are sailors. They've battled much adversity in their days. But something has them spooked. Something has them thinking of mutiny in order to return home. Even though we're a couple hours from the port, a few of them have even contemplated taking the smaller vessels and rowing back to the mainland."

Lightning flashed overhead, and a crash of thunder rattled the deck. One of the crewmembers made his way from the galley and walked toward the captain.

"Sir, we've got a bad feeling about this."

The captain eyed him reassuringly. "Its nothing, mate. Calm the others. It's only superstition, and we are strong men. We've nothing to fear."

"Sir, the candle flickered in our midst, and the flame burned blue. You know the omen. It shall not be good for us there. The night will devour us all... Please, sir. Let's turn around at once."

The lightning flashed again, barely missing the highest mast. More men gathered on the deck. One pointed toward the top of the crow's nest, which was still glowing a fiery ember because of the proximity of the electrical bolt that had just surged past.

"It's another sign. We're heading into great peril."

Hunzuu lunged into the midst of them and drew the feared sword of Tiber. "By the gods, if another of you speak of mutiny, I'll have your head with the finest blade the world ever saw. We are men. We aren't muses, to be frightened and turned away by the song of death. Let it come. We shall meet it with more than a warm embrace. We'll meet it with a vengeance of our own, and if today is the day we die, we die like warriors to receive a warrior's reward."

The captain joined him. "I stand with the one who wields the sword. The gods of Babylon are with us. We have their favor."

The men nodded, still not reassured. However, Hunzuu had put an end to their discussion.

. . .

Hayden looked toward M'ya and chuckled. "If I'd have known all the superstitious power of the sword, I'd never have let it go."

She looked at him curiously, "You don't believe the tales?"

"Of a sword that brings the favor of gods who have always been too selfish to notice me otherwise? I have a hard time fathoming that. Even if it were true, it speaks to the lunacy of Babylonian god-ship. The gods don't care about the people who serve them, but they care about protecting a blade forged from the fires of heaven. Seems rather deficient to me."

"I suppose, but I'd be careful blaspheming the gods when you are walking into a hellhole. You never know what power you might need to call upon."

"Or, what power we might be introduced to."

"Don't tell me you're buying the notion of the one god who has all power," she incredulously replied. "That sounds even more ridiculous than believing in hundreds of gods who bind together to protect an instrument they've placed infinite value in."

"I don't know, M'ya. Perhaps I just like it simple. If a god truly exists, why shouldn't he have all power over the world? Why are some gods limited? How powerful are they really if they can only reign over certain elements but have no authority over other ones? Why do we need a god to bless the seas, another to ensure a harvest, another to control the weather, another to grant fertility, another to bring peace, another to bring war, and another still to grant happiness? Why so many? Is it not easier to believe that one could suffice."

She pulled away from him. "You worry me, Hayden. Please, don't defy the gods."

He moved close enough to her that they were almost touching, and then placed his lips close enough to her ear to whisper.

"Don't worry about me, girl. Gods or not, Hayden Smith doesn't plan on dying today."

. . .

Darius sat alone, a few feet from where M'ya and Hayden were talking. They were preoccupied. He smiled. He'd seen it coming. Hayden wouldn't admit it, probably didn't realize it himself, but it was obvious to anyone paying attention. M'ya, on the other hand, was struggling against the developing feelings. She knew he was in conflict with his emotions and wanted to respect his personal space.

Her feelings toward him were painfully apparent. She tried to hide them, but it was evident. She stared a little too long, stood a little to close, smiled harder, and laughed louder when he was around.

She also acted differently when other women were close to him. There'd been a couple at the Fortress that had vied for Hayden's attention. He hadn't even noticed, but she had. She'd done her best to keep him away from them. Darius had found it most comical.

Even today, she'd suspiciously eyed the captain's daughter, an exotically pretty girl, but another that Hayden hadn't taken the time to notice. Darius drew in a deep breath and whispered to himself.

"It'll happen in time, sweet M'ya, just be patient. He has

eyes for no one else."

He knew the reason, and he respected her for her slow and calculated response to Hayden's situation. Sometimes people just aren't ready for relationships. The last thing a wise person should do is to throw himself or herself at someone who has unresolved emotional turmoil in their life. Attaching to someone who is exceptionally vulnerable can be most treacherous. Relationships that begin with a physical explosion seldom last. Emotional or spiritual instability is the most volatile foundation on which to build. Security and true love are forged slowly, through adversity and trial. He guessed she'd learned the hard way that it was best to allow Hayden the opportunity to grow past whatever demons were haunting him. It's more beneficial to allow a person to heal, then to become a crutch for them to lean on in the most critical moments of change.

Becoming that crutch instead of forcing a person to learn and grow on his or her own is often the most harmful antidote. They heal improperly and forever carry scars and limp through life. Their weaknesses are magnified because they've never confronted the distinct flaws of their own character. At times, alone is exactly where a person needs to be.

Often, personal struggle is the very thing that brings a person to renewed faith in a higher power. Far too many want to be a hero who saves others from failure and heartache. However, in so doing, they keep the one they're trying to protect from ever learning to depend on the higher sources for survival. Faith is destroyed. Legacies are aborted. Eternal kingdoms are ended before they even begin. All because people don't understand that to love, sometimes means allowing a man to deal with his own demons. Sometimes, truly caring means giving a person space to walk alone and define his own values and perfect his own virtues.

Darius smiled at them. Hayden was forging destiny. He was becoming a more balanced man who would do great things. She would be there. She was part of it, and it was obvious that she could feel it. But she was truly a strong woman, pushing her emotional needs aside in order for him to become the man divine providence intended him to be. Darius shook his head watching them. Few men could be so lucky. She was a rarity indeed.

Darius stood and started to interrupt their playful banter but decided against it. Who was he to interrupt a potentially developing romance? He surveyed the deck. The captain and Hunzuu had gone into the galley, no doubt to drink a little wine before going to bed. A few of the deck hands had moved from the galley and were doing their routine labor before turning in for the night. He needed a few peaceful moments to clear his head.

He turned the corner and disappeared around the mid-deck cabin. No doubt it was quieter on the other end of the ship. They'd told him not to leave without them again, but this was as safe as he could be. No assassin could reach him in the midst of the sea.

. . .

The Black Death watched him come. This was too easy indeed. It would be over in a couple of minutes, depending on how soon the aspiring king walked past his hiding spot. Come tomorrow evening, he'd stand before the arrogant King Demsas and demand his reward. If not given, he'd make sure Demsas died before his own life was taken. It's the first lesson he'd learned in the trade school. There's honor in a violent death. Eternity isn't something to fear; it's a calling to embrace.

Darius walked along the deck and stood along the ship's wall, peering over the side into the boisterous waves below. He peered ahead into the darkness. Perhaps the stories were true. The clouds seemed to have fallen ahead, creating a velvety blanket across the ocean's tumultuous surface.

He wasn't aware of the movement behind him. Thirty feet back, the assassin moved from concealment. His best chance would be to cut Darius like he had the slave, remove a lock of his hair for proof, and then throw him over the side. No one would ever find him. The hope of Aksum would have merely vanished. Perhaps they'd think the gods had removed him for pushing into their territory. They'd forever be afraid of the dark rulers of Dahlak.

He drew his famed curved blade, his moccasins allowing him to move without making a sound. He could see it coming. It was perfect, an easy kill.

Twenty feet.

Fifteen.

Ten.

He raised the blade a little higher.

Eight.

Suddenly, something swung from the ratlines of the mizzan mast overhead. It was only a blur, but it had hurt him. Blood pooled at the bottom of his legs. He softly groaned, as he clutched his throat. The groan turned to a wet gurgle.

Darius whirled around. A black man with a curved dagger was on his knees five feet behind him. No one else was on the deck. The man wasn't going to live another minute, his life oozing through his fingers. Darius kicked the curved dagger away and ripped off a piece of his shirt. He placed it around the man's throat, trying to stop the bleeding."

He instinctively yelled. "Hunzuu... Hayden..."

The slave looked into Darius' eyes and removed his own hands from applying pressure. He weakly fumbled with another blade in his waistband and slowly brought it toward Darius' face. Darius stumbled backward, kicking the man away as he fell. The man landed on his back, rolled over, tried to stand up, and then fell face down on the hard deck.

Hayden, Hunzuu, the captain, and M'ya came running from the main deck. M'ya screamed, not fearful but worried.

"Darius, are you all right?" she gasped.

He shook his head. "I'm a little shaken up, but I'm uninjured."

"What happened? How'd you see him coming?" Hunzuu asked, recognizing it was an assassin.

Darius took a deep breath. "I didn't. He should've killed me. Something protected me. He was five feet behind me, and he just suddenly fell, mortally wounded. I turned around immediately..."

He looked at them. "I'm not crazy. I turned, and nothing was there. The assassin was down. Someone was watching out for me."

Hunzuu stooped down and pulled up the sleeve on the slave's right arm. A symbol had been branded into his skin years ago. Hunzuu shook his head, recognizing it instantly.

"You're lucky to be alive Darius. He was the Mamluk, the Black Death."

10

Hunzuu roughly grabbed the slave by the neck of his shirt and drug him to where the fallen assassin lay, forcing him to look at the dead man.

"Is this the man that was hired with you? Is he from the same slave house?"

The frightened man shook his head. "I... I... I don' know dis man. I neva seen him befoe."

Hunzuu forced his head down further. "Are you sure? Take a closer look. Do you know him?"

"No... No... Please. I don' know dis man."

Darius moved to Hunzuu and pushed him away from the worried slave. He turned to face the man.

"I'm sorry. My friends are really worried about me. That's

why they may be a little abrupt. I assure you, you're in no danger. We're not interested in hurting you. We're only concerned with reaching the islands alive."

The man nodded and hurriedly left the deck. Darius approached the group. Leib stood in the midst of them.

"I won't let him out of my sight again. It's painfully obvious that we can't trust him not to go off on his own. Perhaps we should just bind him to the mast and form an impenetrable circle around him."

Darius playfully slapped him on the head. "They'd shoot me over the top of you, gnome."

Hunzuu wasn't finished. "This isn't a game, Darius. You need to quit being selfish."

"Selfish? I lost my wife and son, twice, because of this Kingdom. Yet, I'm still here… How can you call me selfish? I'm here in my father's honor to rebuild an empire and give the people something to believe in. Roman oppression, Muslim influence, and Greek politicians are all they know. It's time for them to have a renewed faith in the future."

"All of that is true, Darius. But how will they have hope if the one they have the slightest belief in dies. This insane notion that you're invincible must cease. You were almost murdered on the deck of a private vessel in the midst of the sea. These people are trained professionals. They aren't playing around. They'll strike when you least expect it. They're skilled at making the places you'd think could never be dangerous your death sentence. They're unlike anything you have ever seen. So quit taking your life for granted."

"Death must come to us all, Hunzuu. I do not fear it."

"Nor should you, but neither should you welcome it. You should combat it with every bit of steel in your soul. Five more feet and you'd have been sent to a warrior's calling. Five more feet and the people of Aksum would have been doomed to the leadership of your brother. That's how you are selfish. You're life is no longer your own."

"I didn't ask for this, Hunzuu."

Leib had been silently observing. He couldn't remain quiet anymore.

"Most heroes never do… He's right you know. Heroes are special, not only because they're willing to make the huge sacrifice of death, but sometimes being a hero means giving them your life; living differently so that others may benefit."

Darius shook his head. "Well spoken, little one. Hunzuu, I accept Sir Leib's suggestion. He shall follow me as a special delegate everywhere I go. He shall, from this day forward, be advisor to the king of Aksum."

The captain whispered near him. "Are you sure that's wise, sir? The people won't accept just any one to possess the king's ear."

"I'm not just any king, and he's not just any man. It has been settled."

"Very well then," the captain winced.

Darius turned. "Captain, make steady the course. We aren't to be deviated from our original bearing."

The captain walked away toward his cabin. His son and daughter stood on the outskirts of the deck, watching the commotion. The girl caught Hayden's eyes and smiled, before shyly looking away. Hayden nodded in her direction and moved toward the galley. M'ya narrowed her eyes and crinkled her nose. Darius gently touched her shoulder and smiled.

"He'll come around, girl. Just wait."

. . .

Ten hours later, someone yelling loudly from halfway up the ratlines alerted them. The crew ran onto the deck to discover the cause of alarm. Hunzuu was the first one to appear on the hard surface. The rain had picked up and was pelting the ship. The wind was whipping the sails in every direction. The fog seemed impassable; forming a line barely above the ship's torrential pull. The man on the ratlines pointed into the expanse of water before them.

"I saw it. There, before us. Land. I saw land."

The captain squinted but saw nothing. Hayden ran alongside him and peered into the water as well. There was nothing there.

The ship suddenly turned sideways in the water like a vacuum had opened beneath them, causing the vessel to uncontrollably slide. The waves slammed against the side of the small vessel, causing it to aggressively lean to one side. The captain's son ran toward the back deck, screaming over the wind,

"We need to get rid of the cargo. We're taking on too much water."

The ship suddenly lurched forward, before abruptly stopping, throwing everyone onto the deck. The man on the ratlines yelled again.

"We've run aground. There's a breach in the hull. The rocks have opened us."

The ship slightly turned again, but wasn't free to move further. Whatever it had lodged against was holding it firmly in its grasp. It was obvious that the watchman had been right. The vessel was taking on too much water and was severely starting to tilt sideways. The men scrambled to remove as much of the crates and supplies as possible, but to no avail. The water was coming in too fast from below, and waves were pounding too powerfully from above. The ship was going down.

M'ya ran toward Hayden and Hunzuu. She was halfway when a wave slammed over the side, knocking her off of her feet and over the slanted side of the ship. Darius was coming from the opposite end and saw her tightly clinging to some netting that had gotten tangled in the mast line. He lunged toward her, just as the mast splintered and fell into the raging sea a few feet away. The force of the mast hitting the water caused the boat to bounce on the waves and then roll even lower into the ferocious surface of the deep. The sidewall was lying parallel over the toiling watery blanket.

Men struggled against the ropes to free the life rafts. The ship was going down. They'd tried everything but were unable to save it. Darius was feeling the same way about M'ya. As the mast fell, the nearest ratline crashed toward him, pinning him against another segment of the battered deck. He quickly removed his dagger and hurriedly slashed at the cords holding him hostage against the floor.

Hayden was also trying to get to her. He'd already pushed through three groups of frightened sailors fighting to get at least one lifeboat on the sea. Their first attempt had failed. They'd cut the boat's binds too quickly, and the small rowboat had crashed ten feet into the water below, landing on its end and quickly being yanked sideways by the strong current. Within seconds, it had capsized and was making its way to the reefs below.

She was still too far. Hayden was certain he couldn't make it in time.

She whimpered, struggling to pull herself back over the side.

No use.

Dangling.

Weak.

Frail.

She was losing strength. Looking over the side of the wall, she saw Hayden running from the opposite end. The ship had turned so much that he was practically running uphill to get to her. The steep incline was making it almost impossible.

Hunzuu tried to join in the rescue attempt, but a large

carton from the cargo bay fell when the ship rolled, striking him on the head. She couldn't tell if he was unconscious, but he didn't appear to be moving from where he'd fallen behind one of the furthest lifeboats.

From the opposite direction, her only hope had been Darius, but he was still bound to the floor, desperately struggling to cut himself away from the restricting bands. There was no one to help, and she was quickly losing her grip.

She pulled with all her might, shifting her weight slightly toward the top, attempting to reestablish her grip on the line. Her calculated change in grasp corresponded exactly with another large wave that rocked the boat, causing it to partially crack in the center. The two movements together weren't favorable, as it slightly altered the position she'd been clinging to. It suddenly moved away from her, breaking her hold, dropping her into the storm below.

She frantically closed her eyes and involuntarily screamed. Only, she didn't land in the terrifying waters. She didn't even fall. Something had grasped her hand at the last second, holding her firmly in place. Now, something was trying to pull her up over the side of the boat, before it completely capsized.

Whoever was pulling her wasn't having the best luck. She tried her best to grasp the rope with her opposite arm. As she caught the side, she pulled herself forward, just as she felt the person holding her other hand tugged from overhead. Finally, she felt something else reach for her, something more definitive and strong. Swinging back over the side and onto the deck, she looked into the worried eyes of Hayden. Sitting beside him and appearing nervous as well, was the captain's daughter. She'd been the one who had saved M'ya, holding onto her until Hayden had been able to get there.

"Sorry, we've no time for sweet gratitude right now," Hayden yelled. "We've got to get off this ship."

M'ya motioned toward Darius, but Leib was already at his side, helping cut away the last of the restraints. She moved toward where Hunzuu had been, but he was no longer there. The captain's daughter urgently pointed into the water.

"Look!"

Two rowboats were moving away from the ship and into the darkness. Three men were desperately rowing in the first one. Hunzuu was lying on that boat's floor, knocked unconscious. The captain, his son, and four of the crew were in the other one, fighting against the squall to stay afloat.

Hayden turned to the girl. "Are there anymore vessels on this ship?"

"No," she frantically screamed over the howling gale. "There are none. They only other two were broken apart when the mast fell."

Darius and Leib met them, finally breaking free from the twisted mess that had ensnared him. The deck cracked for a final time, the floor divided, and the ship was ripped in half. The largest part of the mast crashed headlong into the sea, breaking completely from the sinking ship.

As they plunged into the raging flow, Darius grabbed Leib and pulled him tightly against one end of the beam. Hayden landed a few feet from the opposite end. He grabbed a large portion of the rigging and rolled it around his wrist, essentially binding himself to the floating log.

He searched the water around him. M'ya was a few feet to his right, fighting to stay above water. The captain's daughter was a little further out and to the left. He reached for M'ya first, pulling her hair toward him. She came up gasping for air, and he tied her off as he had himself. Without hesitation, he turned himself to the other girl, but she was gone, having vanished beneath the boisterous waves.

. . .

An hour later, the beam washed against a sandy bank. Hayden exhaustedly pulled himself onto the beach. Putting his arm around M'ya's waist, he helped her stand up. They both laboriously moved further onto the land. Satisfied that they were far enough inland, he crashed to his knees. She fell down beside him.

Hayden heard movement to his right and weakly turned to see Darius and Leib. He painfully nodded toward them and then fell again. He heard someone call to them. Above the waves crashing on rocky embankments, he heard someone faintly calling.

"Over here."

M'ya peeked over him to see who was there.

"It's Hunzuu," she said, "he's alive, and he's with two men

from the ship."

Hunzuu sat down beside them. "We're lucky to be alive. That storm was an aberration from hell. It came from nowhere, wreaked its havoc, and then silently disappeared. Sir, it was death come alive."

"What of the captain?" Hayden asked, ignoring the suggestion about the storm.

Hunzuu shook his head. "We're it, sir. Everyone else was lost."

Hayden tried to sit up but couldn't. "And what of the girl?"

"Gone, sir… She was fighting to reach the mast when she went down for good. The currents were too strong."

Hayden rolled over and looked into the sky. It was a sharp contrast from only minutes before. The sun was large and bright, appearing more vibrant than ever. Perhaps Hunzuu had been right, for no storm could have cleared so quickly.

11

"Where are we?" Leib asked one of the men from the ship.

The man paused for a few seconds, looking toward the sky, as if trying to find answers. Finally, he brought his attention back to the group.

"Honest answer. I don't know. Best guess is that we're on one of the four supposedly uninhabited islands off the southernmost Dahlak stronghold."

Hunzuu winced, "Stronghold?"

The man smiled. "Relax, it's just the name given to the dwelling place of the warlocks and witches. Dahlak is really over one hundred small islands off the coast of Aksum. However, most foreigners only consider Dahlak to be the Stronghold, the literal place the dark forces thrive."

"And why would I relax knowing that?"

Hayden laughed. "You're all too superstitious. There's nothing to be afraid of."

Darius shrugged. "Still not a believer? After what you've just witnessed. How could you not at least wonder if the gods are real?"

An abrupt movement away from the open beach caught their attention. Something large stirred deep in the thick brush that formed an entrance to a larger forest. Hunzuu had managed to keep the Sword of Tiber, despite the shipwreck. He pulled it from its rustic scabbard. Leib removed his small daggers. The others were weaponless, having lost everything in the raging waters they'd almost drowned in.

Suddenly, over thirty people appeared from the brush, wearing primitive native attire resembling ancient spiritual rites. The line was at least fifty feet long where the beach met the trees. A young man stepped from behind the line, momentarily causing it to separate. He marched a few feet ahead of the others and stood, apparently sizing them up. No one spoke for several seconds, until the young man finally broke the monotony of the silence.

"I know what your thinking, and I wouldn't try it. The famed blade of Babylon isn't feared here. You're gods stop halfway across the sea. Our gods rule this domain. Therefore, all you hold in your hand is a common sword, like every worthless man who ever died before you."

Darius recognized the dialect. It was commonly spoken by the younger generations of Aksum, usually the easternmost provinces, if he remembered correctly. He said as much.

The young man replied, "Who are you, that you know us so well?"

Leib eagerly and angrily stepped forward. "Who is he? Who is he? I'll dare you ask who he is! He is your rightful king! You should kneel before him!"

The young man smirked. "We kneel before no man. Our allegiance died a long time ago. We're our own people now."

Darius was furious, not because the young man willingly opposed his claim to the throne, but because the young man arrogantly trampled on the memory of his father. He spoke with hostility.

"How long have you defied your king?"

"How long is unimportant, because what we've heard is that the good king is now dead. Our atrocities against him are buried in the same tomb in which he now lays."

Darius angrily stepped forward. "He was my father. He was a good and fair man. How could you ignorantly choose to resist his rule and defy his kingship?"

"He may have been the King of Aksum, but he was behind the times. His heart may have been kind, but his methods were ancient. It was time for change, time for something radical. The old methods are no longer working. The rules of society have been altered."

"That's absurd. You'd risk being sentenced to death in

order to lead a tyrannical coup against the throne. Why?"

"It's not what we're against that matters. What matters is what we're for, and what we're for is the entitlement of the younger members of society. Why should we kiss the king's hand when he's done nothing but carry a torch that further alienates us because of our youthful inexperience."

Darius was incensed. "That's not the king I knew. If you were alienated, it was because you removed yourself from his position. He was loyal to a fault and always fought to forge the differences between himself and others. He felt his role as the king was to bridge the gap between the throne and the commoners."

The man was indifferent. "Then he should have thought more progressively. Times are changing. His resistance to that fact put our people in a bad light. In an era where the Babylonians, Greeks, and Romans are all thriving and growing in popularity, our numbers continue to dwindle on a global scale. We're less respected and thought more poorly of than we've ever been. The only reason is because of an old king's refusal to follow the trends. He could've modernized our position, but he chose to keep us in the dark ages. Good riddance."

"You do understand that by being rid of the old counsel, you've opened yourself up to the foolishness of tyranny," Darius crossly stated. "What Demsas and his advisors will bring to your lives will be far worse than what you were experiencing."

"The door to progressiveness shouldn't remain closed. It

weakens our families. It disintegrates our future. It destroys our hope for becoming sought out by others who aren't like us."

"You've opened the door, now you'll have to deal with what you'll let in... Some doors remain locked, not to keep you in, but to keep other things out. Some doors are safety measures, meant to protect a way of life that's survived and empowered us since the dawn of civilization."

The young man haughtily glared at him. "Shouldn't the way of Aksum be promoted from the rooftops? Let me answer for you. It should indeed, but what good does it do to shout it when no one listens? And no one listens because our leaders have kept us in the dark."

"Well, what good is it to promote the Aksumite spirit, if its been changed by feeble attempts to keep up with those who do anything to gain popularity, but little to actually advance the wellbeing of their people. Steady may not burn as brightly, but it burns longer than the shooting star. You'd so willingly sacrifice the heritage of the past and the destiny of the future in order to gain attractiveness for today?"

The young man was put off. "You don't understand, do you, son of Adollion? You just don't get it. By making us unappealing as a culture, your father sealed our fate. We'll never achieve the greatness we could have with a more youthful and compelling leadership."

"So, what? You've chosen to be the voice of the people, the prophet crying into the darkness against the wisdom of the ages? The gods have shown you what they failed to show countless others before you? Your relationship, in your few short years, has demonstrated more sacrifice and allegiance to the gods than all the others. So, they've chosen you to be the one who changes Aksum forever? You're the chosen one? What arrogance."

The young leader looked up and down the line of people standing with him. He motioned his hands out to them in a sweeping gesture.

"We're the chosen ones. We've decided together that it is time for change in the landscape of Aksumite history. We'll do what it takes to make sure our children and children's children aren't faced with the same impossibilities and limitations that we were… And they have chosen me as their leader."

Darius' disappointment was highly visible. "Please. Don't leave the protection handed down from the elder generations. Perhaps they saw things that we can't without the experience of their years. Perhaps the largest part of honor is trusting in those who have forged the path before us. Don't you at least agree that they've earned some trust by their valor and sacrifice?"

The young man was stunned. "You only see what you want. Being a privileged child has spoiled your vision. You can see no further than the doors they've closed, and that's all they ever wanted us to see. As long as we stay this way, we'll continue to be a little feared place in the African Peninsula. Rome will tread us. Greece will attack us. Babylon will sanction us. And one of them will one day rule us. Because we're weak for not letting others assimilate into our lives. We must become more like others if we're to get others to respect us."

"We can't lose ourselves." Darius almost pleaded. "Becoming as others may lead to growth, but it doesn't lead to Aksumite maturation. We'll lose our heritage and privileges by doing it the way of the world."

The man scoffed. "We won't. Don't you understand? I'll remain who I am. I'll not stop believing what I do. I'll just stop demanding that others do. We have to loosen up on some of the big issues, despite what the elder tribune demands. There's no reason we have to be against so much that the rest of the world embraces."

Darius firmly stood his ground. "I thought being an Aksumite came with certain responsibilities the rest of the world couldn't understand. I thought it meant we had certain privileges that no one else did. But I guess you expect to keep the privileges and power without making the appropriate sacrifices."

The young man was growing severely disturbed. "Our people have given enough. We shouldn't be known for what we're against. We should be known for what we're for. That's the way it should be."

"Yet, we often find that there's no middle ground. One cannot serve the gods and the things of this world. We're either living for everlasting purpose by establishing eternal principles, or we aren't. It's that simple."

"Absurdity. You are blind."

"No, my friend. I'm afraid it's you who isn't seeing clearly. You do realize that if you continue down this path, small deviations will lead to large divisions. You're attempting to destroy fences when you have no idea the monsters they were designed to keep out."

"Well, others live happy and fulfilling lives. The rest of the world does just fine without the fences."

"And the rest of the world doesn't share our destiny…"

The young man shook his fist at Darius. "I've seen a destiny that's greater than you could ever imagine. While you pretend to have the people's interest at heart, you do nothing but pull them further into bondage. I'm a visionary, and I'll do everything I can to see the doors unlocked, the fences crumbled, and the people set free."

"By unlocking everything, making all our desires and interests a reality, you'll create a place where everything is free except the people in it. We may be free from the bylaws and protective barriers of others, but don't you understand?"

Darius was crying. "Don't you understand, the more free we are from the wisdom of those before us, the more bound we become to ourselves? Every man finds the positives of his own imaginations. All man's ways are right unto himself. We cannot depend on our own intuition when looking forward. Please."

The man looked toward the people on either side of him. He motioned to them again. "What I do, I do not for myself, I do it for them."

He looked at the small group and quickly motioned with his hand.

"Take them to the stocks. We'll hold them there until King Demsas arrives. We'll collect our reward then."

12

Hayden sat on his knees on the dirt floor of the large white tent they'd been carried to. His hands were bound behind his back, and his head had been placed in a wooden stock. The others sat around him in similar fashion. M'ya was the only one who'd been treated differently. Her hands were fitted through two separate holes in the stocks itself, one on either side of her head. None of them could move.

Hayden glanced from one to the next. It appeared that they were sleeping. Good for them. He wished he could, but the experience had proven too painful. He'd been brought into the tent and tied down before the others. It had grown dark outside before his companions had been forced to join him. His best guess was that Demsas would come at first light. They only had a few hours, and there was no way he was going to be able to get them out of this one.

His legs were cramping. He was getting choked up because of the strain on his neck. When he lurched forward, thrusting upward on his knees, he found temporary relief. He could breath more effectively without it hurting his chest and making him feel dizzy from oxygen deprivation. However, as he lowered his legs back to the dirt, to stop the severe cramping in his lower back, neck, and shoulders, he couldn't breath properly. On top of the severe pain, he found that he was growing exceptionally thirsty.

He was startled by the slight sound of something ripping behind him and slightly to his right. He was afraid, because the noise was growing in intensity, but he couldn't turn to see what was causing it. He looked toward the others, but none of them stirred. They didn't hear it.

The ripping fabric stopped after a few seconds, and he heard footsteps in the room. They were soft, but there was no mistaking their approach. Whoever was in the tent was moving right toward him. He braced himself for impending pain.

Only, there was no pain. He heard a gentle voice whisper. He didn't recognize the voice. He would've remembered a voice so clear despite its raspy quality.

"Be quiet. Don't ask questions. I'm a friend, come to get you all out of here. If I let you stay here tonight, you'll all be dead soon after sun-up tomorrow. I can't have that on my conscious."

Hayden strained to turn, but it was no use. He finally quit resisting, as the man struggled to pop the locks off the stocks that held him in place.

"Who are you?"

"We can catch up on all that later, my friend," he hurriedly replied. "For now, just trust me. I've been sent to deliver you from the snares of your enemies."

"But why?"

"Why, you ask? Why not just be content with the knowledge that I've been sent to make sure you don't die? Your life has been placed in my hands. Why is that information not enough?"

"I'm sorry, stranger. You're right. Hurry and get me loose so that we can get my friends free."

The man stopped working to lift the heavy upper stock. "I wasn't sent for them. I was only sent for you. I'm here to get you to safety."

Hayden resisted, "Well, sir, I'm afraid you're going to fail whoever has sent you if you aren't going to help me save them. I won't leave them here to die. If they're going to be punished tomorrow, I shall be punished with them."

"Ok," the man sarcastically replied, "you're definitely the man of whom I've heard. I'll get you and your friends to safety."

"Thank you," Hayden said, as the man pulled against his upper stock again. After a few seconds, the chain cracked and fell to the floor. The man lifted the heavy wooden beam from Hayden's neck, and Hayden gingerly stood up. He took a couple of steps before collapsing, unable to get his feet solidly underneath him.

The stranger lifted him to his feet again. They approached the others and quietly began undoing their stocks. After releasing Darius, Hayden left them to go and untie M'ya from the beam she'd been fixed to. After releasing her, they embraced for a second. Then he shoved her away and made his way toward the others. She slowly followed. After a couple more minutes, everyone was free in the room.

The firelight flickered from a small lamp that had been left burning in the midst of their tent. Hayden looked into the man's eyes. He was a regal man, about sixty years of age, and of Middle Eastern descent. Behind his steely stare, his eyes were sensitive, apprehensive, and kind. He extended his hand to Darius, greeting him with the traditional Roman handshake.

"You're the rightful king of Aksum I presume? Pleasure to make your acquaintance. Your father was an exceptional leader. Your people need someone to believe in again. I've heard that you could be that man."

Darius smiled and let go of the man's hand. "It's an honor to be mentioned in the same breath as my father. For now, let's just get out of this place before we're noticed. Do you know the best way out of here?"

The stranger nodded. "I do indeed, although it will be much harder to slip through with so many of us. Please, everyone stay close and remain calm. We mustn't let them hear us."

The man led them out of the tiny hole he'd cut through the back of the tent. Once outside, they gathered around the opening, and then followed him single file around two of the outermost tents. Once past the tents, they slipped into a shallow ditch running along the camp. The meadow they'd camped in had been an old cornfield that hadn't been used for many years. The shallow line was an irrigation run-off still damp from recent rain. Despite the mud and residual water still in the ditch, they stealthily crawled through, finally falling out of it one hundred and forty yards past the nearest tent.

The man leading them rose to one knee beside some thick brush and pointed to a wall two hundred yards into the field.

"I've got a boat behind that wall. All we need is to wait for the diversion, and then we'll make a run for it. I'm hoping the diversion will be enough to attract the guards away from the gate. If they'll reveal themselves, we should be able to easily avoid them and get to the boat."

"Distraction?" Hunzuu asked, wondering at their strategic position.

The man lightly laughed. "It should be occurring any time now."

As if on cue, a loud scream was heard from inside one of the large tents that housed some of the soldiers. Lamps brightly filled the night sky halfway into the camp. Darius impatiently shifted his feet. The stranger put his hand on Darius' shoulder.

"Wait for it. It's almost time."

Wailing erupted from tents on the opposite side of the camp. Lamps were quickly lit from that direction as well. The stranger pointed toward the wall. One by one, the guards began running toward the campsite, leaving their post exposed. After the last man passed them, the stranger motioned the group forward.

"Run," he yelled, as he leapt to his feet and led the charge. "Don't look back."

Hayden stayed next to M'ya as they ran. He was surprised how quickly she covered ground. Leib was having a hard time keeping up, so Hunzuu picked the small man up with one arm and carried him. His biceps bulged as he lifted Leib from the ground like he was nothing.

They were thirty yards from the large fence line when two guards appeared from the backside. The one on the right was the obvious alpha male. Quickly drawing his weapon, he carefully moved toward them. The other guard warily moved in line behind the first. The only threatening feature of the second guard was the fact that he held the sword of Tiber in his hands. Other than that, he appeared to be a non-factor. Sweat dripped down his face, and he was strangely out of breath.

The stranger stopped running, and the rest of the group caught up within seconds. Hayden looked over their back trail and was surprised to find no one pursuing them. Everyone appeared preoccupied with whatever was taking place in the camp.

The first guard stepped even closer. "Halt, in the name of

our king. Move no further."

The stranger held his hand low. "Please. Lay down your weapon and move away. No blood need be shed today. You can turn around and leave. We have no quarrel with you. You don't have to get hurt."

"I've no plans on getting hurt. I have a weapon. You don't. I may not get you all, but at least two of you will die before scaling the wall. Which two shall it be?"

He pretended to contemplate his own question. "How about the wannabe king and the girl? The elf I'll kill just because he's too small to climb over on his own."

The stranger wasn't rattled. "This is your last chance to leave peacefully. If you don't, your life cannot be spared."

The man held his sword higher. "Well, I have no choice but to…"

His final sentence was never completed. The second guard rammed the sword of Tiber through the man's back, the reason for his apparent nervous becoming obvious. He was a plant, an insider in the enemy's camp.

The first guard fell forward, never fully aware what had taken his life. The insider quickly yanked the Sword of Tiber from the fallen soldier and placed it back in the scabbard. Once sheathed, he unbuckled the belt holding the weapon in place and tossed it toward Hunzuu.

"I believe this belongs to you."

The stranger stepped toward the man and embraced him.

"I see you delivered the contents like I'd asked."

The man smiled. "You are devious for such a holy man. How many snakes did you have in each bag?"

"Ten."

The guard shook his head. "Devious indeed."

Darius stepped forward. "I don't understand. What's going on?"

The guard laughed again. "Your friend here had me turn vipers loose in the camp. I placed the barely opened bags in several tents, giving me enough time to get back here before they all crawled out, starting utter mayhem."

The stranger moved toward the fence. "We can reminisce later, if we all survive. Let's get off this island."

Hayden nodded. "Lead the way. We're a step behind."

The two men turned and quickly scaled the wall. Hunzuu picked Leib up and lifted him high enough that Leib could grab the top and pull himself over. Hayden turned to help M'ya but found that she was already half way over the wall. He waited until the last one of them was over, and then took the sword off the fallen soldier. Once last look indicated that there were still no guards in sight. He reached the wall, climbed over the side, and joined the others in their flight toward the boat.

They gathered around the sixteen-foot rowboat's small frame. The stranger stood beside it and motioned for them to get in.

"Hurry. Don't worry. The waves are higher than normal, but we don't have far to go. The Stronghold is just over the other side of the water. It's only a good hour's row."

"Who are you?" Darius asked, trying to keep his balance while stepping inside the boat.

"Isn't it obvious," Leib replied. "He's the Jew, the one who's been spreading his dogma about the one God."

Realization hit them at once. The missionary had rescued them. They silently stared in his direction, as the would-be guard shoved them away from the shoreline.

A few minutes later, the young leader of the island they'd just been on came barreling over the wall followed by ten soldiers. He shook his head in disgust. They'd checked the prisoners' tents and all of them were gone. It hadn't taken long to find the dead guard and figure out that the serpents had been a distraction. He looked at the lead soldier.

"I'm sorry. We had them."

"Yes, you did have them... Key word did," the leader sadistically replied. "Demsas won't be pleased."

"We're sorry," the man pleaded, and then moved back toward the city.

The leader looked at the man standing next to him. "They've chosen to walk alone... Show them what happens to those who chose to step away from protection. Kill them all."

"Yes, sir," the soldier eagerly replied. "Within the hour.

The leader stared hard into the converging obscurity. He wasn't sure, but deep inside the fog he thought he saw movement. For a second, he thought he'd seen a boat. Then, the boat had disappeared, being swallowed by deeper motion around it. If it had been a vessel, it was in danger. Something dark and vile was closing in on it from behind.

Something wicked.

Something frightening.

Something naturally unexplainable.

13

Torben parked in front of the trendy bookstore and jogged around to the other side of the car. She was already climbing out as he reached for her door handle.

"Thanks, but there's no need for chivalry," she begrudgingly stated.

"Some people haven't lost it," he replied. "A man should still treat a woman with respect."

She warmly grinned. "Agreed, but it's not expected... I'm not a weaker vessel, detective."

"No, ma'am. You aren't. I wasn't insinuating that. Think nothing of it." He shyly looked around. "Habit, I suppose."

He walked to the door and held it open for her. She laughed as she passed through.

"Just can't help yourself, can you?"

"Guess not."

He hurriedly moved to a computer table in the back of the store. A young African-American girl was sitting at the table playing a word game on the screen. The only sound in the area was the folk music coming from the ceiling speakers and the incessant chomping of the young girl's gum. He sat in the chair beside her and placed two twenty-dollar bills on the table. She looked up at him.

"It's yours if I can have this computer for ten minutes," he quietly said.

She moved the arrow on the screen to the black "x" in the top right corner of the open window in the browser. It closed down with the click of her mouse. She quickly pocketed the money before he changed his mind, smiled, and left the table. He scooted to the chair the girl had just vacated and motioned for his companion to sit beside him. She sat in the empty chair and scooted closer.

He emptied the contents of the envelop onto the table. There were a lot of documents and a compact disk. He hurriedly removed the disk from the pile and inserted it into the computer tray. The computer recognized the new software and opened the contents on the screen.

The words were written in symbols he didn't understand. He looked at the girl next to him.

"Recognize this?"

She shook her head. "No. It's not remotely familiar."

He clicked on a few random buttons, hoping something would work. After the fourth attempt, the screen went blank, the computer whined, and then automatically shut down. He quickly reached for the disk, but the computer wouldn't eject it. He tried to reboot, but it was fried.

"The disk must have inserted a virus. The entire system crashed." Torben moaned.

"I see that," the girl replied, "but we've got more pressing problems."

Torben followed her pointed finger toward the front desk. Three men were approaching it, their eyes darting back and forth, obviously searching for someone. Torben fell out of his chair and knelt down beside the computer. From where they were, the men couldn't see them. They were walking around, talking to people in the room. The furthest one was about to reach the black girl he'd just paid to give up her chair.

"We're running out of time," she said, as she started to move away from him. "We have to get out of here."

"I can't leave this disk," he said, while quickly grabbing the papers from the table and stuffing them into the envelope again.

"We can always come back. Please, let's just get out of here."

"C'mon. C'mon." He urged the computer to eject the disk,

as he furiously punched the buttons. It wouldn't respond to his demands.

Finally, he ripped the plug from the back wall and lifted the entire computer from the floor, leaving the monitor and plugs behind. He motioned for her to follow and moved toward the back of the store. The only door had a sign that read *Employees Only*. It didn't matter; rules seldom do when one is faced with danger. He bolted through it, pulling her along. As the door closed behind them, he turned to see if they'd been noticed. The black girl was pointing to the computer corner they'd just vacated. The men aggressively converged on that location.

"Move. Move." He said, as he abruptly shoved her backward, further into the room, stopping long enough to look around. It was an obvious storage area, stacked high with boxes of sealed books. Some new and needing to be placed on the shelves, others old and needing to be properly disposed of. He quickly scanned the back walls, looking for an exit. There was none.

They ducked behind a large crate, just as someone emerged from the rear of the room. The door opened on the opposite end, and one of the men stepped into the storeroom with his gun drawn. He flipped on a switch just inside the door. A few lights flickered, halfway illuminating the previously dark space.

The person who had emerged from the back of the room moved toward the entrance. "You aren't supposed to be back here. What are you do-"

He never finished the sentence, instantly recognizing the outline of the gun as the perpetrator came into view. "Please. Take what you'd like. Just don't kill me."

"It's okay," the man lied. "I'm a police officer. I'm looking for two suspects, a man and a woman. Did they come in here?"

"No, sir. No one here but me."

The man holstered his weapon. "Is there a way out of here, a back entrance perhaps?"

"No, sir," the man anxiously shook his head. "The only way out is through the front door."

The man looked around, unsure if he believed the employee or not. Finally, he grinned. "Okay, if you see or hear anything, you let us know."

"Sure." The worker tensely replied, as the man disappeared back through the door.

After a few moments, the employee walked to the entrance and peered through the window into the main store. He saw the armed man join two others near the entrance. They were still searching the store. The man flipped the light switch back off, removing the little visibility in the room. He turned around.

"You can come out now. I know you're in here."

Torben paused for a second; putting his hand on the girl's next to him. Motioning for her to remain quiet, he released her hand and stood.

"Quickly," the man motioned. "Follow me, before they find out I lied."

Torben's face must have appeared confused. The man smiled.

"If he's with the police, I'm a cosmonaut… There's another way out, howbeit, not conventional. It empties into the alleyway. You better move quickly. They're still looking. It's only a matter of time before they find out you never left the building."

Torben motioned, and the girl hurriedly left her hiding place and joined him near the man. "Show us the way."

The man swiftly moved toward a back hallway. At the rear off the hall was a small office space. On the back wall was an open window.

"Over there." He pointed.

Torben touched the man on the shoulder. "Thank you, sir."

The man nodded and looked at the computer Torben was still clutching under his right arm. "You plan on taking that?"

"Have to. What I need… what they're after… is locked inside. I can't leave it behind."

The man had an inquisitive expression, but didn't ask. "Luck to you," he called, as Torben followed the young woman out the window and into the alley.

14

The boat hit the shore, and the motley crew didn't delay in removing themselves from its diminutive sides. The waves had rocked it back and forth for the past couple of hours. After narrowly escaping the sea, the last thing they'd wanted was to find themselves traveling back across the water in a vessel one twentieth the size of the first one.

As her feet hit the ground, M'ya fell from the boat and spread her arms across the sandy beach. The Jew laughed.

"Tis good to be alive, is it not? That's what I've always said. Rejoice while you may, for no man knows the hour when death will come."

Hayden wasn't in the mood for theological assessment. He weakly smiled, placing his hand on the man's shoulder and leading him away from the group.

"I appreciate you saving us, sir, but where are we going? Why have you brought us here?"

The man snapped his head and glared into Hayden's eyes. "Until this evening, my entire mission hasn't made sense. I knew I had purpose. I knew I had a calling, but never knew why, until today."

"I'm afraid I don't understand."

"And you can't, sir. Not yet, but one day you shall."

"What do you mean?"

The man was somber, as if trying to impart some ancient wisdom.

"All men have purpose, some great and some small. Yet, all have purpose that when knit together forms the tapestry of life. Without the large pieces, the smaller ones wouldn't matter. But without the small pieces, the larger ones would have nothing binding them together. Everyone's purpose matters, Sir Hayden."

Hayden shrugged. "What of it?"

"I've always struggled with that," the man sternly replied.

"Why?"

"All men want greatness, but few possess the inner strength to achieve it. Sure, anyone can become affluent, socially admired, or worldly successful. But that doesn't equate to significance. Significance has a greater value. It's the quality defined by the world's true champions, those brave souls who shutter at the thought of failure and are willing to give anything... everything to ensure that others are given the gift of eternity."

"I don't understand your riddles, Jew. Speak plainly."

"Some men are mere vessels along the river of life, vessels that carry important truths across cultures. Others are merely the flowers that blow in the breeze, reminding us that God works in mysterious ways, choosing to pollinate the land, bringing sustenance and beauty from something so fragile... I'm but such a man."

"I am sure-"

The man held up his hand, immediately silencing Hayden's interruption.

"Others are the oars, propelling truth forward. Others are the dams along the way, cultivating life in otherwise desolate places. And seldom the world finds those... those few who are the river itself, the very essence of what brings life."

Hayden felt a gentle tingle down his spine. The man noticed his uncomfortable expression.

"You felt it, didn't you, Sir Hayden? Revelation; it touched you."

"I don't know. I-"

"You did. You felt it, and the reason is because you are such a man."

"Please, I don't-"

"You are... My purpose, my life, I've always searched for the reason of my existence, but standing here today, I've found it. Everything I've been through. My hurts, my pains, my horror stories, my unfair and unsettling experiences. It's all created me, bringing me into the fullness of what I now am. I'm the culmination of pain, regret, misfortune, prejudice, and the hard persistence of pursuing the One true God. His plan and purpose have been my only ambition. Pleasing him has brought me here, and there's no going back."

"But-"

"My entire reason for existing, Sir Hayden, is so that today, on this day, I can stand before God and declare your importance in His agenda. I'm merely the messenger. He is the message. You are the intended recipient."

"But you've been here over a year. You've converted many to your faith. Surely that counts for something to your God. Surely that means something to him."

"Of course it does. He reaches for all men equally."

"Then why do you declare that I'm so important that he'd waste your life to find me?"

"Because, Sir Hayden, you're an instrument in his hand. You're purpose is still being discovered. Your course is still being set, but your steps are ordered. It's my duty, my honor and privilege, to shed light into your world. Hopefully, it'll be my honor to illuminate your pathway and enable you to freely choose the will of the Father. You must stop resisting what you feel, Sir Hayden. You must give yourself to its pull."

"No. I can't. I'm not sure—"

He knowingly smiled, "No one is ever ready. It's too big. The weight of eternity demands too much. One must forfeit a great deal. The calling is always littered with costly decisions. The path is paved with the sacrifices of many. However, some give all, lay lives down 'til their appointment with death."

Hayden was skeptical. "That sounds painful. Who would do such a thing? Who could pay such high a cost?"

"Those who have unknowingly embraced His heartbeat, been predestined, and have the responsibility of being given a true servant's heart. Only those who have lost themselves in His higher purpose, sometimes without even realizing they've embraced His calling."

"I've never been that man. How can you say—"

"Oh, but you have, Sir Hayden. You fight to save the thieves, when you could have just walked away; your heart in caring for the disfigured and handicapped while visiting the Wards; your selection of slaves, misfits, and rejects to bring Amarsin, himself an outcast, to the Fortress; your laying your life on the line to bring truth to various leaders; even your persistent belief that Abaddon Dearth could change and come to the light. Your entire life betrays you, Sir Hayden. Pretend if you must, but your humble unwillingness to accept your significance makes you such a man."

Hayden was dumbfounded. "So you believe I've been following a god I don't even know."

"You may not have known Him, but Sir Hayden, He has known you. He's always known you."

"And if this be true, as you so fervently believe, what then is my purpose?"

He considered the question. "I don't know. I only see in part. I'm only the fading flower, just a small piece to a much larger tapestry. My duty isn't to see the entire picture. It's too large for my finite comprehension. My only duty is to do my part and make sure that the puzzle doesn't fade because of my irresponsibility. You're the reason I've stayed through the persecution and chaos. You're the reason I'm here."

The man's tears demonstrated his passionate belief of what he was saying. His eyes held Hayden's in a fixed gaze. "My life is meaningful, because I have the distinct pleasure of introducing you to Him."

"How can you willingly lay it all down for one you cannot see?" Hayden struggled to understand.

"How can you not?" The man retorted, not comprehending Hayden's reluctance.

"My emotions preclude me from such commitment to one I cannot fathom."

"But you can fathom Him, Sir Hayden. You've felt anger and animosity toward Him. I've known your rage. You've felt the heavy burden of His resentment and the sting of what you thought was His rejection. You've been there... But you've also felt the warmth of His embrace... you've felt the nervous tingle of His love and the uncomfortable chill of His gaze upon you. Those moments; the unexplained tears, the mysterious nostalgic feelings, and the baffling nearness of a presence you couldn't explain; that was Him walking near. For how can you stand in the presence of such a holy and majestic God and not be thus impacted. His aura demands a reaction from the futile confines of meager humanity."

"I may have felt such feelings before." Hayden sheepishly agreed.

The missionary sounded slightly agitated. "Don't try to fool yourself. You know exactly what I'm speaking of, and that's why you also know the answer to your own question about willingly laying your life down. Our lives, all of us, Sir Hayden, are for His purpose. We live and die, all for the glory of our King. We find true happiness in bringing Him pleasure, for this is where we truly belong. Everything we've ever needed, it's all that He's ever wanted. Man's greatest need is His greatest desire."

"What is that?" Hayden asked, awaiting revelation.

"The answer to all our hardships and heartaches is a relationship with Him, and that relationship is the one thing He's always craved. But we must be willing to individually give ourselves to Him, the way He has given Himself to us. Completely."

Hayden walked further away from the group and knelt down in the sand. The man sat down beside him. Hayden timidly looked into his eyes. "Please, tell me more about this One God."

15

Dr. Poole entered the room. She was sitting at his bedside, slouched over in the chair. Her head was positioned on his bed, next to his right arm. A Bible was lying open on the bed next to them. It was obvious that she'd been reading to him and had unintentionally fallen asleep. He cleared his throat, attempting to softly awaken her. She slowly lifted her head and looked at the clock.

"I slept into the morning, I'm afraid."

"Yes, you did," he worriedly replied. "You should really go home. I'm sure your husband misses you by now. You've hardly been away from this bed the last four weeks except to shower and come right back. I'm sure your husband could use you."

"Pish Posh. He should come here and see our son-in-law if he wants to see me. You would think a man who could help run the country could forgive a young man's transgressions."

Dr. Poole moved closer toward her. "I'm sure he will. Everyone heals in his or her own way and in his or her own time. You know that. He'll eventually come around. Don't give up on him either."

"I suppose you're right, doc. Just hurts sometimes."

She paused, thoughtfully eyeing him. "You know, Hayden is all we've got left of our little girl. She loved him with everything inside her. He was the man of her dreams. She wanted nothing else but to have a family with him and live happy forever. They were so great together. Why'd he do this? How'd this happen?"

Dr. Poole didn't answer. She looked at him for a moment and then continued.

"I know you don't know. I'm asking more just to think than I am to find a real reason. I know I'm asking for the impossible. I guess that's why I'm pulling for him so hard."

"Why's that?"

"Because, she gave him her heart. If he dies, the last piece of my baby girl is gone."

She was crying. "He has to hold on. Dr. Poole, he has to."

Dr. Poole awkwardly put his arm around her shoulder, pulling her near him in a sideways embrace. She turned her head and placed it on his shoulder and sobbed. After a few seconds, she composed herself.

"I'm sorry. I shouldn't act that way. A woman of my stature must demonstrate dignity at all times. Can you imagine what they'd put in the magazines and newspapers if they'd taken my picture just now? It wouldn't have looked good for my husband."

The doctor groaned. "I guess not. Celebrity comes with a high price."

"It does indeed. You have no idea," she murmured.

Dr. Poole looked in the charts to see what the nurse had recorded from the morning rounds. He eyed the notes intently. Finally, he looked down at the woman before him.

"Have you noticed any movement from him?"

"No. Nothing. Should I have?"

"I don't know. There are neurological signs demonstrating that movement has occurred. Has he convulsed or had seizures?"

"No. Nothing like that at all."

"Eye blinks? Feet or leg shifts? Shown any response to touch? Anything?"

"No, Doctor Poole. Why? You're scaring me."

"No need to be frightened. I'm just covering the basics. Make sure to continue reading to him. Hold his hand. Rub his arm every now and then. The more tactile stimulation he receives, the better."

"I'll continue to do those things, Dr. Poole. Keep me

informed of any changes please."

"I will. You'll know everything as it happens."

She nodded in his direction and smiled, as he turned and walked away. The door closed behind him, leaving her alone with her comatose son-in-law. She touched his hand and leaned more closely too him. Her lips were almost touching his ear as she whispered.

"Hayden, I must tell you something. I pray to the heavens that you can hear me. I want you to know that I forgive you for all actions that led to my daughter's death. I forgive you for anything that led to the death of your children… I know you loved them. I can't imagine the hell you've lived with, nor the pain you've carried alone… I love you, Hayden. I love you, because you loved her. I love you, because you were her life, and I cherish every memory of her."

It was so subtle; she thought she'd imagined it. A tear gently glided down his right cheek. She watched it fall from his eyes and land on the white gown he was wearing. He gently squeezed her hand, and then suddenly released it, falling back into whatever far away place he'd been.

She sat dazed for a moment. Had she really felt his hand move or was it just wishful thinking. After several minutes, she was still undecided. So, she took the Bible out and started to read from where she'd left off.

"Yea though I walk through the valley of the shadow of death, I will fear no evil, for thou art with me…"

16

Torben sat in the backseat of the Taxi with the young woman who'd been running with him. He coolly looked her over. She was painfully beautiful.

"I'm sorry. I don't even know your name. Never thought to ask."

"It's okay, because under these circumstances, I was told not to give it. The doctor warned me that I shouldn't speak unless spoken to, and the less others know about me, the better."

"Good advice. What can I call you then?"

She thought for a second, looking around. Finding nothing that satisfied her criteria for a good name, she stared down.

"I don't know. How about... How about-"

"Jane." He interrupted.

She laughed. "So cliché, but sure. Jane it is."

"Well, Jane, it's a good thing we took the computer. I think I know someone who can help figure out what's on it."

. . .

Twenty minutes later, the cab pulled up in front of a small, silver camper attached to an old, beat up Ford pickup truck. Torben removed a few folded bills from his pocket and handed them to the cabbie.

"Thanks, and keep the change."

The man waved as he pulled away, leaving Torben and Jane standing near the camper. Torben sniggered as he moved toward the camper's door.

"Get ready for this. It should prove most interesting."

The door cracked, and a wide-eyed gentleman cautiously appeared between the small gap. His bifocals magnified his eyes more than twice their normal size. His hair was matted in the places he wasn't going bald, and a beard and mustache casually covered his face, making him appear like half the suspects on America's Most Wanted.

"What do you want?" he demanded.

Torben laughed. "Gino, c'mon man. You know me."

"I know someone who once looked like you, but you

could be anyone." He uneasily stated, stammering without looking directly at them. He spoke too rapidly, and his head constantly scanned the environment, as if he thought someone was covertly searching for him.

"Gino. It's only been three years man. It hasn't been that long. Take a close look. It's me." Torben stated matter-a-factly.

"You could be anybody. There's doppelgangers, government cloning, latex masking, and voice modulation."

Torben tried to stifle his amusement, as he reached into his pocket to retrieve his driver's license. "G. C'mon man. Enough of the show already. I can tell ya, this lady isn't impressed by your antics."

Gino leaned closer to the narrow slit in the door, suspiciously eyeing the plastic card in Torben's hand. "Don't mean nothing, nothing at all. Anybody can fake a license these days. Most teenagers have at least one that could fool authorities. You could be anybody."

"Or I could be a terminator come back from time to destroy the world. Have you seen Sarah Conner?" He joked, using his best Arnold Schwarzenegger impersonation.

"Mock me? The real Torben wouldn't mock me. He knows I don't like being mocked. You made a mistake. I see through your clever disguise."

"G, if I wasn't really who I said, why would I be here, right now, talking to you."

"Because, I know your secrets. I know what's going on. I know things, man. I know things you don't want getting out there," he rattled off, apprehensively peering out the window.

"But wouldn't I just kill you, if I didn't want the world to know those things? Why would I drive all the way out here, knock on your door, and ask you to talk?"

"Mind tricks. You… you… you're trying to mess with my head. You want to know what I know. You want to get to the others. You think I'll tell you more. But… but… I won't… can't… not gonna let you get to them. Not me. Not this time… No… not gonna give them up."

Jane shoved Torben over a little and extended her slim hand through the doorway. "G, Gino, whoever you are… look, we're with you. We've accidentally come across sensitive information that we need to access before others move in on us and take it. We've tried, but we aren't able to get it open with our limited computer savvy."

Her impatience was obvious. She stopped and pointed toward Torben. "Mr. Torben here, and this is the real Torben, suggested that we find you for help. He swore that you're the best in the business when it comes to computers. I'm not sure what we need, but I know we need you to let us in."

"No. No. No." He violently shook his head. "Torben Mayes would never come to me for help. He was too good to hang out with me. He wouldn't need the sleek geek's assistance. He used to make fun of me."

She turned to Torben, who shrugged his shoulders. "We

sort of grew up together. Same neighborhood anyway. I grew up tough, and he... well, he just grew up finding a calamity under every stone."

"You brought us to a conspiracy theorist?" She defiantly asked. "Why would you-"

"Because he also happens to be the best computer programmer in the country," he whispered. "He's one of the world's most well kept secrets. He should be working for NASA or something."

She turned back toward the door. "He says he's very sorry, and he wishes to apologize to you in person. Please, let us in, before they find us outside your home."

"You must leave at once. I don't need unwanted attention. Please, if they're looking for you, you'll lead them to me. Go. Go. Go."

Torben stood back in the crack. "There was a day you would've jumped all over this man. What's mellowed you?"

"Know too much. Learned too much. It's dangerous to get involved." He was shaking.

"And what have you learned, G?"

"Can't tell you. Can't tell... won't."

"Why not? Why won't you tell me?"

"Cuz if you're really him... really Torben Mayes... and... and I tell you. I'd be putting your life in danger... if you aren't him... then I would be... would be ratting myself out.

Not gonna... can't do that."

Torben stepped closer. "Think G. If I wasn't me, if I was one of them, would I really come knock on your door and politely ask for help, or would I have already kicked your door in?"

The door closed. A moment later, it opened again and Gino motioned for them to step inside. As he shut the door behind them, he took a quick look around outside.

"Are you sure you weren't followed?" he asked, his fingers moving uncontrollably at his side.

"Yes, G... Do you really live like this? Must be stressful."

"You have no idea. But they're out there, man... They're killing the truth. They want us to stay dumbed down, man. Like stool pigeons... They just want us to believe whatever they feed us, man... But we can't... We gotta stop believing the lies."

Jane shifted uncomfortably. She took a quick assessment of the trailer. The walls were littered with Styrofoam sheets from ceiling to floor. Behind the sheets, tin foil strategically lined the walls as well. Hanging on the Styrofoam walls were small pictures held by pushpins. Several photos of the Apollo Space Missions made a montage in one corner. Kennedy and other famously assassinated world leaders made a nice pictorial assortment in another section. Various images of UFOs randomly lined other parts of the wall. She struggled to bring her attention back to him.

"Who? Who's lying?" She managed to ask.

"The big government, man. They're pushing us over the edge... Getting ready for the end, man... The final countdown... Moving to the apocalypse... Armageddon, man."

Torben sat down on a small couch. "You've been saying the same thing since high school, G. You still preaching that stuff?"

"Noah built the big boat for one hundred and twenty years before the flood came. I'm gonna keep making the people aware... Somebody gotta warn those who'll listen."

Torben shook his head. "I gave up trying to get you to listen to reality a long time ago, G. You really gotta stop and take a look at what you're saying. Your momma would cry to know how far the apple has fallen from the tree."

Gino hung his head low and angrily replied. "Leave her outta this, man. She's got nothing to do with this. She's dying, man. Dying in a hospital room... Dying and I can't even go see her... I can't."

Jane sat down beside Torben, obviously moved by Gino's last statement.

"What's wrong with your mom, Gino?"

"My sister says it's cancer... Breast cancer... Sister been wearing the pink ribbons."

"I'm sorry, Gino. Why can't you go to her?"

"Because, man... They gave it to her. They made her sick so they could get to me. I can't let them find me."

Torben expelled air from his nostrils. "Gino, look how easily I found you. If they really wanted to find you, it's not that hard."

"No... No... How'd you find me? You, you had to ask my sister. She told you where I'd be... I move around... Move around a lot... Never in one place often... Throw them off my tracks... My sister is the only one who knows... You talked to her... But she'd never tell the others... Never... She knows."

Jane placed her foot down hard over Torben's, quietly signaling him to be quiet. She appeared concerned.

"Gino, who made your mom sick?"

"The government. They make people sick. AIDS. Ebola. Cancer. Other so-called incurable diseases."

She was appalled. "Why would the United States government secretly condone such activity? I'm sorry, Gino, but that doesn't make sense."

Gino anxiously shook his head. "It... It does if you... If you're trying to generate money. You introduce a disease and people spend billions of taxpayer dollars and anonymous donations searching for a cure that the government already has. It's a scam. Not to mention the money that's generated in healthcare costs from people who suffer from the ailments. It's the perfect con."

"You can't really believe-"

"I do believe it. I know it." He adamantly insisted.

It was Torben's turn to tap the top of her foot. She backed off her intense inquiry. "Sorry about your mother, Gino. Maybe we could arrange a private visit, without anyone knowing."

"No. No. No." He paced. "You just don't get it, do you? You have no idea how high up this goes. How many eyes they have on us. They're always watching. Always. Everything we do is seen. You know that, right? Nothing sacred. Nothing private. They're always watching man. Eyes everywhere."

"Everywhere? That's absurd. Don't you think you're just a little paranoid?"

Torben cringed and whispered toward her ear, "You shouldn't have. You're asking for it."

"Paranoid... You think I'm paranoid... You just don't know what I know... They're watching everything... All the time... From everywhere," he screamed.

"Okay, amuse me," she lowered her tone, trying to downgrade his agitation." How? How can they see me all the time? Everywhere?"

He calmed, and then looked at her. "Satellite imagery for one. They can zoom in from outer space and watch you anywhere. The images can even switch from thermal to infrared, creating a high definition image of you even under ceilings or behind walls. You aren't covered anywhere."

"That doesn't hap-"

"Street cameras, traffic lights, security feeds, cell phone cameras, computer cameras... It's all networked... They can use your own electronic devices against you... I'm telling you... They're trying to control the world through technology."

"The United States government is trying to control the world, what a-"

He interrupted again, "Oh, no. No. No. You still aren't seeing it. It's not just the United States. No. No. No. It's so much bigger. Global... One world government, man... The beast of Babylon... the spirit of the End Time... Our days are numbered... They don't want us to know."

"If a conspiracy this huge is taking place, why don't we know about it? If a group of people are trying to undermine humanity, why hasn't the public been made aware?"

He looked at her with sympathy, like he couldn't imagine her elementary lack of understanding.

"It's the media, man... They control everything... If they want you to vote for a certain candidate, then they control the outcomes by making one man sound like god and the other look like an outcast. They only give the public the information that will fuel their agenda. Thank God... Thank God the newspaper is considered to be a dying faction... because it's one medium that has controlled us for years. Then there was the television. Now, there's the Internet. Their onslaught never stops... The enemy never sleeps..."

"So you really believe the media has dumbed us down to the point of-"

"Sheeple, that's what we are... Like lambs to the slaughter. We follow and blindly believe the lies. We... We believe whatever they tell us... And they lead us further and further from reality."

"I don't know, Gino. Sounds like you're pretty far out there by yourself."

"No. No. No. I'm not alone. Gino isn't by himself. There are others who know the truth... But we stay away from each other... We don't want to bring others down with us... We communicate when we have to, but we encrypt our data in ways only others in our group could know... We have a system."

Torben interrupted. "So, let's say that someone else created another system, another encryption for communication, could you decipher it for me."

He smiled. "Did the U.S. fake an entire generation into believing they'd put people on the moon?"

Jane disgustedly shook her head. "So you won't help us then?"

He smirked in her direction. "She's green... A true nonbeliever... The answer to that last question was yes."

"Wait, she asked, rather annoyed. "You really believe we never landed on-"

"I have proof... More lies... The photos... The shadows don't match... The flag couldn't have been blowing because the moon has no wind... The pictures were too perfect to have been taken by people in space suits... The American flag is highly visible in every shot, although everything else in the frame is obscured in darkness..."

"Please. You can't be serious."

He sat down in a chair opposite the couch. "You've been drinking the Kool-aid. They have you hook, line, and sinker. Just another lamb for the sheeple."

She shook her head and looked at Torben. "Let's get out of here. This is a waste of time."

Gino put his hand on her knee, as she tried to sit up. "Okay, if I'm wrong, then what's the purpose of Aldrin's tears?"

"What? I don't know-" she confusedly asked.

He challenged her with his stare. "Buzz Aldrin, the astronaut not named Neil Armstrong. He's been asked more than once what it felt like to walk on the moon. He evaded the question every time and even cried because he didn't want to answer. Guilt, I tell you... Guilt."

She knocked his hand away and moved toward the door. Torben stood and quickly grabbed her.

"Please, don't leave yet. He may be a little out there-"

She was mad. "A little. That's an understatement. He's a lot out there. He needs psychiatric help."

"He may. I don't know. But one thing I do know. He's the only person available who can crack this encryption."

17

The missionary and Hayden rejoined the others on the beach. M'ya moved near Hayden and took his hand in hers.

"You've been gone a while. Everything alright?"

"Yes, better than ever right now. I'm starting to see things more clearly."

"That's a good thing," Hunzuu interrupted, "because perhaps you can tell me what that is hovering over the water."

They turned to where Hunzuu was pointing. Velvety darkness hung over the sea's surface, suspended just off the coastline. It appeared to be a dark fog, too substantial to be natural. Its thickness was apparent, more than a vapor hanging in the atmosphere. It appeared to be alive. It had no eyes, but it almost gave the impression of staring toward them.

"What is that?" Hayden eagerly asked the missionary.

The missionary motioned for them to move further inland. He was obviously disturbed. They followed him, running toward the high rocks a couple hundred feet directly away from the coastline.

Finally reaching the rocks, they turned around to observe it still suspended as it had been.

"Look at it," Leib insisted. "The wind is whipping toward the southwest, but it's slowly moving northeast, toward us. It's not an atmospheric phenomenon. It's choosing its path independently of the environment."

Hunzuu moved before the missionary. "Sir, what is that thing? You have to know."

The missionary turned toward them. "I've never seen it. I've only heard the tales."

Hunzuu wouldn't let up. "Tell us what it is."

"I don't know for sure, but the locals call it *dhambi za watu.*"

Darius shook his head. "No. It can't be. I've heard the tales as a child. It isn't supposed to be real."

"Yet, there it is," the missionary retorted.

Hunzuu was growing impatient. "Somebody better tell me what that thing is."

Darius faced him, horror across his expression. "It's the *dhambi za watu;* the sins of the people."

"Speak the proper language, Darius. I don't know what that means. What is it?"

"Folklore. I don't know that anyone has ever actually seen it. It's talked about in the dark myths, forbidden stories told 'round ancient campfires. Stories too old to fathom and too horrific to be remembered."

Leib looked toward it again. It seemed to be edging nearer. He shook his head and looked toward Hayden and Hunzuu.

"I've heard the dreadful yarns. There's nothing we can do. It can't be stopped. It never materializes unless it's threatened, but once it becomes visible, it doesn't leave until it's devoured its target. We're all in danger."

The missionary turned to them. "He's right. It can't be stopped."

Hunzuu leapt forward and stood toward the outer edge of the group, standing closest to the dark cloud. "Anything can be stopped. There's nothing that can't be put down."

The missionary shook his head in a negative response. "Sorry, but this is no such thing. Man's most earnest attempts to defeat it only add to its rage. There's nothing mere mortality can do to combat it."

Hunzuu was livid. "That's absurd. Tell me why mortals can't tame these tendrils of doom."

"Because, sir, you only see the tangible outcroppings of man's despicable heart. The putrid odor ebbing from its bowels are the failings of corrupt humanity. Its blackness is the indelible obscurity of man's soul. Its emptiness, the desolation of human existence."

"But it can still be defeated," Hunzuu insolently continued.

"No. It only feeds off of the flesh, and that's all humanity has to offer. It is most arrogant to assume that man can combat sin alone, and its accelerant of choice is pride."

Hayden watched it grow before their eyes. "You're telling me that this is a visual representation of the sins of humanity. It's alive, and it's coming for us."

The missionary sullenly nodded. "It lives to destroy us all, Sir Hayden. No one is exempt from its vile grasp. It's bonded to our fleshly nature to destroy us all."

"And it cannot be killed?" Hayden asked, still unsure.

"No. People are helpless against it. One cannot will himself to quit sinning. Without a higher power, we cannot defeat the nature we're naturally born into. We're sinners from conception. Even in our childlike innocence, we're still impure, for the flesh itself is unclean."

Leib interjected, "And the cloud grows with every sin that man commits. That's why it spans the ocean as far as our eyes can behold. This is no small matter. The sinfulness of humanity empowers it. It lives, breathes, and thrives off of us. Like a vulture, it lies in wait, swooping in once we've fallen. Man must cease sinning for the Sin Cloud to die."

M'ya winced. "So every sin that's ever been committed is somehow added to this dark presence?"

"Yes. It's a reminder of the shame, regret, and filth of one's past. It's also the continual presence forcing one to prepare for that final day of atonement. Judgment comes for us all, and this only reminds us what's waiting at the end of the line. No man can escape the atrocities of yesterday. Every wickedness is stockpiled."

"But why can't it be stopped?" Hunzuu demanded, still in denial.

Darius interrupted, "Because Hunzuu, it's too powerful. It's reinforced with the wickedness of every generation. Every evil action adds to its stature. From world leaders affecting the masses, to little children who send no ripples across the universe, every one contributes, for all of us are blameworthy. You're staring into the deep abyss of man's unfettered guilt, and there's nothing that can stand against it."

"But there must be a way," Hunzuu continued. "I refuse to accept defeat just because you say it's so."

"There's no way. If feeds on flesh." He paused, and then quietly asked, "Have you ever sinned, Hunzuu?"

Hunzuu didn't hesitate. "Many times over."

"Then you've contributed to its power, and it has a hold over you."

"No, a man can stop sinning whenever he pleases. He can

choose a more holy way. He can, at any time, choose the path of higher living according to the gods."

The missionary loudly spoke. "He may choose to act with more purity. However, purity of actions doesn't begat purity of heart. We're still who we are. We're still bound by whatever actions we've already taken."

Hunzuu was still angry. "This is wrong. Isn't that why we pray to the gods? Some sacrifice their children. Some live in humble reference, standing before the heavens in only sackcloth and ashes."

He looked toward the missionary. "You are a Jew. Your people, they sacrifice animals and routinely bloody altars for repentant purposes. How does that not suffice? Why is hell not appeased?"

The missionary thoughtfully stood, carefully calculating his response. When he finally spoke, his tone was low.

"Impurity breeds impurity. The blood of impure animals offered by impure men doesn't have the power to cleanse us from prior iniquities. It only pushes our punishment backward, allowing us to live peaceful lives."

"You mean, delay the inevitable. One day I'll stand before the gods in judgment, guilty and unable to say anything to my defense. I acted as I was, merely a man, but that shall have no bearing on what happens to me? I'll be tried and convicted solely because I'm human, and the heart of man is wicked and unstable? What's the purpose of life then? We live and then we die to face the wrath of the very gods who've empowered us to fail from the beginning? No... Not empowered us; enabled and encouraged us by our own faulty natures. If justice is such a higher purpose, where's the justice in that?"

"It won't always be that way," the missionary interrupted. "He's coming to save us all."

"Who?" Darius and M'ya asked at the same moment.

"The only one with blood pure and powerful enough to make a difference. One whose very life will shake the foundations of the underworld. His first breath shreds the atmosphere of darkness, and his final breath will topple the evil kingdoms and finally remove the power of death and hell."

"Who is this man you speak of?" Hunzuu asked.

The man stared at them, a faraway look in his eyes. "He's coming. The God of Israel will robe himself in flesh and walk among us."

Hunzuu scoffed. "This one God. He'll save us all? He'll come and walk among common people, throwing lightning bolts into this advancing storm of sin? Then, we'll magically be saved from the wrath of our pasts. Right? His lightning bolts will probably only empower it."

Hayden held up his hand, obviously moved from his prior conversation with the missionary.

"I think I understand now. He's not coming to overpower it, Hunzuu. This God has nothing to prove. He created the world and holds it all in balance. He has power over all things, and all of hell fears him. He's not coming to demonstrate power over the darkness. He's coming to give us that power. He comes so that his light will not only radiate into the gloomy world. It will live in man, and we'll be conduits, exposing his holiness to a sinful world."

M'ya shifted uncomfortably on her feet. Leib looked thoughtfully down toward the ground. Hunzuu was still openly skeptical.

"And what of the dark cloud? What becomes of it? How will we ever be free from its pull, if our sins are continually added to its overwhelming presence?"

"It will be eliminated, Hunzuu. Impurity begats impurity, and impure blood could never atone for the guilt of humanity. However-"

M'ya felt the warm tears trickle down her cheeks. Hayden stopped talking when he heard her voice. "The purity of one God who controls everything, his blood has the power to break the hold of sin on the earth."

She pondered for a moment, and then continued, "But he's not coming to wage a holy war like other gods? I don't understand."

Hayden looked at her, their eyes locking for a moment. "He's not coming to battle it, M'ya. He's coming to stand in our place, to offer himself as the ultimate sacrifice for all of us. Once he comes, we can no longer be found guilty for our atrocities, because the one god of Israel will have paid man's debts completely."

The missionary stifled tears. "It's not flesh and blood that revealed this to you, Sir Hayden. It could have only come from the One."

Hunzuu was visibly shaken. "I don't know if I can believe in such a god, although my heart cries that such a god would exist. Our gods take whatever they desire and display their displeasure by harsh judgments and unexplainable wrath. Yet, you teach of a god who demonstrates mercy and compassion to the most undeserving subjects. How could that be? How could an immortal god die? It's impossible."

The missionary answered, "Because Hunzuu, He'll willingly choose to leave immortality in order to wear the robes of mortal man. His garments will not be the kingly robes of eternity and the crowns of righteousness from the heavens above. He'll come in meager fashion and become the lowest of servants. He'll live in meekness and show kindness."

Hunzuu still couldn't grasp the concept. "So, the most powerful presence that ever existed will come as the weakest man who ever lived? That's absurd."

The missionary moved forward. "I'm afraid you misunderstand us, my friend. Meekness is not weakness. He's coming, not to interject his power into the world, but to interject his power into us, so that we can forever influence this world. If he came and defeated sin, over time things would change. The grass fades, the flowers wither, the mountains wear down, the streams dry up, and generations deteriorate. The old stories of his victory over the underworld would be forgotten, and soon we'd find a way to bury ourselves under the weight of sin again. The Sin Cloud would live, because we'd find a way to revive it."

"And how is this any different?"

"Because Hunzuu, he's not just leaving us a story. By empowering us, he leaves a gift to be passed down through the generations. He leaves something that cannot be forgotten, a power that will forever overcome the world and all evil things in it."

"And what exactly is he leaving?"

"He offers his life to weaken sins hold on humanity. Ultimately, he'll leave a gift we'll carry inside, turning impoverished beings into priceless vessels… He'll leave us… himself."

No further words were spoken. No one knew what to say. They looked toward the oncoming wave of darkness, but its grasp didn't seem as strong. Its presence not so deadly.

18

The oversized carriage pulled to a stop in front of the three-story stone building. The delegates were already inside. A small host of the Fortresses most distinguished members formed a meager welcoming committee along the ornamented terrace leading into the courthouse.

A man leapt from his seat on the front of the carriage and landed by the closed door. He waited for an entourage of ten soldiers to march and stand beside the walkway leading to the porch. After they were set, he opened the door. A few moments later, a short, rotund man stepped out wearing the customary courthouse robes of Babylon. Two soldiers, the king's personal bodyguards, followed him from the coach. They waited for a few seconds, and then the king stepped forward.

He wore the famed crown of Babylon high on his head.

He was sensational, fashionable, tall, and handsome; every bit the presence a king should command. The aura of his presence created a stir. The welcoming party paled in comparison to the king's vast countenance. Their eager smiles faded, as they pretended not to be overwhelmed by meeting the most feared and respected world leader of their era.

As the king approached, the Emperor of the Fortress moved toward him and extended his hand in a warm greeting.

"Welcome to our humble city. We're so glad to have you here. We're making history today, with the merging of our two civilizations."

The king moved past the extended arm without a second glance. The leaders of the Fortress weren't impressive enough to rate an acknowledgement. The first man from the carriage stopped in front of the overwhelmed ambassadors.

"We aren't here for political aspirations. While we appreciate your kindness, we'll be forthright in our purpose for coming. Any time wasted on pleasantries for the purpose of posturing will be deemed as wasteful. Furthermore, it has come to our knowledge that your leaders feel that The Fortress is autonomous from the leadership of Babylon. It's been said that you hold no high esteem of the crown. This will be addressed before we leave your boundaries. According to diplomatic policy, created over two hundred years ago, your meager city is still a landmark of our Empire. Unless you plan on officially declaring independence, which would be an act of treason, you should make the proper arrangements to publicly kneel before your king and kiss his ring."

The Emperor of the Fortress was red-faced, but held his tongue. The others stood with mouth's agape at the arrogance and lack of diplomatic awareness just demonstrated.

"Good then," the small man continued, as he moved past. "Would hate for you to declare war against the most powerful empire in the world."

The diplomats followed the gloried entourage and stepped inside the courthouse. The king immediately made his way across the floor and stepped to the high seat designed for the Emperor and Judge of Babylon. The chair was decorated with emblems of the Fortress. The Fortress' official seal had been placed on a banner and hung over the chair.

The Babylonian king motioned for his two guards. They moved in front of him. One drew his sword and swung it toward the throne. He'd knocked the emblems to the floor in two strikes. The other guard moved to the wall, ripping down the seal of the Fortress. The small man handed him another banner bearing the seal of Babylon. The guard replaced it, and the short man opened a scroll and began his dissertation.

"By order of the King of Babylon, I command you to kneel before his high presence. If you're permitted to speak to your king, you will only do so in one or two sentences at a time. You'll not look directly at him. You'll only speak again if he acknowledges your first response. His ruling is final and shall not be challenged. There are no appeals in his courtroom, and make no mistakes, this is his courtroom. Any questions should be addressed to me. If you speak out of turn, you will be executed. If you challenge the king, you will be executed. If you look at him, and he feels challenged-"

One of the men in the small delegate quietly mouthed the words, "You will be executed."

The movement of his lips allowed the slightest sibilant sound to escape into the tense atmosphere. The words had barely finished being mouthed, when the king's guard nearest him shoved a small dagger through his heart. The dagger had seemed to materialize from nowhere, the movement fluid and swift.

His body hit the ground, creating an uproar in the courtroom. The ten guards who had entered drew their swords and marched toward the assembly of Fortress delegates. A man lurched forward from the crowd, frantically waving his arms.

"Wait. Please. There need be no further blood shed. Please. This is bigger than the people in this room. If this happens, a lot of innocent people will die today... from both sides."

The king motioned toward the man who had been doing his talking. The small man whistled loudly and the advancing soldiers stopped. Two of them turned and removed the dead man from the floor, carried him to the door, and tossed him outside. The door slammed behind him, and the men reentered the room. The king took his seat, and the small man motioned toward the one who had spoken from the

Fortress delegates.

"You must be Amarsin Shamash?" He said, a little too condescendingly.

"Yes, I-"

"You're reputation is indeed most accurate. I seldom meet a rival, but it appears they weren't lying when they told me you were twice my size."

"Well-"

"Good. Good. I shall sit next to you at these proceedings and for once appear small."

Amarsin's face flushed red. "I don't-"

"Perhaps I should hire you to follow me around. An errand boy of sorts… but no, it would take you too long to do the errands. You'd lose your breath before you returned to me."

"What-" he tried to speak, growing more infuriated.

"Oh well. With nothing else to do with you, we might as well get on with your sentencing."

Amarsin shook his head in defiant disgust. He started to speak, but one of the guards moved his hand toward his sword, and Amarsin remained silent.

The man removed another scroll. "Amarsin Shamash, you of Babylonian blood are charged with leading a coup against the throne of Babylon. You caused a man to go free, who should very well have been executed. You helped him escape the grasp of Captain Abaddon Dearth, an appointed official of Babylon. You orchestrated several events that ultimately lead to the death of many Babylonian soldiers at these very gates. Ultimately, your actions led to the senseless murder of Captain Dearth. We, the people of Babylon, deem you and your horde responsible for these horrific atrocities against your Empire. What say you to these horrible allegations?"

Amarsin moved forward and stood beside a chair in the middle of the courtroom. He looked toward the king and held his head low. He bowed in reverence before rising again and sitting down. He looked toward the man with the scroll.

"If I may speak? With all the rules of this court, I'm unsure how to proceed. I mean no disrespect, but it feels as though my grandfather's lessons about the fairness of Babylonian law were greatly exaggerated. How can I defend myself against allegations, if I cannot fairly address the one who'll pass judgment?"

The door suddenly crashed opened and a man stormed into the courtroom. A party of six armed men moved in behind him. The guardsmen drew their swords and formed a defensive line in front of the king. The advancing man stopped, outrage littering his face.

He was an imposing figure and didn't seem in the least worried about the Babylonian soldiers in the room. He removed an envelope from his pouch, an envelope sealed with the king's crest. He tossed it to the small man and moved toward Amarsin. Amarsin stood to his feet.

"Grandfather. What?" Amarsin asked, a shocked

expression overriding him.

"Sit down, boy. Leave this to me. The waters churn differently when forced to swim with the sharks."

One of the king's guards drew his sword and marched toward Marcus Shamash. Marcus stood his ground, and one of his own men drew a sword to meet the king's guard in the middle of the room.

"Wait," Marcus interrupted, "Perhaps you should read what I've placed in your hands before you pass judgment and further blood is shed."

The small man turned to the king. "Your Highness, it does bear your father's shield. What would you have me do?"

The king closed his eyes in thought. Finally he replied, "I'd have you read the words of my father. His noble declarations will always be decreed as long as I'm king."

The small man winced. "Sir, are you sure?"

"Do you question me?"

"No, sir. Not at all, sir. Just making sure I understood your directive explicitly."

"Read them."

The man broke the seal. "I, King Sharukkin, of the House of Sharukkin, by order of all who have gone before me and all who will go after, do hereby grant Parliamentarian Marcus Shamash permanent exemption from any and all crimes in the provinces under my rule. The only excluding factors will be acts of terrorism against the Babylon commonwealth. This is in honor of his family's exemplary service in times of war and political corruption. His leadership, kindness, and commitment have landed him as a most valuable member of my council. His wisdom is renowned, and has been the difference in many of our decisions. Therefore, I do hereby grant him immunity, as a delegate of the Babylonian empire. This document will extend to his grandson, Amarsin Shamash, only now still a child. His father has been lost in the Battle for the Great River. His father's service and Parliamentarian Shamash's loss have not fallen on unsympathetic shoulders."

The man turned and presented the paper to the king. "It does bear his seal, sir, and his mark."

The king read the paper and then stood. "I'm not my father, Mr. Shamash. You would be well warned to know the difference. However, I do cherish his memory and miss him dearly. His wishes will be honored... However, he excluded acts of terrorism from his promissory note. I'll give you this day to present your case. My ruling will be made tomorrow morning at first light. If I find your grandson guilty of treason against the throne, he'll be punished, as would any other man who defied the reach of Babylonian authority."

Marcus calmly looked at the king, but a fire burned in his eyes. "I appreciate your respect for your father's decrees. However, I'm also well aware of what you intended to do here, by having your men force an unwarranted conviction without allowing us the opportunity to present a case to an impartial audience. If the king's wishes are still to use my grandson to send a message to those who would oppose your rule, you'll more greatly dishonor your father's memory than any vagrant opposition from his past. I would implore you to honor his memory with the privilege of an unprejudiced trial. I beg of you."

The king held out his royal scepter. "Your request has been heard and granted. Your grandson's trial will be heard through unbiased lenses. Make sure you have your facts in order though, Parliamentarian Shamash. Make no mistake, he'll be found guilty unless you and he can absolutely prove otherwise."

"Yes, sir. I'd expect nothing less, sir."

The king banged one end of the scepter against the table. "Then let the trial begin."

19

Hunzuu stared further into the dark cloud. "Why's it just hovering there? It's moving so slowly that it'll take hours to get here. Why doesn't it just come on and get this over with?"

The missionary shook his head and sighed. "Sin always brings death. We cannot live the way of our flesh and expect the darkness not to come for us."

Darius looked toward it as well. "My suggestion is to move further inland. Perhaps, since it's taking so long to approach, we can outrun it by heading away."

Leib shot him a skeptical look, trying to stifle his amusement. "Sorry, king, but the thought of outrunning a death cloud is comical, for what man can outrun death?"

M'ya nervously whispered, "Maybe that's our only chance. We can't just stay here and wait for it to devour us. We really have no choice. I agree with King Darius. I think we should try and move away. Stop posing a threat. Maybe it will go away."

It was the missionary's turn to laugh. "It won't just go away. It's here for a reason, and it won't leave until its appetite is filled. Moving further inland won't help, for it can hover over the land just as well as it does the deep."

"But at least we would have tried something," Hunzuu quickly rattled off.

There was a rustling in the brush around them. Hayden had seen them coming. He moved toward Hunzuu.

"There are eight of them. Moving speedily through the brush. Dressed in runic garments. They don't appear to be armed."

The eight stepped from the brush no sooner than Hayden had finished. One of them immediately separated from the followers and moved toward them. His eyes were the deepest blue they'd ever seen. His face was tattooed with several runic symbols. His hair was long and held together in a braided ponytail behind his back.

He stoically looked into the swirling darkness over the water, and then turned back to their group, looking directly toward the missionary. His voice almost screeched. The bitter harshness unnaturally reverberated through the open atmosphere.

"Hello, preacher. I see you have friends, and I see that hell is troubled by them."

The missionary nodded. "It seems I've stirred a bit of trouble. I hope you'll allow us safe passage through your island. We won't be staying."

"Too bad. We've lots to share." The cobaltic sheen of his eyes emanated more harshly. He smiled, his teeth reflecting an eerie, cannibalistic shadow.

The missionary recoiled. "Why, after all this time, has the dark cloud sought me out? I've been here over a year now."

The man devilishly grinned and pointed a bony finger toward Hayden. "It's not coming for you. It's here for him."

Hayden moved toward him. "What did you say?"

"It's here for your soul. It wants to take you home. Kill you here, kill you there."

The missionary interrupted. "No one need die today, priest. Just allow us to pass through your province. Please."

"And why should I grant you permission? You've been coming to my people and proselytizing them with this message of one being who rules all the rest of the earth. It's no wonder the spirits are troubled. You haven't made many friends here. Now you ask for my help? Why not just pray to the heavens and ask your mighty God to work a miracle for you? I mean, after all you've taught and doggedly preached among my islands, you should have to prove it sooner or later."

"Live or die, priest, I do it proudly in the name of the Lord. He could help me if He so chooses, but I could just leave Him alone with trivial matters, if you'd do your part."

"My part? What is my part? You do understand that long after these people are gone, long after you've left to go back to Jerusalem, I will still have to face this people. I won't jeopardize that to save the likes of you."

"Suit yourself. We're gonna have to take our chances alone then. Or will you order your people to have us killed as we cross?"

"My people won't lift a hand against you. You have my word, but they won't have to."

"What's that mean?" Hunzuu demanded.

The missionary shook his head. "It means he knows humans are the least of our concern. These islands are the heartland of paganism in this part of the country. They're protected, not by armies, but by spirits."

The man cackled, "You're aware of our protection I see. No harm can come to us. This island is special. No one comes. No one leaves. Without the spirits first agreeing that it must be so."

Hunzuu leapt toward him. "I'm not afraid of your dark realm. Nothing compares to the power of the gods of Babylon. Let them come and your shadow puppets will be dealt a sting more severe than death."

The man angrily threw his fists in the air. "Your weak gods couldn't even cross the ocean with you Hunzuu, ancient warrior from beyond."

Hunzuu's expression visibly changed.

The man smirked at him. "That's right. We know you well. We know all of you... You sir, have shed innocent blood."

"I've never killed a man that didn't deserve it. I'm no cowardly murderer."

"No. Not a coward, but a killer nonetheless. Just because your king decreed certain people your enemies, that didn't make it right to kill them. Remember the child you left orphaned outside of Coldstone? The little one with the limp you left sitting at the gate. You remember him well, don't you? His cries crashed through the night sky like a volcanic eruption. His heart broke with the same force, as he watched you kill his father... And what, did his mother have to die too, after they had their way with her."

"That was an accident. That-"

"An accident? Hardly seems accidental to me. You don't just misstep into a sexual assault and murder. But it appears you're still making excuses."

"No. I didn't know they were-"

"You didn't have control of your men. They pillaged multiple villages, forcing themselves on whomever they pleased, taking whatever spoils they desired. That's how your gods allow your people to behave? There's not much difference between yours and mine then. A god who teaches his people no restraints; who instructs them to only seek their fleshly desires; who allows others to suffer in order to appease a few; how is this acceptable as truth in your mind, Captain Hunzuu?

"No. It wasn't my fault. I won't accept-"

"It's top down, Captain. You taught your men about accountability, didn't you? Ultimately, you were responsible for every one of them? What they did, what they didn't do, it was all your doing."

"That's enough," Darius demanded. "You can't strike fear in our hearts by harassment. So you know a little about one of us. Are we supposed to be concerned?"

"Darius, Darius, Darius. What did it feel like when your gods allowed your family to be taken from you? When they allowed you to be taken into slavery? When your brothers were murdered in cold blood in front of you at a young age? You recovered well and moved on with life, but surely you can't pretend to not have been negatively impacted. Yet, you still hold to your fictitious belief in gods who weren't there for you. Now that Demsas has killed your second wife and child, how do you feel?"

Darius turned cold, "But the gods were there. They're the reason I'm still alive."

"And what cruel punishment. Take what matters most from you and force you to live without them. What sort of sick god would cause his most faithful servants such calamity? You should join your brother now. He fights on a winning side. He's been introduced to beings who would rather allow you happiness than to watch you begrudgingly sacrifice and create a false commitment."

"And I suppose my brother is happy?"

"Happier than ever, and more alive than ever. There's nothing more liberating than giving yourself to the dark side. Once you do it, there's nothing left to do. It's pure freedom. It's you embracing the role of your creation. Why not just be what we were meant to be?"

"My brother is lost. He murdered his entire family," Darius replied. "How is that living?"

"Your brother has been found, and have you asked yourself why? I bet not… for you're afraid of what you'll find. You're afraid of your responsibility in all of this."

"I'm not to blame for Demsas' failings. Every man must make his own way, independent of the past. We had the same father and mother, the same upbringing, the same beliefs, and the same experiences. He's different merely because he chose a different path. Every man is the architect of his own life. Every man constructs solely on the values he has placed on the flesh or on eternity."

"But yet, you're remorseful… You know your brother could've been different. You helped make him this way. You resisted his ideas. You sought opportunity to present yourself better than him."

Darius was taken back, "He was always different. We knew that from the beginning. He was a problem child, and he turned into a-"

The man thundered the words, "He became what you forced him to become. He had no choice. No one believed in him. Every one accepted his behavior, and he was never asked to change. Your family allowed it and paid dearly for their transgressions. As much as you'd like to pretend that he was naturally so evil from the beginning, you must know the truth. He could've been different. In another life, with a good family, and a brother that cared for him, he could've sat at the right of your throne and been content being number two. How does the weight of that guilt rest on your shoulders, future King? You deserted your family then, and you haven't changed at all."

"No... It's not true... None of it," Darius stammered.

"Then where's your family now?"

He hung his head, "You know Demsas had them killed."

The man seemed to gloat, "That's correct, and it was rather painful and slow. Your wife died after your children. Any idea what they did to her before she died?"

"No," Darius cried. "Please stop."

"I can't, Darius. You chose to put ambition for power over your love for them. What kind of king are you?"

The man abruptly turned his attention from Darius and whipped his head toward M'ya. He smiled at her. She awkwardly stood off to one side, trying not to gaze into his deep blue eyes. He took a few steps to her and reached out, taking her long hair in his right hand. The moment his skin contacted her, she felt cold inside. He moved his hand backward, as if he'd touched a hot stove, and then sympathetically looked in her eyes.

"I feel your pain. You deeply care, but you don't feel cared for in the same way. I see it. It hurts, doesn't it? All your life it's been that way.

Pain.

Heartache.

Regret.

Fear.

And then more pain.

You're wondering now, aren't you? You're wondering when it'll all come crashing down around you. You've stacked the stones and are afraid they won't stand. You feel the end is near; you're only going to get hurt. He'll either be taken from you or walk away... Once more, pretty little M'ya will be left with no one to protect her. It'll be her father all over again. Someone who's supposed to love you but hurts you instead... Doesn't it break your heart every time you remember? How many times he chose your brothers, leaving you alone because he didn't love you like he did them. I know it hurts, M'ya, wanderer, gypsy girl. You've looked everywhere, but on this island, you've finally come home. You belong here with us. A band of misfits finding pleasure in others and in gods who truly care about giving you gratification in this life."

His words were mesmerizing, as he extended his hand toward her. "Come, join me. Embrace me, and you'll be like us. You can stay here, and belong, forever. We're your people, and we'll never desert you."

His stare was hypnotic. M'ya slowly lowered her head. She looked toward Hayden, and then quietly moved toward the man.

"M'ya, don't," Hayden pleaded. "Don't go to him."

The man's smile was intoxicating, his voice low and steady. "Come on over, M'ya. No more rejection; you'll always be loved and accepted."

Hayden wanted to move, to push her away from whatever was binding her, but he couldn't. He was paralyzed. The others seemed lost to what was taking place. He tried to speak, but the words couldn't be forced out. She was almost to the man. The man smiled, ready to take her in. Hayden didn't know what the touch meant, but everything inside knew that she didn't need to make that connection. He looked into the distance. The darkness abxiously shuttered with every step she took, obviously pleased with the promise of her acceptance.

Hayden's voice quivered, as he tried to force it out.

Nothing.

Gasp for air.

Breathless void.

Empty formulation of protest.

His mind was screaming at her. "No. M'ya. Stop now. Don't move closer. Stop."

The man's hand was just out of reach. She hesitated, and

then turned again to look at Hayden. He was trembling, trying to break whatever was holding him. She closed her eyes and took a step backward, nearing the man behind her.

She opened them again. A single tear rolled down her cheek.

"I'm sorry," she mouthed, as she moved nearer to the man's embrace.

Hayden tried to shake his head, but all he could do was stand there, watching the darkness celebrate, as one he cared about was pulled into its snare by the promise of a better life. She wiped the tear from her cheek and momentarily stared into Hayden's tender eyes. There was something there. Something almost imploring her not to do what she was contemplating.

But why?

What could it hurt?

It was true. She'd only get hurt again.

Why not surrender to a higher power that offered more than she'd ever hoped for? She could feel its warmth calling her. She could hear the hope in his words. She could see the heart of true acceptance. She was being completely embraced, something she'd never felt anywhere else.

No judgment.

No second guesses.

No hurtful evaluations of her character.

No appeasing others.

She took another step. One more and she'd be in his arms. She turned to the man. His blue eyes were oddly misshapen, and his mouth was arched at a strange angle. His eyes were almost glowing with a dark intensity.

He gently spoke again. "One more step delightful girl, and you'll embrace this better life forever. Give yourself to us. One more step is all it takes to be free."

She froze, as if her body was trying to refuse the commands her mind was sending.

His voice stayed low, "I can't come to you, M'ya. You must come to me. Come and enjoy the sweeter life. It's yours. It's at your fingertips. Your friends will even have safe passage across the island as a token of my loyalty, our loyalty to you."

The missionary spoke. He was the only one who seemed to not be stuck in the evil sorcerer's spellbinding trance.

"You don't have to go, M'ya. It's long been assumed that the grass is greener. It never is. You know that. You also know that you've already found a home. You're already accepted. You have no need to throw yourself away because you fear history will repeat itself. Mya, Hayden is not your father."

"I can't go through it again. I can't-"

"You're strong, M'ya. You're resilient. You'll find another way. This isn't it."

"Don't listen to him, girl," the man hissed. "He's trying to destroy your chance at happiness. He's jealous because what I'm offering has the power to change your life, while he has nothing to offer but more of what you've already received, empty promises from broken gods."

"No, M'ya. Don't fall for his lies. Don't-"

She looked at Hayden again and tried to force a smile. It wouldn't fully come. "I'm sorry," she mouthed, tears flowing down both cheeks.

She turned and took the last step. As he wrapped his arms around her, the darkness swirled in the distance. It swarmed, a blackened madness charging toward them. Within seconds, it had engulfed them with an overwhelming intensity.

Hayden was knocked off his feet, a scorching pain devastating him. He blindly struggled to see through the cyclonic haze. Regaining his senses, he tried to stand against the wind, but found himself being driven back to his knees. He tried to crawl toward M'ya and the man. Squinting his eyes, he tried to peer through the whirling hell on the beach.

There she was, barely visible. He crawled further. The man still held her tightly in his grasp. Her demeanor appeared peaceful, but her eyes betrayed the fear inside her.

"M'ya," he yelled into the storm, but his voice was drowned out by the vociferous wind that mocked him, seemingly laughing as it churned.

The man looked in his direction and locked eyes with him. He suddenly lost his human shape and morphed into a nightmarish figure. His long cape whirled around M'ya, completely covering her from Hayden's view. The darkness exploded in an upward motion, and then crashed down full force into the man holding M'ya under his garment. There was a terrible explosion.

The sky cleared, as the last echo reverberated over the waters before them. The darkness was gone, but so were M'ya and the man who'd been holding her.

Hayden stared into the emptiness. Hunzuu wiped his eyes.

"What just happened?" Hayden screamed.

Leib came from the brushes he'd been blown into. His face was bloody from the abuse of hitting the wooded area. His left arm was loosely hanging, as he grimaced from the pain.

"Where's M'ya? Did she do it? I couldn't get to her. I tried." He whimpered.

Darius was visibly shaken. "I couldn't see or hear anything. I don't know what happened. Where is she?"

Hayden was too hurt to speak. Darius touched his shoulder. "Sir Hayden, where is M'ya."

Hayden appeared dazed. He flabbergastedly turned to the missionary. "It lied?"

"Hayden, that's what he does," the missionary stated. "One cannot trust the darkness, ever."

"But we all believed him. He said it had come for me. It

didn't."

Leib exhaled loudly. "Yes, it did, Sir Hayden. There are some fates worse than death. By taking her, he got to you. The darkness has won… The darkness always wins."

20

"I've got to get her back." Hayden loudly cried.

Leib reached out to him. "She's gone, Sir Hayden. There's no coming back from that. She made her choice, giving her life to save us and give us safe passage. The sin was appeased by her sacrifice."

The missionary sympathetically looked at him. "And you should take full advantage of it, Sir Hayden. You need to make haste and utilize the advantage she gave you."

"No. No. It can't end like this. It's not supposed to end like this."

"It was her choice, Sir Hayden. We can't take that back."

"No. It's not real. It can't be real."

He fell down and sobbed uncontrollably. "I didn't get the

chance to tell her how I feel. I didn't even know how much I did until now, and now it's too late. It's not fair. It's not supposed to be this way."

Hunzuu sat on a rock a few feet away. His lack of compassion wasn't uncommon for a hardened Babylonian soldier.

"Life is never fair, Sir Hayden. That's one truth we know most assuredly. One day to the next, we never know what will happen, and we must not take anything for granted. None of us know which day will be our last, or even which breath... At least she got to choose how she left this world. That's more than most of us will get."

Hayden turned toward the missionary, hatred burning in his eyes. "I'm going to destroy it. You... You have to know a way."

"Hayden, every man has a choice concerning sin. If you willingly give yourself, you'll die. That is the way of things. She embraced it. It doesn't matter the reason. One cannot give himself to sin and expect life to end with happily ever after. Sin corrupts and destroys. There are no exceptions, and there's no coming back from that."

"It deceived her into believing she was getting everything she ever desired. Please. There must be some way to get to her, to save her. She can't be gone. She can't."

Darius urgently approached them. "I don't mean to break this up, but we need to worry about this later. We can't help anyone if we don't get off this island. Look over the water."

They all turned, expecting to see the cloud reemerging. Instead, several boats were making their way across the divide. Demsas' men were closing in from the other side.

"Follow me," the missionary replied. "We must make haste."

Hayden got up on one knee. "Let them come. I no longer desire to live."

Darius grabbed him by the shoulder and tried to pull him from the ground. "We knew this would be difficult when we came. We've all lost a beloved friend today, but this is about more than us. We have to remember that. We're working for the betterment of an entire nation. It's not about me. It's not about you. It wasn't about M'ya, and she understood that. Don't belittle her sacrifice by not taking advantage of the chance she has given you."

Hayden's bitterness was apparent, "You're right. It's not about us. It's not about anything… I quit… I'm done."

"Hayden, you know M'ya wouldn't have wanted you to quit. You must stay strong. For her."

"For her? Darius… king… there is no her."

"For her memory then. Please. You know this is not what she would've wanted. She didn't give her life so that you could turn around less than twelve hours later and give yours for nothing. Let's move."

"You can go without me, Darius. I would rather take my chances and face them alone."

"It's a death wish, Sir Hayden. I can't allow you to stay."

"And how do you propose to stop me?"

"I don't know, but I will. Don't make me," he sternly replied.

Hunzuu knelt down beside Hayden. "Sir, I'm with you 'til the end. If you die today, then I shall die with you."

"No, Hunzuu. You've served me well. Now, allow me the privilege of dying alone."

"Okay," Hunzuu said, as Darius hit Hayden over the head with the hilt of his sword. Hayden fell down and was out.

Hunzuu smiled toward Darius. "You hit him. You're gonna have to deal with him when he comes to."

They both smiled and picked him up together, quickly moving away from the rocks and deeper into the island.

21

Gino moved toward the window and slightly opened the blinds. He peered outside with nervous anticipation. *How is it that you have such vital information, but they haven't found you yet? It doesn't make sense. I know they're coming. You better prepare yourself.*

Torben smiled. "Gino. Come on. We've been careful. Once they followed us to the library, we knew they had to have some sort of tracker on us. We ditched the car. We changed clothes. Even got rid of my electronics and bought a go phone. I'm virtually untraceable."

"You're never untraceable. Good computer guys can have you located in just a few hours by tying into the traffic cams and video surveillance in the area. The more you use your phone, the better chance they have of matching your voice through high frequency analysis. Once they find you, they'll be able to close in on your position. You can't hide from them. You must understand that, Torb. There's nowhere to run."

"Well, then you better make good use of the short time I've got left, G. What have you got for me so far?"

Gino closed the blinds and went back to the computer he'd connected to a large monitor in his living room area. He blankly stared at the screen.

"Nothing yet. It's only been three hours though. These sort of things can take days. You gotta learn to relax, man. I can't just work magic. It's not like pulling something out of a hat. The program I created is running analysis after analysis looking for any match. If I can find any chink in the armor, the program will work from there to find a way in."

"I thought computers were fast," Jane interrupted.

Gino glared at her, obviously offended. "They are fast, faster than you can imagine. However, someone built a firewall around this that isn't letting go easily. It's gonna take a little work. Without my program, you wouldn't have a chance. So, unless you know someone else that can do this, I'd suggest you just chill, man."

She laughed. "You're telling us to calm down. There's the definition of irony."

"Hello, pot." Torben humorously offered.

"Cute," Gino deflected. "But this isn't the pot calling the kettle black. This is you getting off my back so I can effectively do the job you've asked me to."

"Seriously, G, what takes so long?" Hayden asked.

"Think of it like this. Someone has created a complex maze. However, the solution to one maze only opens the door to another network of mazes that must also be solved. Sort of a layered puzzle, man. The solution to one only leads to the realization of another."

"Okay. Got it. Never mind," he offered. "Just do your thing."

Gino exhaled deeply, "Breaking this encryption is difficult. I must not only find one key that'll help me solve it all. I must find a different key for each individual level. Every layer offers a new challenge, and every challenge is only more difficult than the previous. The program can't work any faster. I'm sorry."

"That sort of makes sense. I suppose… Just how many layers into this are we?"

Gino paused and stared at the screen. His reluctance to answer was obvious. "Still working on the second."

"And each layer will take longer to crack than the first one? That's the basic synopsis of what you're saying?" Hayden worriedly deduced.

"Well, that depends. If the program picks up a lot of keys along the way, it could move quicker, even though the layers are designed to be more difficult. This program is self-learning. It adjusts on the fly to any changes in the process designed by the defense experts to block us."

He suddenly looked deeply into the screen. "No. No. That can't be. It can't be."

"What is it?" Torben asked, as he moved around the computer to see what Gino had noticed. There was nothing but a lot of unrecognizable symbols."

"What's going on, G?"

"This programmer's skills are sick, man. He knew some high tech stuff, stuff that most of us have only talked about. This is new. Technology that shouldn't be accessible yet. If they have it, they have to be working with the government, man. You've stumbled across some classified info. High-end knowledge."

"How do you know?"

"Because, man. Look at this.'" He pointed to a small bleep on the screen.

"What is it?"

"It's a signal, man. It's sending a homing signal. The whole time it runs, it sends a wireless tracker through cyberspace about every half hour. It's so small I almost didn't notice it. Clever."

He vigorously pressed buttons on the keyboard. "I can't block it. Nothing is working. I can't mask it. We're gonna have to move. One of us gonna have to drive this metal bucket and keep us on the go. Maybe they won't be able to peg our location. That might buy us some time."

Jane walked to the front. "Keys in it?"

"Always keep it ready, girl. Never know when I'm gonna need to move fast."

Torben started to follow her when Gino stopped him. "You trust her? I never seen her before?"

"She seems okay so far. Why?" Torben asked.

"I don't know. There's something about her. I don't trust her, man."

"You don't trust anyone, Gino. You've known me since childhood, and I still had to prove myself. Give her the benefit of the doubt. I think she'll be alright."

"We don't have that luxury, man. People will kill for what I have right here. There's no doubt that this is top secret. Nobody wants this to get out. They're gonna be doing whatever it takes to stop you. You must know that."

"So."

"So what do you have to fight them with?"

"What do you mean?"

"Weapons, man? What's in your arsenal?"

"Don't have any, G. Had to give my gun up when I went on leave from the force… Why do you ask?"

"Check under the couch. Lift the cushions and pull the small rope binding upward."

Torben did as Gino instructed. He shook his head and closed the couch back, replacing the pillows.

"G. What were you expecting? You have enough weapons in there to supply a small army."

"You never know, man. World War Three, the zombie apocalypse, Chinese overthrow, civil war, the new American Revolution. One can't be too careful these days. Anything could happen."

"G. Half of those guns are illegal. Where'd you get them?"

"Here and there, and it's a good thing you're here in a non-official capacity. If not, I guess you'd probably confiscate my belongings and arrest me. Probably send me to Gitmo for acts of terrorism. But I'm no terrorist, man. I swear to you, I'm one of the good guys."

"No doubt, Gino." Torben chuckled, "No doubt."

"Take one, man. At least one. You might have to defend us later. Would be better for you to have the hardware ready before the shooting starts; don't you think?"

Torben reopened the couch and removed a Glock 9mm from the stash. He found two clips and a box of ammo. He filled the clips and put one in the gun. He racked it, the loud clank got Jane's attention from the front seat.

"What was that?"

"A last resort," Torben called. "Let's get this thing moving. If G's right, we need to get on the road."

The engine loudly roared, and a second later the large vehicle lurched forward.

. . .

Hayden rolled over and groggily blinked his eyes. His memory was momentarily fuzzy, but came back to him in an instant. He struggled against the physical cobwebs to rise to his feet and stumbled to his knees before regaining his balance and standing wobbly. He turned around to find them all watching him.

The firelight danced off of tall clay walls that surrounded him. A steady, cool breeze made the hair on his arms stand on end. He moved away from the fire and pointed his finger toward Darius. "I should kill you myself. What's wrong with you?"

"Sorry, Sir Hayden. It was the only way to get you away from there. She wouldn't have wanted you to die. We all know that. Perhaps you should honor her by staying alive. I just wanted to give you a chance to think more rationally before making such a final decision."

"Okay. I've thought more rationally, and I'd still prefer to meet them in battle. M'ya would still be here if not for them. If they hadn't taken us hostage for your brother, we'd all be sitting around a campfire laughing."

Hunzuu spoke up. "Sir Hayden, listen to yourself. Life is full of 'what ifs.' It doesn't matter. We cannot go back and undo what's already been done. We cannot correct the mistakes of others, and we cannot correct the mistakes that we ourselves have made."

"Wait a minute. You can't be insinuating that we're to blame for this. They're the reason she's not here." Hayden demanded.

"Sir Hayden, if we would've never come, she'd still be alive. If you'd never have crossed her path that day they'd stolen the fruit in Babylon, she could very well still be alive. If she would have stayed at the Fortress with Amarsin, she would very well still be alive."

Hayden slammed his fist into the solid wall beside him. "And did you see her die? Did any of you actually witness her last breath? I didn't... I saw the evil encase her, but I didn't see her die. Until I see her remains, I'll not believe it. And until I believe it, I'll never stop looking."

Darius sadly frowned, "Listen to yourself, Sir Hayden. You must learn to let things go. Sometimes life is hard to accept. Sometimes death is the hardest thing to understand. But we must all learn to embrace it. Death is just as much a part of us, as well... life."

"She's not dead, Hunzuu. I can feel it."

The missionary stood up. "Shh. This place is a hallowed place of solitude. You can't just act any way you'd like. You must respect the sacred nature of this consecrated ground."

"Where are we?" Hayden asked.

"We're on an island off the coast of Aksum. A few miles away from where M'ya was killed. We're-"

Hayden interrupted the missionary. "Taken. From where

M'ya was taken. How can you all just give up on someone so easily? If anyone of us could have survived, it would be her. She's pure and strong. The goodness of her heart wouldn't have been devoured so quickly."

The missionary nodded. "There's nothing wrong with hope, Sir Hayden. A man should be allowed his dreams. Often they are what keeps him going when all else says he'll fail. They are the foundation on which a man stands while the rest of the world sinks into oblivion."

Hayden nodded. "And I'll hold onto the hope of her until the end... Now, why are we here?"

"We're here because we had nowhere else to go. These are my people."

"Jews?"

"Yes, mostly, and a few proselytized Aksumites. They've established boundaries to keep the others out. They've made the proper changes to make sure other lifestyles don't stop them from inheriting God's blessings. Because of these changes, they are safe. This is the best place we could be right now."

Hayden inquisitively looked around. "What makes this place so special?"

"The wall you see stretches around the entire city. It's highly fortified. No one goes in and no one leaves unless approved by myself and the city councilmen."

"How many people live inside these walls?"

The missionary proudly boasted. "Over two hundred, but it's so well fortified no one has been able to break in and defeat us. I have plans to change those meager numbers in the near future. We'll grow when others embrace the idea of changing their lifestyle to be more like us. There are a few who are currently contemplating such moves."

"And how long has your numbers remained steadfast near two hundred?"

"Since I came. Most of the people here came with me to spread the word. Since that time, there've been a few converts."

"So, you only allow people inside the city who have changed to fit your criteria of how a person should live?" Hayden inquisitively asked.

"Yes. If a person wants to live under our blessings and protection, they must prove themselves capable of living our lifestyle. If they can't demonstrate basic conversion, they have no place at our tables."

Hayden nervously chewed his lip. "How did we get here?"

Leib crinkled his nose. "Ship… A rough lot of ship hands agreed to transport us across because we were out of options. They knew leaving us alone would be a death sentence. So, they helped us."

"And where are they now?"

The missionary placed another log on the fire. "They're just outside the gates. They'll be okay. More than likely, if our pursuers find them, they won't know they're the ones who helped us."

Hayden angrily stood before them. "I don't know if that's the way your God treats those who have helped his people or not, but it's not the way I repay kindness. Bring them to this fire at once."

The missionary waved his hand, dismissing them from following Hayden's directive. "I'm afraid that here, I am king. You have no authority."

Hayden stood up. "Then I'll take my chances out there, with them."

The missionary was wroth. "Why would you do that? Why would you risk being exposed in order to commune with a few men you've never even met?"

"Why would they risk their lives for a few men they'd never even met? What goes around comes around."

"They aren't welcome in this city. Don't you understand, if we start opening the gates to just anyone, we essentially invite the darkness into our midst."

"Do you not possess the light?"

"Of course we do. It's the bond that joins us."

"Is there a better place for the darkness to be expelled than in the presence of the light?" Hayden demanded.

The missionary was upset, "But you've witnessed it first hand, Sir Hayden. Sometimes the darkness wins, and when it does, it's usually devastating."

"And what of the inhabitants, they don't wander far from these gates? They have no connection to the outside world?"

"They've been instructed not to. It's a dangerous world out there. Evil waits; always wanting to destroy the very gifts they've been given. It's better to give up a few things out there, than to lose the precious gifts most valued."

"I don't wish to hurt your feelings, but you're wrong my friend, on so many levels. This can't be the way your one god has designed for you to live."

"And why not? You know nothing of him, yet you presume to know his thoughts for his people."

"No offense, sir, but it can't be his design. It's too exclusive."

"Well, he is the god of the Jews, is he not?" The missionary quipped.

"Yes, but on the beach, you told me of a god who was coming to give his life for all our sins; a god who would defeat the iniquity of all of our lives. Were those promising narratives only a precursor to more Jewish bias? One can only be loved and accepted by this God of yours if he or she loses all connection to those who're of different mindsets? How could that be the way your God has designed to spread his agenda? I'm sorry, but I'm afraid that way of life makes no sense, not if you intend on revolutionizing a culture."

"Pray tell then, if you are so wise, what would you do to

influence the masses?"

Hayden immediately continued, "Embrace diversity and allow your god to bring unity from the division that exists. It should be the higher calling that unites, not lofty ideals established by one man's intuition. Your God should at least be given the opportunity to change a man, before the man is asked to change."

"You mock my rules?" The missionary stammered.

"Not at all, sir. Rules keep the world in order. Without them, we'd be most lost. Yet, too many rules without balance doesn't bring liberty, they bring more guilt and condemnation. What if your god actually had the chance to cleanse from within, allowing change to be perpetrated on a deeper level? What if the end result mattered more than the beginning? What if you allowed people to serve your god based on their experiences with him, rather than their commitment to new ideas they've never heard before a stranger introduced them? What if people felt loved and accepted instead of judged and rejected? Wouldn't the changes be easier to accept?"

"We must all make sacrifices, Sir Hayden. That's the way of life."

"It is indeed, but wouldn't those sacrifices be more bearable if people had the chance to embrace them with the knowledge that a higher power was still in control. To walk blindly seems irresponsible."

"Yet, to walk blindly is the epitome of faith."

"But faith with nothing connected to it is dead. What do the common people of Aksum have to believe in other than a concept, if you've not demonstrated to them the power of your god's great love? If they aren't good enough to sit inside the walls of your city, why would they be good enough to be loved by a god as mighty as the one of which you speak? Your words say one thing, but your actions demonstrate another. I, along with countless others, find no reason to pursue your way of life, for it's too bothersome."

"Without commitment, surrender, and faith, you could never be accepted anyway."

"So, the onus of responsibility for acceptance is on man's shoulders? That goes against the very nature of the loving God you described. How can you have it both ways? Either He loves unconditionally and will come to destroy sin for us all, or He'll remain distant to everyone but the Jews."

"He'll come for us all," the missionary shouted.

Hayden genuinely couldn't understand. "Then, how will you be able to spread His love and message, if you teach your people to hide behind these walls? What does that demonstrate about the power your god possesses, when his very people are afraid to engage the secular world, for fear they'll only return to life before conversion? Is the change that occurs not worth keeping? Is it so easily replaced by the world around us?"

"No," the missionary passionately continued. "But the flesh is attuned to the things of this world. You must know that. We fight everyday to keep our flesh in check. Inviting the world into our midst in any form would only lead to disaster. Moving outside these walls would only be a way to lose those we've already gained."

"But don't you see, sir. The longer you remain barricaded behind your walls, the longer the world cannot see the beauty of what you shared with me. The longer they feel alienated and unsure of your position; the longer they feel inferior to your higher spiritual mores; the longer they feel punished for not having the strength to make the commitments you have through deeper knowledge; then the longer they'll remain disconnected from your cause. You have no common ground with them, and no reason for them to join you. You must give them something to believe in, not just teach them on the veracity of faith itself. People only believe in what they've been conditioned to. They only change those beliefs when something comes along that's more powerful and compelling than what they've been shown. You must give them something more to trust in."

"Not at the risk of my people," the missionary brashly responded.

"Sir, the walls aren't keeping you safe. They're keeping you isolated."

"No. My people will never be like the people out there."

"They're not your people. They belong to Him, and from what you've told me, He's well able to keep them from the dangers of the world."

"We must battle to keep the evil at bay. We must commit to fighting that Sin Cloud at every turn. You've witnessed firsthand its destructive fury. How can you suggest I send my people into the world where that exists?"

"How can you not?"

"Why-"

Hayden ardently interrupted, "You know it's out there. You know the hold it has, the power it wields over them. You also know that you possess the knowledge of one who has power over it. You know the destruction and calamity it brings. You know the broken hearts it leaves in its devastating path. How can you not be there to help those who know nothing of your god?"

"It's not that simple. We must preserve and protect our inheritance. We must keep all things away that aren't like us. We possess different qualities than the rest of the world, because we've chosen a different path for ourselves. We've chosen a more difficult journey because it enables us to survive the daily barrage of darkness."

"But by hiding, you've learned to fear it. That doesn't sound like the lessons of a god who controls all things."

The missionary paused a few seconds, and then continued. "We have the reputation of being people who live above the mere laws of the land. Our way of life protects us from things that others are corrupted by. We have the reputation of being spiritually awakened and pure."

"But doesn't your god empower you to possess changes on the level of your heart? Isn't that where he does his greatest work? Shouldn't a heart change come before a life change? Shouldn't-"

"Sir Hayden, our reputation-"

Hayden stopped him, "There's a danger when your spiritual reputation is more esteemed than your spiritual condition. How can you claim to demonstrate a loving and compassionate god, when you show no real love or sacrifice toward others?"

"Your argument makes no sense," the missionary groaned.

"But it does. It's easy to love those who make me comfortable because they encourage and uplift me. It's much more difficult to love those who offer nothing in return and could possibly cause harm. Yet, it seems that your god has chosen to love us all. How can his followers do less?"

"You're mistaken, Sir Hayden. We do love. We love completely. We just choose to love from a distance."

"Is that even possible?"

"Of course it is. It's-"

Hayden didn't believe him. "*True love* is active, a fervent and continual expression of an emotional condition. It's more than profession. Without active exhibition to reveal the confessed feeling, love is nothing but an empty declaration. The world isn't moved by narrative, they receive enough of that through politics. Movements that spread deeds that go beyond the cultural norm move the world. If you're going to love, you must love in word *and* in deed."

"We've survived this way for decades. There's no need to change."

"Survived. Your god doesn't sound like he's into survival. You said he's come to empower, to equip people to overcome the adversity around them. How can they overcome the world if you've removed them from it?"

"I must remove them from the world for their own protection."

Hayden stood firm, "But you can remove the world from them without removing them from it."

"No. There's no other way. We must battle the Sin Cloud and keep it from reaching into our holy and sanctified realm."

"Be careful lest in battling the cloud so fervently, you become the cloud."

"That's blasphemy. God will protect us from such assaults."

Hayden slapped his hand against his leg in frustration. "When you continually shove others away, you make enemies of every one. You cannot offer yourself to the world if you aren't willing to embrace its differences of opinion. You can't offer love while living defensively. You can't expect others to be receptive to you, if you aren't willing to open yourselves to them. You're so afraid of the thorns that you hesitate to smell the rose."

"We'll fight until the end."

"You have no choice but to wage war. It's the atmosphere

you've created. You live in a way where you appear defensive, mean, unfriendly, arrogant, and self-centered. We've never been introduced, but I hardly doubt that's the plan your god intended. There must be more to it than this."

"But I'm right. This is the way to live."

"You don't have to always be right. How can you truly help others when they feel there's no way they can stand before you? Why must there be such quick lines in the sand? You're supposed to be a witness of God, not just a person who can testify for Him."

"And you suppose there's a difference?" the missionary asked, not understanding how Hayden could fathom such an opinion.

"A vast one. Anyone can testify for your god. It takes no special effort to communicate one's beliefs. It takes an entirely different mindset to actually be his witness, to live in such a way that you aren't forced to tell others to help them see, because they can see him and feel him in you, that's what your god must truly long for. By keeping yourselves in and others out, you protect yourself from the influence of others, but you remove your influence as well. Your god is big enough to meet people's needs where they occur, in their own world. Is he not?"

"He is most definitely."

"Then why do you not allow him to be god there? Why do you only allow him to be god where you feel safe and protected?"

"I must keep my people from being violated."

"A greater violation is to cause them to sit outside of their true calling. If they are to engage a lost world, how can they do so if they have no activity in it? If you are to be his hands and feet on this earth, how can he move among others when he's locked behind the walls of the places you've made sacred?"

The missionary was visibly upset. "You can do anything you'd like, Sir Hayden, but my people and I will remain as we've always been. Surely you understand."

Hayden stood up and moved toward the city gates. Darius got up to go with him. Hayden shook his head, as he walked away.

"No, sir. I don't. A god as powerful as yours doesn't need to be hidden… for any reason. Perhaps giving your life for him means more than wasting it doing nothing but turning yourself into judgmental bigots. Perhaps truly living for him means embracing those you said he'd embrace. Perhaps it means loving the outcast and sick. Perhaps it means loving the unlovable and reaching the unreachable. Perhaps it means demonstrating a love that's unbreakable, only because it's unconditional."

. . .

"I've got something. Torben, I've got something," Gino excitedly leapt from his chair.

"It's about time," Torben dryly retorted. "We've only been driving for the last five hours."

"We're gonna need gas soon," Jane called from the driver's seat.

"No. No. Flip the reserve tank. We're good for a few more hours. According to my calculations, they'll have a fix on us in five minutes. We can travel another twenty, then fill up the tank that just emptied. By the time they lock onto us, we'll be moving again."

"What did you find, G?" Torben eagerly asked.

"My program found the first key to the encryption. It took it a while because the reference it had to use is ancient."

"Ancient?"

"Yes. It's Sumerian."

"Sumerian, as in one of the earliest forms of writing? Mesopotamian. " Jane hollered.

"Yes, and *the* earliest, I believe," Gino called, obviously impressed with her knowledge. "No one uses it anymore. Except... uh..."

"Except who, G?" Torben inquired.

"Except people associated with the occult or the One World apologists, man. Crazy, but that's the only people I know who still have the propensity toward this language that's been dead for centuries."

"What does that teach you, G?"

"So far, nothing much. But I can tell you this, Torb. You're getting into something you may want to stay away from. You're entering deep waters, man."

"What makes you say that?"

"Because the encryptions and symbols I've been getting up until now are all layered with multicultural pseudonyms. Everything my program has unburied has been symbols of high-ranking government agencies. I've been able to read the heading of the file. It's labeled *The Affair*. By all accounts, the affair is a government initiative."

"C.I.A? F.B.-"

"No, Torben. Global. The executive branch of the United States, Sunni and Shiite Muslims, the CCP, the Vatican, and the United Nations. There's also another one that I don't recognize. But it's clear, man. Whatever you're getting into, it's dangerous."

Torben looked at him. "You can get out of this anytime you'd like. You know that, don't you?"

"Are you kidding me. I've waited my whole life to be part of this. I'm gonna help uncover the conspiracy, man. The people need to know."

Torben laughed. "This symbol that you're unsure of, what's it look like?"

"It's bizarre, man. Spooky."

"Okay."

"It's got a large serpent coiled around an inverted, bloody cross. There's an inscription penned on the top of it. It's an obvious twist of the words that St. John described. *IESUS NAZARENVS REX IVDAEORVM."*

Yes. Jesus of Nazareth, King of the Jews." Jane answered.

"It now says, *NAZARETH SCRIPTOR REX DEBET MORI."*

Torben chuckled, "Sorry, I must be the only one not up on my Latin."

"Nazareth's King Must Die," Gino ominously stated.

"Wow," Torben shook his head. "That's sick."

"Yeah. And that's not all. I've been able to determine that there are five distinct layers. This unknown emblem with the other governmental frameworks is embedded thoughout all five layers."

It was obvious that Gino had something else. Torben anxiously waited for his next explanation. Gino finally surrendered, realizing Torben wasn't going to ask for it.

"Yeah, man. The five layers are collectively labeled. They're called… Iscariot."

22

Hayden and Darius walked outside the gates. It didn't take them long to find the men's camp. They walked into the midst of the tents. A few of the men sat around a small fire. One of them stood and marched toward them. He laughed, as they came into view.

"The one who sleeps has come for us."

The others laughed; obviously amused that Hayden had been unconscious so long.

"How long was I out?" he asked them.

The man who'd separated himself replied. "Oh, a good two days. You slept more than I've ever seen any man sleep. If we didn't see you breathing, we would've thought you were dead."

"There's no way I slept that long." Hayden snickered unbelievingly.

"Well, you started to wake up on the evening of the first day, but the little man, he put you back to sleep for a while."

"He hit me again?" Hayden asked, his face glowing with resentment.

"No," the man chuckled. "He gave you something while you slept, some potion from the apothecary. Whatever it was, it worked. You slept another day and a half, and didn't wake up until after we landed here."

Hayden smiled, but he wasn't amused. "I guess I'll have to speak to the little man about that."

The men around the fire thoughtfully studied him. One of them asked, "What brings you out here with us, causing you to leave the safety of the city?"

"They told me that you all risked your lives to get us over here. I'm appreciative. I also don't see the sense of making anyone stay outside the gates. You risked yourself for me. The least I can do is decline special privilege if it's not afforded to all."

"Thank you, Sir, but that kindness isn't necessary. Although your sentiments are extremely appreciated."

Hayden noticed an elderly, black gentleman right inside a tent flap motioning for them. They cautiously made their way toward the open flap. As they stepped inside, the man knelt down and bowed his head in reverence.

"My king. I've called upon you to give you fair warning."

Darius was concerned. "Yes, what about, sir?"

"My king, two men were here just today asking for your whereabouts. We told them we weren't aware of your location, but I know they'll be back. We were told if you showed up to let them know immediately when we saw them again."

"Who were they?"

"I don't know, but from the looks of it, they're not looking for a friendly chat; they mean business."

"Thank you," Darius replied. "You may have just saved my life."

. . .

Several tents away, a large man watched through the folded flap. He clutched his sword tightly in his hand and motioned to another tent across his position. His brother motioned back, sword also in hand.

The ambush was set nicely. The target would be moving through the walkway between the tents. It was the main path in and out of the makeshift campsite. It hadn't taken them long to convince the crew of the ship that they should be hired on. Their considerable size made them perfect hires for the aggressive and physical labor of a deckhand. In a world where one crew would challenge another for a job at any moment, having tough men capable of fighting was a necessity. It was obvious that these two men were well able to handle themselves in combative situations.

From the moment of their hire, they'd plotted the best plan of attack against the future king of Aksum. They'd formulated several scenarios, attempting to cover every option. When he walked into their camp, it wasn't a total surprise. They weren't expecting it, but it was something they'd already discussed and planned for nonetheless. They'd drawn their swords and each taken a position in tents opposite one another. The walkway was narrow. If they both charged from opposite sides at the same time, he'd be an easy victim. Another notch on the hilt of their swords.

. . .

Darius moved away from the group he'd been talking to. He looked at Hayden and spoke uncharacteristically low.

"I'm not comfortable here. You're point has been made. I think it's safer to go back inside the walls. I don't want to die just to prove you believe in what you speak."

"Then go. No one is stopping you." Hayden unemotionally responded.

"Come with me, Sir Hayden. I don't want to go back without you."

"You'd do well to go back. There's no way you can defend yourself out here."

"And what of you? What are your plans? Just give up and let them win? You're so eager to let her death be in vain?"

"I'm going to find her. I pray that your journey lasts long

and brings you all the peace and joy you've ever dreamed. But, I'm not going to rest until I'm holding her in my arms."

"She's gone. You know that. Deep down, you know I'm speaking truth. You must let it go and move on."

"I can't. You should go in peace, Darius."

"Hayden, we need to finish what we started. After we're done, I'll be in a great position to help you in your quest for her. You must see the logic in what I suggest?

Hayden pondered the sense of his statement for a moment. Finally, he embraced Darius. "Brother, I'll finish what we started, but tomorrow. For tonight, let me grieve in my own way. I wish to speak to these men and find out if they know of a way M'ya could've survived. I need to know if they think she could've been taken somewhere. If she has, she'll know I'm coming for her. I can't disappoint such passionate faith."

Darius nodded. "I understand. Take your leave. Return to us in the morning. I shall return to the safety of the city at once, for there's no protection outside the walls."

Hayden tapped him on the back, and the two men separated. Hayden moved back toward the men sitting around the campfire, as Darius made his way through the tents, carefully walking along the dirt path they were built around.

The walkway was uncomfortably narrow. Darius clutched a small dagger, the only weapon he'd been able to recover since the shipwreck. He felt extremely exposed without the security of his bow and arrows. He tucked his head low and consciously willed himself forward into the darkness. The shadows from the distant fires danced like stalking silhouettes along the white, pitched tents.

The large man attentively watched him come. His heart wanted to beat more quickly, but the discipline born from years of training overrode his body's initial physiological response. He breathed deeply a few times, his eyes narrowing in nervous anticipation. This was it; the time was coming.

He'd been through this same routine too many times to remember. He'd lost count. That's why they'd started carving a simple mark on the hilt of their famed blades. One mark for each kill, and both of their hilts were running out of room.

Only four tents separated the black man from their position. He leaned close to the flap again and motioned for his brother. This time, there was no signal back. He motioned again.

Nothing.

Three tents.

Where was he? He couldn't have gone, the target was too close. There's no way he would've left his post. They'd plotted too hard, and they never deviated from a plan once they'd settled it. If one of them was out of place, it meant the other would be compromised. They'd survived this long because they trusted one another completely, and they always had each other's backs.

Two tents.

He was getting nervous now, a feeling he wasn't acquainted with. For once, he didn't know what to do. The plan was foolproof, if they could both charge at once. It wasn't that he thought the smaller black man could take him, but in his experience, deviations always led to disaster. The easiest way for good men to die is to alter plans in the midst of a struggle. That's why you plot ahead, when no emotion or fear gets in the way. Once you've established protocol, it must never be broken.

One tent.

Again, he frantically motioned. Again, nothing stirred on the other side. He clutched his sword more tightly. His brother knew the plan. When Darius was between them, they'd both lunge forward and the target would be cut down between them. The fact that Darius was alone only made the kill that much easier. He had to trust his brother to be there. He would be. He always was.

The man waited until Darius moved directly in front of him, and then silently lunged forward. His sword was already in mid-swing before Darius realized he was being assaulted. He had no time to lift his dagger, and even if he would have, the dagger was no defense against a sword as large as the one being swung at him. Instinctively, he fell back into the dirt. The blade missed his head by two inches, as he fell underneath it.

The attacker quickly countered with a downward motioning, stabbing his sword toward Darius' midsection.

Darius rolled just as the blade sunk into the earth. He lifted his feet into the air, pulled them slightly toward his stomach, and then shot them back out again. He simultaneously bent his knees and arched his back, the momentum rocketing his upper body forward, launching him to his feet.

He squared off against his unknown attacker. The man was huge. Scars covered his upper body and face from previous battles. The fact the man still stood was a testament to his skill as a warrior. Darius knew immediately that he was facing one of the gladiators. Fear suddenly riveted him, sending chills down his back. The gladiators were a team. Where was the second one?

The killer was sharing the same thoughts. Where was his brother? Something was definitely wrong. His brother wouldn't have wandered off knowing the target was in the area. They'd waited days for a target before. With no food, only a little water, and no allowed movement. They'd had to urinate and defecate through their clothing and pray the wind didn't shift enough for the target to smell them before they could make their move. This one was supposed to be much easier. There's no way he wouldn't have been there unless something had happened to him.

However, he was a professional. He refused to panic. He didn't know the meaning of the word. He held his sword high, both hands clasped around the hilt. Slightly tilting it from side to side, he prepared for his final attack. The black man only held a dagger in his right hand. He obviously possessed no other weapons, and he was too stupid to turn and run. This was still going to be easy.

He swiftly and powerfully swung the sword around to the right. Darius countered by holding his dagger vertically, parrying the quick swing. The impact of steel on steel reverberated across the night sky. Darius was knocked backward by the force of the larger man's thrust. The smaller blade flew from his hand and imbedded in the earth a few feet to his left side. He feigned like he was going to move toward it, but the attacker was prepared for that and cut him off by stepping in that direction. The man lifted his sword high, a smile pursing on his lips.

He often knew the final moment when it came, the one right before he delivered the kiss of death. He could see it in his opponent's eyes. They always knew it too, a mixture of fear and uncertainty, not knowing what was waiting for them in the afterlife. He saw it now on the black man's face. He knew he was about to die.

He held the hilt in both hands and thrust it down toward Darius' chest. Something slammed into him, lifting him from his feet. His sword fell harmlessly at Darius' side. He landed three feet back, his head slamming just inside the tent his brother should have charged from.

His head was swimming, and he wasn't sure why. He tried to get up, but something kept him down. He felt it then, a searing pain penetrating his chest. Impulsively, he grabbed at the spot and felt an arrow burrowed near his heart. Turning his head, he saw his brother lying there. There was no doubt he'd been killed. Someone had managed to reach him from behind and silence him with a garrote. The wire was still tightly wound against his neck.

He reached for the dagger at his side and managed to lift himself to his knees. His brother was dead, and he wasn't going to let the target walk away from here. He tried to stand but felt something grasp him from behind. A searing pain dumbfounded him, as a blade penetrated his back. He fell face first in the sand. He rolled quickly to see his attacker. Whoever… Whatever had been there was gone.

Darius leapt to his feet. He'd seen a blur. His attacker had been about to kill him, when an arrow had shoot through him. The man had fallen into a tent and had been attacked by something lightning fast.

Darius picked up the oversized sword that lay at his feet and charged toward the tent. As he opened the flap and stepped inside, he noticed two things immediately. The two gladiator brothers were both dead inside, and no one else was in sight. The space was curiously empty. There appeared to be no rear exit. Whoever… whatever had been there had simply slipped into the night.

He heard footsteps rushing toward him and abruptly turned the sword in their direction. Hayden was running through the sand with three other men at his side. Darius fastened the blade through his sash.

Hayden was out of breath, "Someone came running up, said you'd been attacked. I thought they'd gotten you."

Darius grasped Hayden's bicep and pulled him away from the others. He leaned in closely and whispered.

"They would've killed me, but something happened… again. Just like on the ship. They had me dead to rights and somehow they both wound up dead before they could touch me. It was closer this time, but I'm alive because-"

"You have a guardian angel," Hayden said, as he stared unbelievingly into the darkness.

"I must. I can't explain it, but I should now be dead twice over. I don't know what to think. Last time I saw nothing. This time I saw movement, but no discernible features. Someone is helping me, and I'm not even sure they're human."

"Well, just be glad they're on your side and not working against you. Two assassin teams have been taken down; so that also leaves two. The bouda still lives, as does the decorated Roman guardsman. You aren't out of the woods just yet, Darius."

He weakly shook his head. "I know, and if I survive them, I'll most surely have to endure an encounter with my brother."

23

Two hours later, Hayden and Darius huddled around the small fire with several of the sailors. The men had identified the two fallen brothers as the ones that had been looking for Darius. The story of what had happened had already been told and retold around several other campfires surrounding the city. One of the men slapped Darius on the shoulder.

"Tis how legends are born, sir. Darius, future king of Aksum, one who walks with ghosts."

They all laughed, although Darius' laugh was slightly less intense than theirs. It wasn't the alcohol they were consuming either. It was more his malfunction than theirs. He simply did not find it funny.

The truth was that something had saved him twice. Something he couldn't see or hear. He'd always considered himself a realist, but he wasn't sure anymore.

The truth was also that his savior could be human. It could've been someone who'd taken the assassin's creed and learned the art of invisible killing. However, both events had been incredibly swift and in tight confines. Most assassins like their kills to be methodically planned out. For someone to be following him around without detection and fighting for him without the benefit of a battle plan was preposterous. That left only a few shocking options: A ghost, a god, an angel, or a devil; and none were appealing.

Finally, one of the men drunkenly scooted close to him.

"If I draw my dagger to stab ya in the throat, would your great protector come flashing from the sky for us ta view, or would ya just be left ta die because it don't wanna be seen?"

Hayden shoved the man backward, knocking him slightly off balance.

"He doesn't need protection from the likes of you. That's what he's got me for."

The sailors laughed, picking the man up and giving him another drink. One of them was sitting a little away from the rest. He was young, no more than fifteen. He had blond hair and blue eyes, stood about six feet tall, and was stronger than his small frame suggested. He wasn't drinking like the rest of them. He locked eyes with Hayden from across the crowd.

"And what 'bout you, sir? You got protection?"

Hayden touched the hilt of the blade stuck in his belt and warmly smiled at the young man.

"I've got all the protection I need these days."

The youngster nonchalantly smiled back without looking up. "Didn't protect her from him though... did it?"

Hayden's smile faded instantly. "What did you say?"

The boy continued staring at the ground. "M'ya. I believe that was her name. Didn't stop him from taking her away from you... did it?"

Hayden took a step toward him, but Darius intervened by extending his hand.

"Hayden, don't. It's not worth it."

Hayden fiercely looked at the boy. "What do you know about that? Choose your words wisely."

The boy stopped staring at the ground and lifted his head in Hayden's direction. He didn't smile.

"I know she still lives."

Hayden gasped. It felt like someone had punched him in the stomach. He was emotionally overwhelmed and couldn't gather himself to speak. Darius faced the boy.

"You'd better not be fooling around, son. We both take this matter seriously. She was our friend."

The boy laughed. "To some more friendly than others, no doubt," he stated, glancing at Hayden with a sarcastic wink.

Hayden leapt forward. "Where is she, boy? You'd better not stand in my way."

"How should I know where he's taken her? Your guess is as good as mine. I'm not his watchman or her keeper. They could be anywhere... nowhere... or not at all."

Hayden drew his weapon and charged toward the boy. The clank of several weapons being drawn got his attention. Awakened from their drunken stupors, the boy's shipmates obviously had his back.

"Looks like I've got some protection of my own here," the boy condescendingly replied.

Hayden didn't back down. "You'd better not be messing with me, boy. I'm not in the mood for games. Whether King Darius' protector comes raining down or not, one thing is certain, you won't leave here alive. You shouldn't torment a man hell-bent on revenge."

The boy's smirk was irritating. Darius scowled, "If I thought it would help, I'd bend you over my knees, remove your trousers, and beat you with a thorny switch."

"Ah, spare the rod, spoil the child, that's what mother used to say before I killed her with my own hands."

He smirked again. "Everyone just sort of blamed it on daddy. Said he shouldn't have left us when I was but a lad. Didn't have discipline in my life, so I turned out mean. How's that sound? Accurate?"

Hayden was angry. "A man chooses his own path. You don't have to be the way you are. Your heart has been encased with evil. Your mind's been clouded by the darkness. However, if you truly wanted to, you could change."

"How clever... Manipulation... Trying to cause me to change my mind about my actions. Perhaps I will feel a tinge of guilt and just tell you the information you're longing for."

"Perhaps I'll beat it out of you," Darius threatened.

The boy chuckled again. "C'mon, ole man, if ya dare. You'd find killin' me not so easy as killin' the feeble slave that traveled by your side to tha Fortress... Doesn't it scare ya to remember that ya were with him all that time and never really knew who he was? All those nights, he just carried around his plot to kill you all. He was just gonna do it for tha money."

Hayden shook his head. "No. He chose his path. We won't feel guilty for something that's beyond our control. It was kill or be killed. At times, that's life."

"Did it really have to be? I mean, have you pondered if you could have saved him? What if you would've given him more personal time, would you have recognized the danger signs and been able to prevent his final meltdown. Perhaps your recognition could have saved him from his one-way trip to hell. He was perfectly honest about one thing; he really didn't want to die. But Hayden, you let him, and Darius, you killed him. You should both be sentenced under the strictness of the law. "

Hayden groaned. "What about the girl? Where is the girl?"

"You only ask about her because you're selfish. You want her for yourself. You aren't concerned about her at all."

"How do you know she still lives?"

"I know. That should suffice."

"No. I need to get her back."

"Need. Such a strong word, Sir Hayden. You need to keep breathing in order to live. You need to eat and drink for nourishment. You need your heart to continue pumping blood. However, life goes forward with or without her. There's a huge difference. Desire and necessity are mutually exclusive."

"If she's gone, my heart has been taken with her. All men must die, only a fortunate few know the beauty of being alive."

"And therein lies your problem, sir. She's your fatal flaw, the one thing that keeps you from reaching your potential. She's what holds you down. The beautiful apparition of peace that only creates chaos, bringing the storm instead of the calm."

"No. You've gotten it wrong. That's not her."

"Isn't it? You're here for a higher purpose. Are you not, Sir Hayden? Yet, she was content to selfishly weigh you down with the mere emotions of mortality. How can you reach eternal destiny while trying to possess fleshly promise? Those concepts vary too deeply."

"No. She wasn't like that. She isn't... She... She gave herself for us at the island. She stood in the vortex of the Sin Cloud and took it head on. She surrendered her life to make sure we were given safe passage."

"And you allowed that? What kind of man are you?"

"No. I tried to stop her. I couldn't... I couldn't move."

"Or, did you not want to because you knew it wanted you instead."

"I'd have gladly given myself for her. In an instant."

"But you didn't. What does that say of your devotion? What kind of love do you think you possess. Look at yourself honestly, Sir Hayden. You don't truly love her. You can't, because your love is too selfish and self-appeasing."

"No. No... What do you mean?" he stammered.

"If you truly loved her, you would've let her go, so she could safely develop away from you. Instead, you kept her close, knowing full well the cost that would have to be paid. You knew, and you egoistically let it happen. Then, when the end comes, you want to cry and wonder how it got to this point. It's the little steps along the way that matter. You kept her near, and now you're suffering for it. Now, fate has removed her from your life, the way providence intended."

"So, this is my fault? No. It can't-"

Darius grabbed him. "C'mon Hayden, stop... He's just a kid. He doesn't know anything about life."

Hayden turned his back to walk away with Darius. He abruptly stopped. The boy's words caused his body to quiver.

"I know where she is. I'll never tell, but I know where she is."

Hayden whirled around. "I'll kill you."

The boy laughed. "You already did her."

Hayden grabbed his dagger and hurled it toward the boy. It flew from his grip and headed straight toward the boy's head. Right before it sank into his flesh, the boy laughed, and then disappeared. The knife sunk into the wooden tent pole he'd been leaning against. The fire hissed, lapped loudly for a second, and then was extinguished. The boy was gone, leaving only the remnants of a dark cloud where he'd just been."

24

The shipmates stared into the shadowy haze that still lingered around the center stake. It had been five minutes, but the smoky residue wasn't weakening. Hayden was spellbound, and Darius silently left him to his thoughts.

Finally, one of the sailors broke the hushed ambiance. He didn't address Hayden but looked toward his companions.

"Who was that boy? How'd he-"

Another one interrupted. "Said his name was Tyre. He'd only just joined us. That's all-"

"But how'd he do that? How'd he disappear into the haze? Why's it still there?"

The one who had interrupted stood from where he'd been sitting and walked toward the fog. It seemed to ripple as he moved near. It turned toward him, as if threatened by his presence.

"Don't," the first man called out, as the other one reached his finger toward it.

However, he continued moving his hand forward until it was buried in the black smog. Suddenly, he screamed, as something lifted him from the ground and hurled him thirty feet through the air. He landed across the walkway on the side of one of the tents. People scrambled from inside, unsure what had just caused their makeshift shelter to collapse. Darius reached him first and bent down, feeling his neck and wrist for a pulse.

The man was dead.

He turned and shook his head. A low murmur started among the onlookers. The cloud rose twelve feet in the air and continued to hover.

Hayden moved to Darius. "It's watching us. I don't know how, but it's alive. It's measuring us. We have to find a way to defeat it."

Concern was written over Darius' face. "I don't think there's a way, Sir Hayden."

"There must be a way. Surely someone around here knows of this cloud and how it can be defeated."

An older black man loomed over them. He was massive, his shoulders broader than both of theirs together. His neck was extraordinarily thick, biceps and forearms bulged, and legs were solid as tree stumps. His head stopped only three or four feet under the blackness.

"I know one tha' may have da ansaas ya seek. She hard ta find, but if we leave now, we mite make it to her 'foe dark."

Darius politely smiled. "Who might you be, stranger?"

"I jus' anotha Aksumite ship slave, suh. Pay me no mind. I jus' know sumthin' 'bout tha cloud. Seen it b-fo'e. It ravaged tha whole village. Kilt em all, suh. Men an' women. Even tha lil' ones, suh. They come in and took 'em. Threw sum in tha' riva. Hurled otha's ova tha cliffs. Otha's was jus' lef' ta die out by tha roads. Dey left them there for tha gods to decide dere fate."

"The cloud... How'd the cloud do all that?"

"Sorry, suh. Ya misundastood. The cloud led the attacks, but it had hands and feet. It wuz real, live flesh and blood humans tha' did tha deeds, suh."

Hayden was appalled. "How could anyone kill a child? That's barbaric."

Darius lightly touched his shoulder. "Hayden, be careful. Ritualistic sacrifice of children is common practice on this side of the world."

"That's absurd, Darius. That's one thing I could never understand."

"Relax, you don't want to offend anyone for their customary beliefs. In my country, twins are considered evil and are both executed immediately after birth. If the parents try to intervene, they're terminated as well. If a mother dies during childbirth, it's considered a bad omen. The baby must be buried alive in order to make sure the evil spirit that killed the mother dies with it."

"And… You're honestly okay with all of that? How, Darius? You're a wise man, with good morals. How can you not see the lunacy in this?"

"It's what we know, Hayden. It's all we know."

Hayden disgustedly shook his head. "There comes a time when you must change what you know, a time when truth transcends knowledge and reason supersedes tradition."

"You mustn't try to combat every belief not like yours, Sir Hayden. It's not going to win you any friends here."

"I'm not in the business of winning friends, Darius. What kind of man would I be to weaken the resolve of my beliefs in order to appease those who I don't believe in."

"Why is it so hard for you to grasp? The entire world lives with various convictions concerning this subject. Even in Babylon, your people annihilate the handicapped and feeble. Infanticide is a common practice in every kingdom of the world. There's no corner that isn't influenced by this exercise."

"It shouldn't be. The Cloud kills children. We kill children too. How are we different?"

"There's a big difference, Hayden."

"And what would that be, Darius?"

"We do it to further the human race. The Sin Cloud does it for mere pleasure."

"Try telling that to a grieving mother whose child you've just thrown into the river. I doubt she'd recognize the difference."

"Perhaps we could do a better job of comforting those who mourn," Darius conceded.

Hayden looked as if he'd just been slapped, "Or, perhaps you could stop the mourning all together. Do you not place infinite value on human life? What if it were one of your children who developed a debilitating sickness? You'd so easily have them executed? Or, you'd demonstrate compassion and understand that even the weak can contribute something. Every one has value and deserves to be loved."

"You've asked a hard question... I... I don't know if I can honestly give you an answer."

"If your child's life is worth saving, King Darius, perhaps you'd do well to remember that so are your people's children."

The massive black man spoke up. "He be right, suh. I wuz lef' out by dah road from Carthage. Sum people found me and raise me as dey own. I glad dey did, or I wouldn't be heh."

Darius stared at the ground. Hayden turned to the black man.

"Where do you suggest we go to learn about the darkness?"

"Follow me, suh. I show ya tha way."

Hayden started to follow, as the big man walked away from the tents. The Sin Cloud moved away with him. Darius grabbed Hayden's left arm so hard it spun him around. Hayden jerked away from him.

"Look," Darius pointed. "It's moving. That can't be a good sign. And we don't know anything about him. You can't just blindly follow into the unknown. That's not wise."

"Perhaps you should come with me then. Your secret protector would no doubt make sure we're kept safe."

"No. We can't risk it, Hayden."

Someone moved in from the brush nearby. "Maybe there's an alternative."

They both turned to see that Leib had joined them.

Leib continued, "One of my connections here sent word that you'd been attacked, King Darius. I really cannot remove my eyes from you for more than a few seconds without finding out there's been another attempt on your life."

Darius was mildly agitated. "I'm more than capable of taking care of myself. I wouldn't be doing the right thing if so many people didn't want to watch me die."

"Well, we must keep you alive... Hunzuu is interviewing the people to see what he can turn up. He should be here any moment. He's going to stay near you to make sure that no further attempts are made against you. There's no one else we can trust who knows the way of the assassin. You should be more than fine with him at your side."

Leib paused and looked at Hayden. "I shall travel with you to discover the truth about finding M'ya. Together, we should be safe."

Darius chuckled. "You aren't exactly warrior material, short one. What makes you think he's any safer with you."

"Even the elephant fears the mouse, my king. I have more to offer than it appears."

Hunzuu briskly rounded one of the tents and slowed up to them. He removed a pack from his back and handed it to Darius.

"Had it made just for you. It should be the right size. It's made from famed cypress. The artisan said it should shoot straighter than any bow you've ever owned."

Darius lit up when he saw the bow and quiver. It was made a deep mahogany and had ancient emblems carved into the framework. He smiled and nodded toward Leib and Hunzuu.

"Tis truly a weapon fit for a king. I shall be more careful not to lose this one."

Hunzuu removed the scabbard of the famed blade of Tiber and handed it to Hayden. He showed Hayden the two small swords strapped to his back.

"These will do me just fine. It's time to place this blade back in the hands of its rightful owner. It's been a pleasure holding it, but I've got a feelin' you'll get more use out of it than I shall. You and Leib go now, make haste. Watch your step. Especially if the Cloud stays with you."

The enormous man interjected. "It be safe. Tha cloud not gonna be no botha'. It already know where I take ya, and it can't stop ya from goin' dere."

"Then lead the way," Hayden motioned, as he and Leib fell in behind.

. . .

The journey was more difficult then either had planned. They'd been making their way through the rough terrain of a desert. The heat was sweltering. Neither had water, and both were growing irritated from thirst.

The man leading them hadn't slowed down. He hadn't stopped to drink, not once. They'd both emptied their pouches a couple hours ago. He'd never noticed.

Hayden's shirt was drenched in sweat. The material hugged his figure like he'd just step from bathing in a cool lagoon. Leib wasn't faring any better.

"How much further?" he finally asked. "We need water."

"We almos' dere. Don' stop now. We gotta keep goin'."

"You don't understand," Leib panted. "If I don't get water soon. I'm gonna faint. My body wasn't made for this."

"Nor mine," Hayden seconded, trying to appear as if he wasn't complaining.

"Once tha trip begin, it cannot be ended 'til we arrive. She wuld know, and she don' want no one comin' ta her that don' wanna make tha sacrifice to be dere."

Leib whined. "You aren't making sense, giant. What does it matter if we're dehydrated or not? That can't be a prerequisite to meeting her."

"It be hers, suh. I don' make dem rules. I just know dem, suh. Tha's all."

He stopped walking and pointed to a huge tree in the midst of the next valley. Vultures circled overhead, scanning the area for food. The top of the lone tree was a magnet for the large scavenger birds, as hundreds of them filled the small branches.

"Dis be as far as I go. I not welcome ova' dere 'less she acks me, and she didn't. So, I stay right heh. I wait 'til ya get back."

"Wait. There's nothing but a tree over there. Where will we find her?" Leib asked.

"Little man, jus' go stand by dat tree an' wait. She be showin' up soon enough. She won' disappoint'cha."

Hayden motioned to Leib, and the two of them warily left the black man sitting cross-legged in the sand. After a couple minutes, he looked back. The man was still sitting as he had been, watching them walk away.

The minutes slowly rolled by. A quarter hour later, Leib turned again. He could barely see the man sitting in the distance. He stumbled and fell to his knees.

"I can't go anymore. We're only halfway to the tree. I can't do it," he groaned.

Hayden picked him up and slung him over his shoulder. Leib tried to resist.

"Put me down. You won't make it carrying me. Go yourself, Hayden."

Many of the buzzards moved from the branches overhead to circle above them. One drifted downward, slowly hovering above the injured Leib. Leib made a sudden movement, and the bird lifted back into the air, never removing its eyes from Leib's weakened body.

Hayden stumbled his way to the tree and looked up to its high branches. Over three-fourths of the tree was a solid trunk. The remaining top portion was full of uneven branches.

He sat Leib down beside the wide base. "It's the Baobab Tree. This one is huge. Its trunk must be at least thirty-four feet thick."

Leib leaned against it. "Wonder what we're waiting for. I didn't see anything around."

"Nor did I, dwarf."

"He's no doubt brought us here to die. Neither of us will be able to make it back with no water," Leib complained.

The birds continued to circle overhead, waiting for one of them to draw their final breath. A few landed nearby, warily moving back and forth, measuring Leib's awareness and strength.

Hayden moved next to him and sat down against the tree's soft bark, nervously looking into the distant twilight.

"It's gonna be dark soon. The temperatures are going to drop extremely low. We're gonna freeze out here."

Leib sullenly looked at Hayden. "There's too much at stake. You must go back without me."

"Not an option. You know I'd never do that. We'll figure something out. We always do."

"Not this time, sir. Its hours back to civilization. We're out of water. We've got no food. There's no hope in sight. We're not gonna make it out of this one… Not together… Alone, at least you'd have a chance."

"If one of us dies here, we both die here. That's just the way it is, Leib. I'd expect nothing different if the situation were reversed."

The tree suddenly trembled. Leib and Hayden stumbled away from it, looking back to see what had caused the unexpected movement. A section in the center of the trunk was separating, slightly protruding from the rest of the bark. Then it slowly rotated outward, leaving a gaping hole in the core of the tree.

The opening was approximately five feet tall and two feet

wide. It wasn't an even split, more like a jagged tear. An ember light emanated from inside, casting a ghostly illumination on the ground. Hayden stood and slowly moved toward the fissure.

Leib reached out and touched Hayden's leg. "Don't. It could be dangerous."

"Or it could be what saves our lives, Leib. A man gains nothing if he fears risk."

"Help me up then. I'll go with you," he weakly begged.

A few seconds later, both men made their way toward the sudden, makeshift opening. They were five feet away when the light became blinding. Leib fell to the ground, holding his hands over his eyes. Hayden stood firm, but squinted against the light, trying to see what was creating the brightness.

He could see movement, but it was impossible to recognize anything more. The shapes were oddly distorted and moving toward them rather quickly. He grabbed Leib and pulled him, as the figures were almost to them. He'd taken five steps when he lost his balance and toppled over backwards. He looked into the light again. Strangely enough, it seemed to be dimming, finally fading until the only obstruction to their vision was the orange and green spots that remained from looking directly into the light. It was as if the sun had scorched their pupils, causing a temporary blindness.

Hayden blinked against the spots, rapidly closing his eyelids several times. Leib closed his eyes and held them shut, hoping the effect would go away.

This loss of vision was worse than merely stepping into the darkness. There's nothing as painful and repugnant as being blinded by the light. It's amazing how too much of either yields the same result. Man wasn't designed to live in the extremes.

A scratchy voice emanated from the area in front of them. It was unfamiliar and seemed to be that of an old woman. Hayden cleared his vision further to find that his assumption had been correct.

She was average height but appeared older than any woman he'd ever seen. Her skin was porous and wrinkled. The lines in her face told a story of heartache, sacrifice, and pain. But there was something else, something he couldn't quite explain. He could feel it, rising to the surface of his senses and causing the hair on his neck to stand on end.

She beckoned, "Hayden, he who travels from worlds beyond, why have you chosen me? What have I done to deserve a visit from you?"

He shook his head toward her and held out his hands. "I was led here. I didn't come seeking you on my own.""

Her expression was a mixture of nervousness and fear. "The gods couldn't have brought you to the likes of me. You must leave."

Hayden was confused. " What have I done to offend you, dear woman?"

"Offend me? It's not your actions that I find offensive. It's your very nature that's distasteful."

Hayden was puzzled, "I'm sorry, but I know only how to be what I am. I don't know what you've heard, but-"

"What I've heard. By the gods, this isn't about what I've heard. I've heard nothing. This is about what I've seen. I've witnessed your pollution firsthand."

"Pollution?" He was seriously perplexed.

She almost screamed the words, "Pollution is too kind a word. You're an insurgent, causing others to drift against the natural order of our world, a rebel who revolts against our lives. Your antics will get them all killed."

"Who will-"

She fiercely interrupted, "Those you love. It will destroy them all. You can't be called and chosen and live like everyone else. You have to decide..."

She paused and then harshly slammed the words toward him. "If you love her, let her go. Let her go, Hayden. Let her go."

"I can't... I won't... She means too much to me. I mean too much to her. We're nothing if we're apart."

"Yet, your destinies are not interwoven. You've created a synthetic truth. It's real to you, but it's not real to Him. He created you both for a purpose. In Him, Hayden, your purpose is in Him. Don't you understand?"

He was hesitant, "No. I don't. Why can't I have both?"

"You weren't brought here to develop an attachment that

could devastate your life. You'll destroy her. You have to let her go. You must willingly make the sacrifice."

"It can work," he demanded.

"No. It never will."

"What do you mean? Why not?"

"There is no merging of worlds. There's no satisfaction there unless you choose wisely here. It's the way of things. Every decision you make along life's journey leads somewhere. You must remember that. There are no meaningless steps. Every footfall matters."

Hayden was crying... There? Here? It didn't make sense. Yet, he somehow instinctively knew. The nightmares... There? This life... Here?

He looked at her, "You really believe we're-"

"We are the sum of our parts, the compilation of major falls and minor lifts, the offspring of a union between natural appeasement and spiritual fulfillment."

"I can balance the two. I've done quite well thus far." He strongly stated.

"To you, you've done well. Yet, you have no real discernment. If you did, you'd understand that to feed your fleshly desires starves your spiritual man. There's no middle ground. You must choose whether you'll serve the flesh, fulfilling your own lust, or serve God, giving your desires to him."

THE SIN CLOUD

"There must be. I can choose it anyway I'd like," he yelled.

"No. You aren't in this journey by yourself. It's not about you. It's never been about you. You're part of a much bigger world, a world held most sacred, a time and place that depends on you for its survival. You are the key, Hayden. You've always been the key. You must submit to your calling. You must embrace your destiny."

"But the choices are mine to make. They have to be. I can have both."

She lowered her head. "No. That's not the way of things. Never has been. From the beginning, man has tried it his way, yet has never learned that it cannot work."

"Why would He not want me to have both, to possess what truly makes me happy? Why does everything have to be a sacrifice? Why does it all have to hurt so much?"

"It doesn't."

"But you just said-"

She firmly interrupted again. "I said that you must learn the proper order of the universe. Placing your desires above your calling only leads to devastation, long-term failure, and chaos."

"It would bring me such peace to have her by my side. She completes me," he cried.

"Maybe for a moment, but there's no peace outside of His presence. That's what you must learn."

"But I can have both. I insist its true. He'd want me to have both."

"Yes. He does."

"Then why not? Why can't I-"

"Because He wants you to have Him first. You give Him everything, all you are and ever hope to be. Give him every piece of your heart, mind, and soul. Lay down every burden. He'll make sure you're cared for. He'll make sure you get the desires of your heart. Try your way first, and it always comes up empty."

Hayden vehemently resisted, "Life with her would never be empty. I'd rather leave the promises of higher fulfillment and live in the Dregs if we could be together. I love her that much."

She nodded, understanding his sentiments. "If only it were that simple, but I must make you aware that there's much more at stake. So many lives hang in the balance."

"No. I never asked for this. I don't accept it. I just want life to be normal. Why can't I have a normal life?" Hayden wept again.

"You're life is normal, much more so than most, and you fail to realize it. It cannot be more obvious, and you can't be more oblivious. You've grasped the real world. What you see every day is only a fragment of reality. What's in your heart, sir; the powerful grip on your soul; the beautiful yearning in your spirit; Sir Hayden, that's what is real. It goes far beyond what others know, for you've been chosen."

He was visibly upset, "Reality is not what you or anyone else has designed for me."

"No. Reality is what He's created you for. Reality is all about Him," she gently replied.

"And how do you propose that I tell the difference? How can I know when a choice is reality or just my own carnal desires rearing their ugly head?"

Her reply shook him, "Eternity. What matters there? If it doesn't matter in His big picture, then, Sir Hayden, it does not matter. It never did. There's a world that exists beyond what you hear, taste, smell, see, and feel. You mustn't sacrifice the eternal to make the temporary more satisfying."

Hayden was crying more fervently. "I weep for her. How is that not real?"

"Your feelings may be thus real, but they don't serve the purpose of the actual world. You must discern the truth of what I'm saying, or you've lost. Too many other lives are at stake."

"No. I'm my own man. I'm not affecting the lives of others."

She anxiously continued, praying he'd understand. "Hayden, when you stand between an infinite calling and a finite decision, you can't see the value of what hangs in the balance. You can't afford to choose based on feeling alone. If so, man would choose selfishly, and the eternal would be lost every time."

"But how can I be asked to choose, when I know what my heart truly desires?"

"You walk in the now, Hayden. You're only focused on what your heart sees before you. But you were designed for larger venues than today. You must open the horizons of your soul. You must be willing to journey beyond the recesses of your own emotion and intellect. You must be willing to embrace the truth that's out there, waiting to be discovered... Today is all you see, but the future lies ahead."

"I can't do it." He wailed. "I can't. I won't let her go."

"Then your fate is sealed, and you've limited the potential that lies before her. You've broken the Creator's design. You've trampled the lives of many."

"No. My life has little impact. I'd rather it that way," he contested.

She forcefully sighed, "But you still have no choice about the impact. Your decisions have influence, one way or the other... You just don't get it. When you fail to engage His purpose and selfishly persist in your own will, you crush the dreams of those who've paid the ultimate price before you. Life is bigger than you. Your surrender would be a tragic blow felt through the ages... It's more than just a choice; it's a calling, and there's a high price to being selected by the King of Kings."

He shook his head, wiping away more tears. "How so?"

"Your life is a meager page in a much larger script. The Master Scribe has already penned it long before the earth was formed. The story was complete before time even began. When your page is opened, you either embrace the unfolding story, or you rip the page from the book. Although you fail to realize its affect, the story is then somehow incomplete. Sure, it moves on without you, but a missing page affects the whole. It alters the story."

"You mean... everyone?"

She nodded. "Every believer who ever fought before you, every martyr who gave their all to make sure the truth was known, every man or woman who ever cried to the Heavens for His will to be performed, and every old saint who ever whispered weakened prayers for mercy and compassion to come to the earth. You take a little piece of their heart when you alter His story. You make their sacrifice a little less meaningful than it was before... Believe me, your loss is felt."

"Those martyrs are gone anyway. What does it really matter?"

She sullenly winced; worried she wasn't getting through to him. "If you're not moved by the past, then what of the future, Sir Hayden. They depend on you as well. The unborn and today's small children, the entire future waits. Some who would have been impacted by your life may not receive the chance, if you fail to make the choice. How can you be happy with the knowledge that you're the reason others fall?"

Hayden's crying had grown uncontrollable. His tears soiled the barren ground. He fell face down and sobbed into his hands.

She gently continued, "You know what must be done, Sir Hayden. When you find her, you know what must be done."

He picked his face up from the sand. "So she still lives? Please, tell me she still lives."

"She does live, Sir Hayden. She's captive to a king. King Apollyon of Tyre. He's holding her there."

"Thank you," Hayden painfully stammered.

Leib moved toward her. His eyes held resentment, as she'd obviously caused his close friend such pain. She turned to him.

"I haven't forgotten you, Sir Leib. Come with me, please. Leave him be for a few moments. He must collect his thoughts."

Leib reluctantly followed her into the entrance of the tree. He was amazed at the inside. Someone had carved a space for her. The small opening was larger inside, at least fourteen feet wide and twelve feet deep. The "ceiling" was eight feet high all the way across.

"Amazing," Leib said. "Purely amazing."

"Welcome to my home," she offered, as she tossed Leib a satchel. It was strapped closed.

She smiled. "For the road. Bread and honey for you both. Also, there are two fresh pouches of water. It should be plenty for your trip back. And warm blankets to combat the cold."

"Thank you, ma'am."

She knelt down in front of him, now at eye level, and pulled him close. He started to resist, but was calmed by her warm embrace, as she squeezed him tightly. A tear fell from his eyes. He'd never felt anything like this before.

Love. Pure love. She was holding him, because she loved him. She didn't know him and had never seen him. Yet, he couldn't deny the powerful emotion overshadowing his psyche.

It was too much. He abruptly pulled back. She smiled anyway.

"You must make sure he knows what he's getting into. He must be prepared to fight this next battle. I'm not sure he's ready for such an adversary as the King of Tyre."

"Who is he?"

"Officially, the king of a province near the homeland of the Jews. Unofficially, Hayden has already encountered him twice."

"When?" Leib quizzically questioned.

"The young man he tried to kill in the camp, and the man who took M'ya into the Dark Cloud."

"How? How could he have-"

"Have been both…" She laughed. "He's a powerful man. Some know him as the Sorcerer… Don't be mistaken. His power is much deeper than that. He's no man of magic. He's much more evil. Many believe he's a manifestation of darkness itself."

"But how? Who is he?"

"I don't know for sure, he could be many things... Many cultures have many different names for him. I don't know which is correct, but one truth is certain, whatever he is, he's no man."

Leib shuttered. She quickly interrupted his thoughts by handing him a ruby amulet. She then removed a lambskin pouch and placed the amulet inside.

"You'll need this. It represents the blood of innocence. Possessed by one of pure heart, it's the only weapon against the power of the Sin Cloud."

He appeared confused.

Her nose twitched. "That's why you've come isn't it? You want to know how to defeat the Sin Cloud?"

He gave an affirmative nod. "The blood?"

"Just keep it, you'll know what to do when the time is right."

"Why me? Give it to him. I don't know-"

"He needs you. More than either of you realize. He needs you all. But his stubbornness will bring deadly consequences. You must be willing to pay the price. You and the others must be willing to surrender everything. It's his only salvation, and the only way this world will be saved... Stay with him. Make him find his way back to reality. We're depending on you," she stated, desperation evident in her intonation.

"Who?"

"You must keep Hayden focused on moving forward."

"Who?" He repeated.

"Don't let him settle for the present. There's another world he must live for. If he sells himself short here, it will kill his purpose there. Don't let him sell himself short. He has much too high a purpose."

"Who?" He emphatically demanded. "Who is depending on him so completely?"

She slightly tilted her head and sadly frowned. Her answer created chills over the length of his body. He was tangibly shaken.

"Who?" He had asked.

"All of us, Sir Leib. All of humanity."

25

Only a few candles burned in the windows surrounding the southernmost part of the room. The black man entered alone, carefully measuring his movements. He was uncharacteristically nervous, and hadn't felt this way in years, not since the big race against the other young boys of the city. Of course, his elder brother had won, and his father had rejoiced over another victory for his young hero. One of many such events he could readily recall. It's no wonder he'd learn to hate so passionately.

He stepped further into the room and saw the four of them waiting. He tried not to smile… Four of the most powerful men on the planet, and he had made them wait. They'd been interested enough in what he had to say that they'd stayed, even though he was purposely twenty minutes past the appointed time.

He moved to the head of the table and sat down, hoping they couldn't see his insecurity. He'd spent most of his life trying to hide his weakness. He'd secretly wished many times that he'd been born with the courage and conviction of his elder brother. Yet, it seemed he'd been given the coward's heart. He'd failed to realize that the only difference between them wasn't bravery or spinelessness. The only difference had always been that one was egocentric and the other selfless.

Many people often mistake unselfishness for bravery. However, unselfish people are just as afraid as anyone else. They've only made up their minds to pay the highest price for others. They move forward against the fear, because once a man's made the decision to give his life, there's nothing that can stop him. He'd never been such a man.

He held his hands out to the group, "Thank you for joining me here today. I trust each of you have found your accommodations acceptable. If not, please, speak with me afterward, and we'll straightway get your situation rectified."

He looked from one man to the next. "Has each of you been introduced? I can't think of a time since the Babylonian Pact when every major nation in the world has been represented at one table."

The men looked around, eyeing each other suspiciously. Demsas introduced himself first.

"I am Demsas. The new King of Aksum. I've called this meeting because I believe it's high time to act against the indecency of the world."

He pointed to the first man and nodded his head toward each as he stated their name and position. "Emperor Cassius Augustus of Rome, glad you could be here today. Emperor Khu of Egypt, you will be pleased at what you'll hear. Emperor Farooq, leader of the powerful Orient. And Emperor Narcisso, famed leader of the Persians. I'm honored to have all of you here."

Emperor Narcisso was annoyed. "We've all traveled a long way when we could've just sent delegates. Then, you keep us waiting. Our time is valuable. You may be new at this game, King Demsas, but I'd suggest you learn proper etiquette before calling another of these preposterous meetings."

Demsas dismissed the man's agitation with a polite smile. "Emperor Narcisso. I think you'll have a change of heart once you realize the purpose of our face-to-face encounter. This topic will greatly affect us all. I personally feel its best to eradicate a potential problem before it spreads, influencing the world like a disease."

"I hope so. You mustn't call meetings on a whim. If it's not of world importance, it's not worth calling us for."

Emperor Farooq nodded an agreement. "I'll be away from home over a month because of these arrangements. Pray tell, you discuss what could justify sending me across the globe."

Demsas smiled. "I requested you because there's power in a name. You're truly known as one who distinguishes truth from lies. I want you to help me today. Your role is vital in our negotiations."

Emperor Augustus slammed his fist into the table. "I hate to bring up the obvious, but we must be wise here. We're all aware that there's one nation that should be represented, who you've conveniently left out. This meeting isn't complete unless we've invited the Babylonians. They'll be sorely offended if world policy is created or altered without their input. What shall we do then?"

Demsas appeared appalled. "Does the heart of Rome beat in the hands of Babylon? I'm sorry, I didn't realize the Kingdom across the sea held your honor in its bosom."

Augustus stood. "That's an outrage. Rome fears no one. You should be more careful Aksumite dog. If I remain thus offended, masses of Roman soldiers will overrun this place. They'll kill every man, woman, and child within your borders. I could have your entire civilization blotted from memory. Don't forget that Rome is the second most powerful kingdom in the world, and the most powerful in this hemisphere."

Demsas shook his head. "And obviously the most easily offended... I meant no disrespect. On the contrary, you're here because I carry a great deal of respect for your people. I want you to help lead us where we're going."

"And where are we going?" Narcisso demanded. "Persia will be joining no cause that doesn't demonstrate immense reward for itself."

Demsas smiled. "What I'm proposing has a threefold purpose that can't be broken. The way will be difficult, but the reward will be most prosperous."

Augustus was curious. "What are your purposes, King?"

"First of all, unite the eastern provinces. It's time we take back what's ours and quit being dictated to by an Empire across the sea. The Babylonians have no right to rule us and no real recourse if we suddenly stop behaving as if we fear them."

"Bold," Narcisso declared. "Risky, but you could be right."

Demsas was gaining confidence, "The second goal of this meeting is to devise a plan that will lead to the overthrow of the Babylonian way of life forever."

Augustus was concerned. "An assault against Babylon would be highly costly, if it could even be done."

"Costly indeed," Demsas chuckled, "but with five nations involved, the manpower and sheer numbers guarantee our success. Aksum is home to one of the most respected naval forces in the world. Rome has the most advanced infantry in history. Persia's way of doing battle is completely unequaled in terms of death. The Orient also has their reign of terror. Egypt has always been feared since the days of the Pharaohs. Together, Babylon stands no chance. Apart, we continue to be subjected to a power that none of us observe and less respect. It's time to end the oppression imposed by those we never see."

Augustus moved on. "And what's the third item on your agenda?"

"The biggest has been saved for last. I want to destroy

Jerusalem, to demolish the Jews and rid the earth of their filth."

Narcisso narrowed his eyes, his forehead crinkling in thought.

"They're but a small and relatively unimportant nation. Why would you be concerned with their annihilation?"

Demsas was angry. "They may be small, Emperor Narcisso, but they are most deadly. I'm sure you've heard the stories of their coming King."

Augustus laughed. "You've made your most poignant thought for our deliberation about a bedtime story told by Jewish mothers to help their babies sleep at night... Why would you bother?"

"Because, our spiritual advisors say something has changed in the atmosphere of the earth. They feel it's more than a story. It's possible the king could've arrived as long ago as last year, and His presence has altered everything we know."

Emperor Farooq quickly stood up. "Our magicians and medians tell us the same. They feel that last year's star carried great significance. They believe it was stationed over a small town in the Jewish nation."

Narcisso shook his head. "I can't believe this is happening. Our prophets have viewed that day with dread since it occurred. The underlying elements of the earth were rocked with revelation the moment the star appeared. Stories have been told of angelic visitations within the Jewish borders. There've been whisperings of a miracle child."

Augustus was disturbed. "You can't be serious. You want to eradicate an entire population because you think a baby has power to… what… change the world?"

Emperor Farooq turned to him. "Augustus, this is an urgent matter, a matter of international security. The gods have been troubled deeply by his arrival. Our historians checked, and never before has an event troubled our spiritual ministers so deeply. From our witches covens to my own fortune tellers, all are bothered by what transpired last year in the Holy Lands."

"Likewise in Egypt," Emperor Khu interjected. "Our historians researched as well. We've not seen this sort of upheaval in the spirit realm since the Jewish prophet, Moses, had his people apply blood to their doorpost. There was something about the blood then, and our leading occultists keep saying there's something about the blood now. Only now, it seems more potent. They've advised me to find a way to stop it, unless we want another Passover on our hands."

He thoughtfully paused, as if reluctant to speak further. Finally, he overpowered his caution and continued,

"I've had spies looking for the child. They've narrowed his location down to Jerusalem. The Day of Atonement is near. Many families will be making their way to Jerusalem to celebrate at the temple. I've gotten it on good authority that the child's mother and father are already there."

Demsas clapped his hands together. "Perhaps that's it then. We have one chance to end this properly. All of our armies should march against Jerusalem on the Sabbath of Sabbaths. Every man, woman, and child shall be killed in the streets. After that, the rest of the world will fear the alliance formed on this day. Shall we complete this with the seals of each Emperor?"

They all stood in agreement. Augustus was the only one still reluctant. However, he rose and joined the others.

"I don't do this to murder a Jewish child in cold blood. I have no problem doing so, but I wish it to be known that I don't fear such a child. Nor does Rome. With that stated, I will still fulfill this pact, because after we march against Jerusalem and the other Jewish provinces, we shall sail for Babylon."

The other Emperors cheered, and each stamped their seal on the pre-written treaty Demsas had drawn up.

Aizan slipped outside, as they were signing the papers. He ran through the dusty streets and made his way to the shipyard. Scribbling something on a piece of cloth, he sealed it in the scroll's container, and ran toward a ship about to set sail.

He ran up the peer and onto the loading dock. Several sailors moved to greet him. It wasn't going to be a favorable meeting. Babylonians didn't particularly like foreigners around their vessels. He recognized their aggressive stares and knew he'd stepped into a problem. Trying to isolate the quiver in his voice, he spoke,

"Please. I need to speak to your captain immediately. It's urgent."

"Perhaps he'll want us to take you out to sea. Every successful voyage should offer something to the gods in exchange for safe passage home."

He took a step backward, "No. Please. This is desperately urgent. I need to get a message to your homeland security advisors."

"Of course you do," the obvious leader laughed.

Aizan took another step back, "I'm serious. This is an official governmental vessel. Is it not? I know there are high-ranking officials on this boat. I need to speak with the captain."

A man was walking down the walkway from the ship's deck. He heard the commotion and paused to listen. His men were closing the gap, aggressively getting closer to Aizan, who was nervously trying to move away. He couldn't; the sailors had him surrounded.

The man yelled from the wooden walkway. "Let him alone. He wishes to speak with me, let him be. Any man lays a hand to him will be left on the dock to fend for himself. Anyone want to be here alone when his friends come looking for him?"

None liked the idea of fighting alone. One by one, the men slowly made their way back to work, defeated by the destruction of their mob mentality. The captain moved toward him.

"Sorry for the inhospitality. The boys can get a bit antsy at times. Nothing personal."

Aizan brushed off the apology, "Sir, pardon my intrusion, but I don't have long. I hope what I've heard is correct. This is the vessel used to transport Babylon's highest clientele, is that correct?"

"It could be."

"I know this vessel has a secret technology you activate once in the open water."

"Perhaps."

"Sir, this is serious. How quickly can you make it to Babylon?"

The captain sensed his urgency. "Six days tops, five if all goes well. Why?"

Aizan handed the captain the parcel. "This is a matter of Babylonian national security. Don't open it. I need this delivered to your King as soon as possible.

The captain clasped hands with Aizan. "It will be in his hands within the week."

"Good, because the Sabbath of Sabbaths is coming up in a month, and all hell is about to break loose in the world."

26

"Dr. Poole, how's he looking?" she called to him from her chair in the corner.

Dr. Poole smiled and closed the chart he was looking through. He placed the folder on the patient's bed.

"Well, not much has changed, but I see a couple of positive signs. It appears he's grown more restless over the past couple of days. He's been stirring a little. Nothing significant, but it's more than he's been."

"A cloud the size of a man's hand. I'll take what I can get, doctor."

He laughed. "As will I."

"How're the pneumonia-like symptoms? Does he seem to be progressing?"

"No recent signs of the pneumonia. His x-rays came back clear. The nursing staff turns him every two hours... I don't think it should be a problem... That's nothing short of a miracle. I'd say God is continuing to work on him. And, if the other signs are real, he may be out of the woods sooner than we think."

"Good. I think our prayers and your care have finally started getting through. God has heard us, and Hayden's life will be restored."

Dr. Poole nodded his agreement, "Your being here for him has probably been one of the biggest positives that's helped him through this. You must understand that. Somewhere deep down, he feels you near him. He needs that love and devotion, someone to believe in him, to love him enough to want him to make it. You're all he's got left."

"No." She didn't want to acknowledge the powerful role she was playing.

"Yes ma'am. You're partially responsible. You've read to him for hours, talked to him when no one else has, prayed with him, and been there almost every step of the way since you came here. When he comes out of this, there's no doubt he's gonna remember you with a heart of sheer gratitude."

She stifled tears, "I hope he does. For my daughter's sake and in her memory, I hope he never forgets."

27

Hayden saw Darius among the men of the city and hurriedly approached him. Leib waited at the gate, along with the large black man that had escorted them to and from the Baobab tree.

"Darius, she's alive. I know she is."

Darius tried to hide his agitation. "And how did you come about this knowledge, Hayden?"

"I spoke with someone in the wilderness. She knew things, things she couldn't have known unless she has a spiritual connection."

"A witch?" he asked, skeptically.

"No… Not a witch. I don't know what she was. But she was no worker of darkness. She was kind and welcoming, warm. A bright light exuded from her being."

"The darkest forces sometimes come as angels of light, Hayden. They are deceptive, like chameleons, forever blending in to bring devastation."

"Why are you so eager to not believe? M'ya is special. Why are you so eager to just let her go?"

"Hayden, you must learn to exercise caution. There are those who would play on your emotions. You're a wise man. You're just refusing to see it."

"No, I see it clearly Darius. It's you who've placed the blinders on."

"Hayden, my friend, I love you dearly, but you're an easy mark now. Your desire to believe is making it simple for the enemy to trouble you. A man must be careful in his quest for truth. Often, he finds that he unknowingly influences revelation because he wants to see so badly. One must make certain that the truth being discovered is actually eternal truth and not something created by his own desires."

Aizan hurriedly ran to them from around the corner. "Darius, we must talk immediately. I've been looking for you everywhere."

Darius looked at Hayden, concern on his face. He looked back to Aizan and recognized the sheer panic in his eyes. He shifted his attention to Hayden again.

Hayden sadly shook his head. "Go ahead. Do what you must. I'm leaving."

He started to walk off, as Darius yelled to him. "Wait. Where are you going?"

"To Tyre. She's in Tyre," he said, as he continued walking toward the gate.

Darius ran and grabbed his arm, spinning him around. "Stop. We've been through too much to leave each other's side like this. Come with me. Let's speak with Aizan. Help me address his concerns. Then we shall sit as men and logically discuss our next course of action."

"Our paths are diverging, oh great king. Perhaps we're no longer meant to be together."

"No. It's not that way, Sir Hayden. I'm meant to be with you, and you with me. We both know that to be true."

"I only know that I'll pursue M'ya until there's no life left in me. I also know your pursuits must be different, and rightfully so. I don't expect you to be weighted down with such trivial matters. You've a kingdom to rule."

Aizan neared them again. "This won't wait, sirs. And, it affects you both."

Both men reluctantly followed him. As soon as they were far enough away that no one could overhear them, Hayden turned to Aizan,

"What's so important that you-"

Aizan extended a hand for them to remain quiet, "Please, just listen… Darius, your brother has united the armies of the world to destroy the Jews. He's planning an attack on

Jerusalem around the time of their feasts. The Sabbath of Sabbaths is the date that he's sworn to destroy every Jew from the earth."

Darius was skeptical. "He couldn't pull that off, Aizan. The other Emperors would laugh him out of the war room. In this era of peace, none would go for such a preposterous idea."

"They already did. He presented it to them this afternoon. They all embraced it… His plan is two-fold. First, destroy the Jews. Second, wipe out Babylon."

"He's gone mad… How'd he convince the others to follow such revolting ideas?"

"He made a valid case about why the Jews must be destroyed, because they all fear the child King, the one they say will one day rule the world."

Darius was still reluctant to believe, "And the other countries dropped what they were doing and rallied around this ridiculous notion?"

"Yes, they openly acknowledged their fear of the Godchild."

Hayden mumbled under his breath. "How does this affect me? Right now, the Jews, the Babylonians, the rest of the world, doesn't even register. Until I find M'ya, nothing else matters."

Aizan took a crumbled piece of parchment from his pocket. "I think you should see this. Both of you."

He laid it on the table. Hayden studied it. It was a map of the territories surrounding Jerusalem. The Kingdom of Tyre was founded directly to the north. Lines had been drawn, headed from Tyre through the heart of Jerusalem, and into the southern most regions of the nearby provinces. Other lines were drawn from the east toward Jerusalem's center, while others were plotted from the south. Jerusalem was being strategically surrounded.

"This is Demsas' battle plan. I've heard him discuss it before. He mentioned it again in the meeting with the other Emperors. He plans on using this to wipe out the Jews."

"Why does that concern me?"

"Because, Sir Hayden, things are not always as they appear."

"What do you mean?"

"There's a faction that's been waiting for years for something like this to occur. They've secretly been plotting for an opportunity to make their presence felt. They want to turn toward one governing body that controls the entire world. Both Hemispheres."

"So. How-"

"There are rumors. I've heard them resurface lately. Demsas is unaware of them. Rumors have it that they already have a leader in place. He's just waiting to take over once the world falls to shambles during times of war."

"Who is he?"

"Legend has it that he'll come to the world during time of deepest crisis with a public decree to implement global change. He'll captivate the hearts of the people with his charm and quick wit. However, behind his smile and steady demeanor is an agenda that leads to supernatural chaos."

Darius chewed his lower lip. "There's no one person who could unite the entire world."

"The man responsible will be powerful… feared even. The prophecies say he'll rise to power at the time of a great wedding celebration. He's destined to wed one from across the sea. This union will unite the rebel forces from both hemispheres."

"Who is it?"

"Most enchanters believe the King of Tyre is such a man."

Darius quickly turned to Hayden. "If that's true, M'ya may very well be the girl he plans to marry. She'd meet the prophecy's criterion."

Hayden's face turned red. "I'm heading to Jerusalem. My fate, and the fate of the world, may very well be there."

"I'm going with you," Darius answered. "There's cause for us all in Jerusalem. The battle is there."

28

Leib stepped from the ship first, making his way out to the dock. Hunzuu was a few steps behind, separated by a few crewmembers unloading crates from the deck.

Leib's only possession was the dagger at his side and the lambskin bag strapped over his shoulder. He turned to speak with Hunzuu as soon as his foot touched the ground. However, the first word never escaped his lips. Someone slammed into him from behind, knocking him to the ground.

He quickly stood and brushed himself off. Hunzuu helped him the rest of the way up.

"Slippery isn't it?" Hunzuu mocked. "Appears you're still on your sea legs."

Leib brushed himself off, knocking the sand from his clothes. Suddenly, his expression turned from slightly embarrassed to maddeningly worried.

"Hunzuu, did you see who hit me? Someone stole the bag."

Hunzuu frantically looked around. He hadn't noticed who had hit Leib, but he knew what was in the bag, and they had to find it.

He motioned toward a rapidly retreating movement from further down the dock. Hayden and Darius topped the ship walkway just in time to see Hunzuu and Leib running away from them toward the city.

The captain chuckled as they walked by, "Some kid stole the little one's bag. You'd have thought he'd stolen a fortune."

Darius fearfully glanced at Hayden before looking back toward the captain. "He just might have, sir. We must get back what's in that bag."

. . .

Thirty minutes later, the four men met in the town square. The boy was gone. They'd found the lambskin pouch on the ground between two adobe storefronts, but the amulet was missing.

Leib dejectedly shook his head. "All I had to do was hold onto a bag. I couldn't even do that. I'm sorry."

Darius tapped him on the top of the head. "It's okay, little one. We'll find it. This city isn't that big. He's got to be here somewhere, and there's still six hours or so before nightfall. Go back to the ship. Give the sailors a description. Tell them their king will owe the entire crew a favor if they find the kid for us. The more eyes searching, the better."

Leib left them. Hunzuu faced Darius and Hayden, keeping his voice low.

"Have you noticed the peculiarity of this city? Something is off. Can't quite put my finger on it."

Hayden's expression was stone cold. "The people here are different. It's obvious in their mannerism, dress, and attitude."

"This is Mji Wa Radhi." Darius matter-a-factly stated."

"What's that?" Hunzuu asked.

"Most of mankind's dream, an urban utopia. Whatever you desire, you can have it here. Nothing is forbidden. Nothing is off limits. There are no taboo subjects. Anything and everything goes. What happens here stays here. People come from around the globe to take sanctuary in this private sector."

A man walked toward them and extended his hand. "Withhold no good thing from yourself. That's our motto."

They all just stared at him, as he boisterously giggled. "Sorry, I'm the elected mayor of this place. Welcome to Mji Wa Radhi, the City of Pleasure."

Hayden awkwardly moved past the customary pleasantries. "We're looking for a child. He stole something very valuable to us. Can you help us find it?"

"No. There's been no crime committed," the man rudely stated.

"Please, sir. It's important, and there has been a crime committed. He stole something of value from a visiting dignitary's entourage. That crime is punishable under international law."

"Not here it isn't. This place is free from the oppression of the law. Here, stealing doesn't exist. He saw something he wanted, and he took it. That's the way of things. There's nothing wrong with people following their primal instincts. If there were, why'd the gods see fit to fashion us with such desires?"

"You can't just take what doesn't belong to you." Darius groaned.

The mayor politely smiled, a little too friendly. "Nothing belongs to anyone. That's our belief. Everything was created by the gods and thus belongs to them. If you see something you want and are capable of getting it, then by all means, do so."

"That's absurd. Hasn't that led to lawlessness?" Hayden retorted.

"Of course we have more violence than many cities. But we also have fewer long-term health concerns, less stress, and better financial flexibility."

Hayden was appalled. "Sir, I've seen the faces here. There

aren't many of them who look happy. If indulgence is so liberating, why are there not more smiles on the people's faces?"

The mayor continued demonstrating his charismatic grin. "You see their daily routines. That's the mundane and necessary parts of life. We don't live for that here. It weighs us down. It is mandatory, for we have to keep up the city, but you should see those same people when the sun goes down, and they're no longer employees, but able to do as they please. They do whatever they want to put smiles on their faces. Never a dull moment."

"But-"

The mayor cut him off, "We believe in the finer things of life, embracing the forbidden fruit, as did our mother and father in the beginning. Their eyes were opened, purged from their desire for better things. Our eyes have also been thus enlightened. We're more pure than we've ever been. You should embrace the truth and live in the limelight of this city for just a few moments. Relax. Take it all in. Soak it up. Live a little. You won't leave disappointed, and I guarantee you'll always come back for more."

"So there are no crimes? No punishment? No rules? No checks and balances," Darius confusedly asked.

The mayor returned Hayden's whimsical stare. "Why should there be? We all live for each other's pleasure. That's why we're here. The world is better that way. You want something from me; then freely take it. For, if I desire something of you, it's my right to take it as well. Here in this city, resistance is futile. The only crime is failing to cave to someone else's strong desires. If you don't willingly participate in someone's freewill fantasy, you could be punished, or banished. We all exist to please each other; makes the world a much brighter place."

Hayden was incredulous. "Don't worry, sir. We'll be leaving as soon as we find the boy and retrieve our missing item. We won't be a bother."

The mayor looked worried. "I'd be careful if I were you. That boy had every right to take the item. You make too big a deal about this and the civilians won't be pleased."

"Have a good day," Hayden stated, as he walked away to search for the lad.

Darius and Hunzuu followed. Hunzuu pulled them close. "I'd suggest staying together. I've a bad feeling about this place."

The mayor followed them a few steps. "I'm serious, gentlemen. I wouldn't suggest you continuing this manhunt. You'll only upset the residents. They don't take kindly to outsiders who don't understand or respect their way of life."

Hayden's agitation was apparent, "Respect? You demand respect for something so outlandishly foolish. You allow your people to live any way they want, without regard for their fellowman. You've created a system wherein your people are destined to fail."

The mayor's smile faded, his warmth was swallowed by a sudden fury. "It's not about success or failure. It's about happiness and peace. We yearn for it. Through the years we've discovered that this is the better way. When we have a desire, we fill that craving however we can. It works for us. We aren't unsatisfied."

"Yes, I'm afraid you are; You're just too intoxicated on carnality to see it."

"We pursue bliss. There's nothing wrong with that."

"Oh, but there is… You only fool yourselves… Happiness is not an event. It's not something you find by pursuing childhood fantasies or following fleshly longings. Passion is a powerful thing, but when the fire always burns hot toward lustful ambitions, it's dangerous… Happiness is a lifestyle."

"No. A life of happiness cannot exist outside the continuum of pleasure," the mayor argued.

"Sir, you're most definitely wrong. Pleasure has no bearing on true happiness. Happiness, as you define it, is merely an emotion. It's fleeting. That's why you must pursue it every moment you're alive. That, in itself, is taxing… True happiness isn't that way."

"Then what is true happiness? Since you are so wise," the mayor mockingly questioned.

Hayden thought back, conjuring word from feelings he remembered, although unsure of their origin. He was momentarily confused, feeling something he knew he'd felt before, but unable to place where. He tried to bring his thoughts to life.

"You don't have to feel the emotion at all times to be happy. Happiness is an attitude, a mindset. At times, you can be down and still possess joy. True joy is peace. It's knowing that you're doing the right thing and in the right position, even though at the moment it doesn't seem to be working."

"You're more disturbed than we are. You tell me that one can be happy while not in high spirits. That's preposterous."

"Ask a mother who's giving birth. The last few weeks aren't comfortable, but they're part of a process that brings utter joy. Labor pains aren't exhilarating, but they're prerequisites to the greatest pleasure one can find on this earth… Sometimes, pain is a necessary part of pure fulfillment. True peace is not being happy in every moment; it's knowing that each moment is working to bring a greater reward down the road. It's being able to enjoy the journey for what it is, completely trusting that it will end in an indescribable destination."

The mayor vehemently refused to accept Hayden's explanation. "We're creatures of desire by design. You can't deny or change that fact. The lust of the flesh and the lust of the eyes are ever before us. Man's pride is his greatest asset."

"Or his easiest downfall," Hayden quipped. You don't even see it, do you? Man only grows inward and stagnant. Each bit of pleasure only creates a bigger need to pursue another one. Like a drug, the high gets harder to find, until you overdose on self and are destroyed. You're killing your people, and you can't even see it."

"Your analysis is skewed. It's not like that at all. We're free from oppression."

"Free from oppression? You've created the worst kind. You're bound to your own natures. There's no oppression so hard to overcome than the corruption of the flesh."

"We are free because we have no laws to obey, no decrees to follow."

"Obedience doesn't bind you, it liberates. It's a precursor to peace."

A large crowd had started to gather. They were listening to the heated argument and growing restless. Hunzuu tugged at Hayden's arm.

"Sir, we need to get out of here and retrieve the item."

Hayden looked around, noticing the highly enraged mob for the first time. The mayor looked at Hayden, no concern in his eyes.

"It appears you're inciting a riot. I should have you arrested, but I won't. You've got precisely thirty minutes to be outside our borders before I allow them to do whatever they desire with the lot of you."

Hunzuu slightly moved toward the mayor. "Sir, this is the King of Aksum. You can't just-"

"It's because of him that I've shown you this kindness. You've offended our people and criticized our way of life. Now, get out of my city before my people follow through with what's in their heart."

Hunzuu and Darius turned to walk away. Hayden stayed behind a moment longer. Not out of disrespect, but pity.

"Are you sure there's nothing I can do to help you see the light?"

"You can help by leaving us the way you found us."

Hayden's voice saddened, "All things left alone eventually deteriorate. It's an immutable law. We live, grow old, our bodies break down, and then we die. The mountains eventually erode. The lakes and rivers eventually dry up. The grass fades. Nature consumes itself. It is the way of things."

"It is indeed. So, we might as well enjoy the moment while it's before us. We've learned to bask in the sun before it finally sets."

"Or we could live placing our trust in a higher power. We could live for eternity instead of for the moment."

The mayor shook his head, dismissing Hayden's final attempt at persuasion.

"You now have twenty-five minutes to be away from my city."

"We can't leave without recollecting our item," Darius insisted.

"Then I wish you luck finding it in the next few minutes. After that, I wish you luck surviving."

They looked at the crowd again. Men had gathered carrying chains, garden tools, swords, and other makeshift weapons. Their faces were full of hostility. Hayden, Hunzuu, and Darius dejectedly moved toward the outskirts of the city.

. . .

Cowered behind one of few stone buildings in the center of town, the thirteen-year-old boy removed the ruby amulet from his pocket. He tossed it between his hands a few times, fascinated at how the sun reflected through it, casting red sparkles on the surrounding walls. There was a brief movement to his left, just down the alley he'd avoided. She was there, coming toward him, head bent low, wearing the same veil as before. He discerningly looked, but couldn't see her eyes.

She sat down beside him, and he curiously looked up at her. Finally, he decided he was more interested than afraid.

"Why are people so scared of you?"

She avoided his gaze and emptily replied, "People always fear what they don't understand. It's the way of things, child. Harmless things appear much more dangerous in the dark."

"But you don't seem dangerous to me. You seem kind."

"Looks are deceiving, boy. Don't believe them moving forward. Let that be the one lesson I teach you."

"Don't trust my judgment?"

"Trust no one," she flatly replied.

He smiled and tossed her the ruby. "But you could trust me. I got it, just like you asked me to."

He couldn't see through it, but he could tell she was smiling beneath the veil.

His smile faded, as curiosity won again. "Are you truly the bouda?"

"That's the rumor, kid. Just don't stare too long to find out."

Something else moved down the alley on the right side. He turned quickly to find who was there. No one was there, just an alley cat that had knocked over a can. He turned back around to talk with her, but she'd disappeared, leaving him alone in the darkness. He sat there for a moment, thinking of her.

Cold.

Empty.

Quiet.

Gone.

29

Hayden and Hunzuu sat on the hillside slightly out of sight of the stream below. Hunzuu motioned to the tall trees in the distance.

"You hear that?"

"Hard not to. Whoever it is, they're not even trying to conceal their whereabouts."

"There are two of them, judging by the footfalls. One is heavy, the other not so much. Maybe a man and a girl. We'll know in a moment, they're coming right toward us."

Hunzuu removed both of the blades from his back. Hayden moved his hand near the Sword of Tiber. The footsteps moved extremely close. Finally, they stopped before a wall of trees and greenery too dense to see through.

"Come out," Hunzuu demanded. "Or I'll have to come in after you."

The greenery grew apart, and Leib suddenly emerged, the massive black man from the ship trailing behind him.

"We've been looking for you? Did you find the amulet?" Leib excitedly asked.

"No. We were kicked out of the city. We've got to find another way... What's he doing here?"

"He wanted a chance to serve his king. Said he'd rather make sure King Darius was taken care of than continue as a deckhand. Didn't figure we'd mind the company."

Hunzuu dryly quipped, "Welcome to our little band of misfits. What's your name?"

"Thank ya, suh. Erebody jus' call me Big."

They all laughed.

"What's your birth name?" Hunzuu asked.

"My fam-lee name me Bennett."

After a moment, Leib broke the humor, noticing that Darius wasn't with them.

"Where's the king?"

Hayden motioned with his head in the direction of the hill. Leib and Bennett followed his head movement.

"He's on the other side. Decided he needed to bathe in

the river. Asked for privacy. We're gonna give it to him."

"What are we gonna do about the amulet?"

"Wait 'til Darius gets back, and then we're gonna discuss it."

"I'm going back in tonight," Hayden replied. "We've got to get it."

"Let's sleep while we can," Hunzuu sharply replied. "Darius will return soon, and they'll be no rest once we start moving again."

. . .

Darius dipped his head into the cool water and let it flow past his face. It felt crisp and clean. A few seconds later, he lifted his head above the water and whipped it around, letting it fly from his face.

The water was chest deep, and he was enjoying it immensely. He closed his eyes again and dove, resurfacing moments later a few feet from where he'd went under. He wiped the water from his eyes and scanned the surroundings.

The atmosphere had changed.

Too quiet.

Too still.

The songbirds had grown silent.

Nothing moved, except the gentle rippling of the water's surface.

Nothing existed but the isolated lagoon he'd discovered. He knew his companions were just over the hill, but he wasn't going to call them. He'd look foolish if they came running to his aid and there was no trouble, and if something was off, he didn't want them running blindly into an ambush. For now, he was on his own.

What was wrong? he couldn't quite put his finger on it.

There are times when man gets a premonition, something is disturbed inside him, causing him to take a closer look.

Perhaps it's a subtle change in the environment, some element that's out of place. When one is used to living off the land and surviving by instinct, he learns to notice things that others simply wouldn't. He naturally commits every aspect of each situation to memory, and any unexpected alteration causes silent alarms. At times, it may take a few moments of conscious thought to realize what's wrong, but usually the senses send the alert before the full revelation is achieved. This was such a moment.

Darius tried not to panic. He was in deep water, which meant his movement was severely restricted. If someone wanted him dead, he couldn't have given him a better opportunity. If he were an assassin, this was the type of scenario he'd have planned for. It would be all too easy.

He realized that his best chance of survival was to pretend he wasn't aware of danger. He closed his eyes, took a deep breath, and dove under the water again.

This time, he opened his eyes underneath and tried to peer through the surface for any sign of movement. If anyone were trying to get close to him, they'd surely approach while he was under the surface. That's what he'd do, but then, he was no trained assassin. He squinted his eyes through the shimmering waves above him. He needed Hunzuu.

Running out of breath, he rose to the top again, wiped the water from his eyes, and turned in a full circle, searching for anything out of the ordinary.

There it was. He wasn't sure if it was what he had noticed the first time, but now it was painfully apparent. Leading to the water's edge, by the stony embankment, were a fresh set of tracks that hadn't been there when he'd entered earlier.

Human tracks.

Soft tracker's boots.

Military issue.

Roman, by the look of them.

One of the two remaining killers was here, and by the look of it, he was already in the water.

Darius looked around again, fear overwhelming him, as he tried to appear calm. The sunlight danced off the rippling water. There wasn't anything that appeared to be off.

He was uncertain of his next move. He could make his way toward the rocks where the footprints had entered the water, but the killer may be hiding there. He could head toward the reed bed to the south, but the killer could've anticipated that and be easily hidden there. He could merely return the way he'd come into the water, but that would be the most obvious place an assassin would wait, especially since that's where he'd left his bow. Perhaps, if he just waited in the center long enough, Hayden or Hunzuu would come to check on him, and he could motion for help.

He tried to force logic to override terror. Often, a level head is the only weapon against an unexpected attack. Chaos creates panic, and panic causes confusion. Confusion leads to irrational behavior, and irrational behavior can get a man killed. He had to make the right choices if he wanted to stay alive.

Rationally, there's no way someone could be in the water with him because they hadn't surfaced.

He'd heard tales of trained assassins who were skilled in water kills. The legends told of men who could hold their breath for seven or eight minutes. Men who'd grab a victim and pull them into the deep, rolling them like a viscous crocodile from the Nile. The victim would run out of air long before the skilled warrior. Those kills were all too easy for this elite type of soldier. However, those were supposedly just stories told round campfires to interest teenage boys.

If the man hurting him wasn't of such pedigree, then he must have some sort of breathing apparatus, something providing oxygen from the surface while he remained under water.

Darius immediately turned and looked toward the reeds. There was a slight disturbance among them. Something had stirred them. Something large. Something beneath.

He heard the sound before he could respond. The reverberation chilled his insides.

It was soft.

Barely audible.

But there was no doubt what it was. He'd heard that familiar sound often when practicing to become skilled at his craft. It was undeniable. The bow makes an incredibly distinct noise when the drawstring is released, and the arrow violently seeks its target.

He swiftly pivoted to his right, hoping to avoid the arrow if it had been aimed true. However, nothing landed near him.

Instead, a few feet away and to his left, there was a sudden splash. The arrow hit the water's surface. However, it didn't sink or deflect. For a moment, it seemed to stay right there, half in and half out of the water. A second later, he understood why.

The Roman soldier emerged eight feet away, a dagger in both hands. The arrow still protruded from his neck area, but he was still coming, trying to clear his head enough to reach his intended target.

Darius quickly moved away from him and yelled for his friends, just as another arrow sank into the Roman's chest.

Darius turned to where the bowstring sound was coming from. His bow bounced to the ground by the rocks, as someone disappeared into the greenery of the forest. He'd been saved again, and his protector had used his own bow to help him.

Hayden and Hunzuu topped the hill first. Darius quickly pointed in the direction his protector had fled. Moments later, he was out of the water and running through the woods in the direction of the movement ahead of him. He ran in a full sprint toward the sound. He had no fear. If this person wanted him dead, they could've killed him several times already. He didn't know why, but he had an unknown ally.

Suddenly, he saw a flurry of movement before him. The figure's clothes blended almost perfectly into the surroundings. He pursued.

"Wait. Come back. I mean you no harm," he hollered, as he ran.

The figure continued to flee, as Darius continued to give chase, with Hayden and Hunzuu close behind, loudly tearing through the underbrush.

The forest gave way to rocky terrain. The plush greenery disappeared, opening into a steep, almost mountainous incline. At the top of the slope, a lone figure stood, the echoing sound of raging water was behind and below.

His protector. Small frame. Quick. Deadly.

Hayden appeared to the right, and Hunzuu suddenly emerged from the forest on the left. Darius was coming up the center. There was nowhere to go, the assassin had run toward a forty-foot drop from a harsh, rocky embankment. He was completely boxed in.

The trained killer drew a blade from behind the back. It was unlike any they'd ever seen, a single blade, slender and curved. The warrior held both hands at the hilt, slightly protruding the sword from his body. Hunzuu had seen similar blades from the Orient. Those swords were known for their extremely sharp edges. If this was such a sword, only an exceptionally skilled warrior could wield it.

Darius held up his hand. "Please. I mean you no harm. Put your weapon down."

The assassin looked toward Hayden and Hunzuu. Both stopped approaching, but had the only escape routes blocked.

Darius took another step forward. "Just put your weapon down. I just want to talk with you. Please."

The assaassin looked at each of them again, and then looked the only other direction.

"No," Darius screamed, as the figure lunged off the backside of the cliff.

Darius ran the rest of the way up, meeting Hunzuu and Hayden at the top. The figure had disappeared, plunging into the raging water below. He searched for several minutes for a sign of life.

No one emerged.

Nothing moved.

His protector had disappeared again.

THE SIN CLOUD

Maybe this time forever.

30

Gino stepped from the restroom and nervously looked around. He was always apprehensive in public. It's why he hated going out. He'd tried to convince them that he shouldn't be the one to do it, but they'd insisted. It was his turn.

Reaching into his pockets, he felt the twenty-dollar bill under his fingertips. Drinks and food. That's what he'd been sent for.

They'd filled up with gas a couple hours ago. That station had been too crowded, so they'd left without going inside. Now, they'd seen this little station below them. Torben had stopped the motor home on the side of the road and instructed him to make the short jog down the hillside for the supplies. It made sense. Their vehicle could remain out of sight on a little used country road, while he'd jog down to the main highway, get food, and slip back up to them. So far, the plan had worked to perfection. As nervous as he'd been, he was certain that no one had seen him that didn't need to.

He stood in front of the cooler and peered inside. So many choices. It was water for Heaven's sake. Why were there so many brand names? And, why in the world would anyone pay three dollars for one liter of a liquid the government supplied for free?

Unless his theories were true. He'd believed for years that the government was putting chemicals in the drinking water. That's why he'd built a purifier. Perhaps others instinctively knew the truth. Without his resources, they just naturally chose to purchase purified items over the counter. That was plausible, except the government could eventually corrupt the bottled water supply as well. It was too controlling. There's no way one governing body was ever intended to be so powerful.

His thoughts were interrupted by the clerk's voice from behind the counter.

"No, sir. I ain't seen nobody looks like either of those two. I'll make sure to keep an eye out for ya though. You got a number I can call should they show up?"

Gino peered around the corner to find two men in black suits interrogating the young attendant. One of them handed the attendant a business card, and they both turned around to leave.

He tried to move, but it was too late. They'd spotted him.

"You," the first one called. "Come here."

He had no choice. The authorities didn't have his description yet. Hopefully, they weren't aware of his assistance. He reluctantly stepped from behind the counter.

The larger man approached him, extending a paper. It was two photos blended onto the same page. The man sternly held it in front of Gino.

"Recognize either of them?"

He wanted to play it cool, but didn't quite know how. Calm was never part of his repertoire.

"Yes, that's my sister and grandfather. How'd you get that photo? Haven't seen that since the house burned down and the old family photo album was destroyed."

The large guy grunted, shoving the paper into his jacket pocket. The second one moved toward him, as the first stepped away.

"What's your name?" he demanded

"Why you asking?" Gino softly replied.

"Because I'm with the authorities, and I have a right to know."

Gino was stumped. "I have a right to my privacy."

"Then you shouldn't come out in public. Show me some identification, now."

Gino fumbled in his pocket. "Sorry, must have left it at

home." He nervously smiled.

"Then I need your name and date of birth, sir."

"For what? I didn't do anything wrong. I'm not guilty. This is harassment. That's what this is. It's harassment."

"What are you so nervous about? If you've got nothing to hide, tell me your name."

"Show me your badge. I demand to see some identification too."

The guy pretended to search his pocket. He wryly smiled. "It appears I've misplaced mine as well... Problem is I know who I am. He knows who I am. The department knows who I am. But no one knows who you are."

"I'm nobody, sir. I prefer to keep it that way. Please."

"Well... Nobody... You should have kept your mouth shut. Because now I'm curious what you're trying to hide. Why are you so nervous?"

He took Gino's hand and twisted it, pulling a set of cuffs from his side. He locked one cuff over Gino's left wrist. Before he could fasten one over the right, there was the sudden sound of glass shattering, and then a car alarm blaring outside.

The first man stepped to the window and peered out. He motioned for the second, as he ran toward the door.

"The window is smashed. Someone's breaking in to the car."

The second man pointed at Gino. "You wait here. I'll be back for you."

As soon as the man disappeared outside, Gino ran to the back of the store, found the rear entrance, and opened the door. Someone grabbed him as soon as he exited. He swung his arm, but the blow was easily blocked. He breathed a huge sigh of relief. It was Torben.

"Gino, we've got to move. I broke their glass, but it won't take but a minute for them to realize it was a diversion. Let's get up the hill."

The first man approached the car and peered through the shattered passenger window. A large brick was lying next to the car door. Someone had intentionally set off the alarm.

The second man whirled around, realization hitting him. He ran back inside, but the half handcuffed man was gone. He looked at the clerk, who hesitantly pointed toward the rear of the store.

Both men headed in that direction, guns drawn. The back door was agape, and they ran through it to search the area. There was no one in sight.

The one who lost his cuffs punched the side wall.

"He knew something. We were close. Very Close."

The first one was already on the radio giving the location to someone on the other end of the line.

"I want satellite imagery of this area from thirty minutes ago until thirty minutes after. I want it yesterday."

31

Marcus Shamash stood before the council. His grandson sat in a chair slightly behind him, surrounded by an entourage of what amounted to an expensive legal team.

"You didn't give us much time to prepare. Amarsin is lucky that I foresaw such an event and started building a defense before your arrival, my King. I don't plan on being disrespectful and certainly hold no grudge against your crown. However, blood is blood, and I shall be most pointed in the case to have my grandson freed."

The king held the gavel in his right hand. "You'll have to be," he said, and then hammered the ornamented, wooden desk before him. "The trial has begun."

The king's overweight assistant stood and walked before the panel in the makeshift courtroom. He glared toward Amarsin, as if his eyes would strike panic, resulting in a full confession. Amarsin slightly reclined in his chair, smiled, and then waved his hand toward his opponent in a mock *hello*. The man snapped back toward the panel.

"Mr. Amarsin Shamash is on trial this morning for acts of treason and terrorism against the powers of Babylon. He's an anarchist, and should be punished as such. He and his gang of rabble spread their filth across the land, corrupting the common people, and willingly breaking countless laws. We find these acts distasteful, and not in the interest of the same Babylon that Mr. Amarsin took an oath to preserve and protect. He was also involved in actions that took one of our primary military leaders away from the main Babylonian provinces, ultimately ending in his death. Mr. Abaddon Dearth was a highly decorated and respectfully distinguished soldier. Mr. Shamash and his band are responsible for the loss of man-hours of all military personnel involved in the pursuit, as well as the horror caused by losing one of our most reputable strategists. The punishment should be equal to the crime. Mr. Shamash and his merry crew should all be crucified."

He smugly looked back toward Amarsin and took his seat. Marcus Shamash rose and walked toward the judiciary panel.

"I am Parliamentarian Shamash. I too am a reputable citizen of Babylon. I am many years Mr. Abaddon Dearth's senior and served with many of your fathers in battles to preserve our way of life. My family has long since spilled its blood for the purpose of protecting Babylonian heritage. To suggest that my grandson, Amarsin Shamash is guilty of doing anything less goes against the Shamash code of living. Amarsin may violate some political principles, but he'd never go against the passions of family. Without family, we have nothing, and he would certainly never violate the code of law established by our forefathers."

He turned and peered in the direction of the prosecution. "They are going to make a case for Amarsin's guilt based on nothing but speculation. I have come to present the facts. Please, for honor, for Babylonian pride, make your decision today based on truth. Unless your integrity has already been compromised, you will have no choice but to find Amarsin innocent of all charges."

He turned to take his seat again. The king cleared his throat.

"Moving speech Mr. Shamash. Let's move this trial right along. Why don't you present your first witness?"

"The prosecution hasn't even made their case yet, Your Highness."

"Their case is well documented. All in this room are well aware of your grandson's shortcomings."

"So, we won't be following the procedural edicts of the high courts before us? Your father's protocols have been amended?"

The king stood up. "Parliamentarian Shamash, may I remind you yet again that my father is no longer with us. While I do respect him more than anyone could possibly understand, I am your king, and however I decide to run this proceedings is my business. I'm not an elected official who can be impeached. You'll do what I've declared, or I'll have you reprimanded, and this case will move forward without you. Are we clear?"

Marcus nodded, unsuccessfully attempting to conceal his anger. "Yes, Your Highness. We're clear."

"Good," the king said, as he sat back down. "Now, please call your first witness."

"The defense calls Aikan Sansman to the stand."

The overweight follower of the king flipped through a scroll and whispered to the men around him. The king summoned Aikan closer.

"Who are you? And why are you here?"

Marcus Shamash spoke first. "He is brother to a tracker who served as a private contractor to Abaddon Dearth. He's here to testify of his brother's private admission concerning Captain Dearth's frame of mind during the manhunt for Amarsin and his friends."

The fat prosecutor stood to his feet. "Objection. That's absurd. Captain Dearth is a victim here. He's not on trial. We shouldn't be allowed to stain his memory by dragging his reputation through the mud."

Marcus was hot. "This witness can give a vivid description of Captain Dearth's uncharacteristic behavior at the time. It will help prove that my grandson and the others feared for their lives. That's why they were heading to the Fortress."

The king thoughtfully peered around the room. Finally, he looked at Marcus.

"Objection sustained. I know you're trying to build a case, but turning this into a witch-hunt against a former decorated officer must be prohibited. You'll have to build it another way."

"But-"

"But nothing, Parliamentarian Shamash. Your king has spoken. Abaddon Dearth is a war hero. He deserves our respect."

Marcus' face was flush. He paused, before continuing, "Not at the expense of falsely condemning the living. It's a travesty to live so much in the glory of the past that we fail to face the future by protecting the present. Nevertheless, you've spoken, and there's nothing I can do. So, may the defense call the second witness to the stand?"

The king reluctantly nodded, "Of course."

"Then the defense calls The High Priestess of Baal. Surely her testimony will be permitted. She commands respect because of her power and walk with the gods."

A pretty young woman stepped forward. The King smiled as she approached to stand before him and the others.

"Priestess. Thank you for coming. Do you mind to state your reason for being here today?"

Marcus interrupted again. "She's here to testify how Captain Dearth secretly hired her outside of Babylonian authority to find my grandson and the group he traveled with. Captain Dearth was so desperate that he invoked the gods to aid in the pursuit of them."

"Objection again... King, it's evident that Parliamentarian Shamash's only recourse is to smear the name of a fellow officer. I won't allow it."

The King looked at Marcus. "You're on thin ice already, sir. Now, what exactly does your witness intend to state on the record?"

"The truth, sir. She intends to tell everyone that she was privately employed and asked to use supernatural means to aid Captain Dearth in battle. She'll also testify that the Captain was very much alive when he left her three miles from the Fortress."

"Objection. You can't consider allowing this testimony. Again, sir, Captain Dearth is not on trial."

The king stared at Marcus. "My temper is growing most shortened. You'll defend your grandson, without attacking the character of one of our greatest war heroes."

"I can't build a case, sir, if I'm not allowed to discuss the one person who has placed him in this position. It's not Amarsin's fault that the person who caused this entire dilemma is now dead."

There was an audible gasp around the courtroom. Marcus disbelievingly shook his head,

"Fine. The defense calls an unknown thief to the stand. I don't know his name, nor will he give it to us."

Three of Marcus' men entered the courtroom leading a

bound man into the center. There was more loud grumblings from those in the room. The king yelled over the noise.

"And who might this be?"

"This is a common thief, sir. We don't know his name, and he refused to give it for fear that we might retaliate against his family."

"Why is he here?"

"This man was with a crew who savagely attacked Captain Dearth near his childhood home site. He was the only one left alive. The Captain hewed the others down when they tried to rob him. He has agreed to testify in exchange for leniency. Please, let his story be heard."

The king was visibly shaken. "Is this true?"

The man reluctantly nodded. "Yes, my king. It is true indeed. We'd been looking for food when we happened upon him. He seemed wealthy, and we knew him to be a Babylonian Elitist... He didn't wish to be robbed, and drew his weapon."

The king was agitated. "So you and your men killed him like a dog in the street?"

"No, sir. I was there. I fled when they attacked him. I wanted no part of it."

"So you're a coward who only preys on the helpless and weak."

The king motioned for the guards in the courtroom.

"Take this man outside at once. Treat him the way he treated your fellow officer. Show him what happens to one who stands against Babylonian authority. Then crucify him and leave his body hanging along the road. Let others be warned that their king will not tolerate such craven and cruel behavior."

Marcus stepped in front of him. "But he's my witness, sir. Without him I don't have a case."

The king angrily snapped back at the guards, "And have Parliamentarian Shamash treated the same way if he interferes with what I've ordered."

Marcus backed off. They all watched as the man was brought screaming from the courtroom. The king waited until the doors closed, and then loudly stated.

"If you don't have any witnesses left, I'm afraid I have no other choice but to find your defendant, Amarsin Shamash-"

"Wait," Marcus demanded. "You've left me no other choice... I must invoke our right to the Royal Babylonian Voice. Under that decree, the defense or prosecution is able to call a leader to the stand."

The king didn't waver. "You're never allowed to place a Babylonian leader on the defensive. Tread carefully, Parliamentarian. This court will not be merciful in the event that you bring charges against authority."

"I have no intention of bringing a charge against authority. I'll only have him give testimony to aid in Amarsin's defense."

The king rolled his eyes. "Careful, sir."

Marcus shook his head. "The defense calls King Sharrukin of Babylon, to the stand."

32

Dr. Poole looked up when his door opened. One of the evening nurses stood in the doorway. She was off and should have been on her way home since the morning shift had arrived. A young nurse, she'd only been at the hospital for a few months. By all reports, she was good, got along well with others, and handled the patients with care.

He shot her an awkward glance. It was unusual for the nurses to intrude without a knock. She stepped inside and closed the door behind her, fidgeting to lock it. He quickly stood.

"Selena, what are you doing?"

"Sir, something's going on that I think you should know about. I'm scared."

"What are you afraid of?"

"The coma patient. He-"

"He's going to be fine, Selena. Every caregiver struggles the first time they're asked to oversee such a tragic case. You've been handling it quite well from what the other nurses say. Now-"

"No. Dr. Poole, it's not that at all. We need to talk. Please."

He nervously looked at the locked door. It bothered him to be in an office with one of his younger, more attractive, female employees. It wasn't that he didn't trust himself, but if anything were ever said, it wouldn't look good for his Christian reputation. He'd witnessed more than a few good men get in trouble because of meaningless accusations. Even more had been in trouble because the accusations had turned out to be true. There's a reason so many primetime television dramas use hospitals as their backdrop. It's the perfect breeding ground for infidelity. Long hours, close quarters, and plenty of adrenaline rushes were a dangerous combination. It's more than an over-hyped stereotype; the facts support the idea.

That's why he'd sworn to never allow himself to be placed in a compromising situation. Yet, here he sat, with the alluring Selena Rodriquez in the chair across his desk.

However, despite his resolve, something caused him to sit down instead of making the walk over to open the door. It wasn't her attractiveness. It was the panic in her eyes. He motioned for her to sit down across the desk from him.

"What's on your mind?"

He fully expected some variation of the usual. One of the other nurses had said something offensive. Someone had gotten territorial. Two employees had found out they were having an affair with the same doctor. Of all the possibilities, he wasn't prepared for what she presented.

"Someone is going to try to kill your patient… Tonight."

"What? That's ridiculous. Where'd you-"

"Dr. Poole. I can't tell you. You just have to trust me."

"Selena, you can't make those sort of allegations with nothing to substantiate the claims. Who told you that?"

"No one told me… I overheard a man on the phone."

"Where?"

"Dr. Poole, please… I can't."

He curiously looked at her. "Were you doing anything illegal or against hospital policy?"

"Nothing illegal, sir. Possibly against policy. I'd say a gray area."

He nodded. "I see. I don't need to know who you were with Selena. I do need to know where you were."

She hung her head, obviously ashamed. "In the supply closet on your floor. He said he'd locked the door. We were in the back. Both of us were on break. We only had a few minutes."

Dr. Poole held up his hand. "Don't need the grizzly

details. Just need what happened concerning my patient."

"Someone fidgeted with the lock just long enough for us to jump down from the table and hide under it. I couldn't see who it was, but someone was on the phone. He looked back in our direction but thought the room was empty and continued his conversation."

"What was said?" He eagerly asked.

"He said he was sorry to not have completed the task already. He promised that he'd finish the job tonight. He apologized and stated that he hadn't been trying to make excuses. Then he told whoever he was talking to that it would be much easier if they'd get their wife out of the room."

The doctor's eyes widened, "Did you tell anyone about this?"

"No, sir. Wanted to talk to you first."

"Selena, make sure whoever you were with understands that this can't be discussed. Ever."

"Yes, sir. I'll talk to him."

"Thanks for letting me know about this," he said, as he stood and moved toward the door.

"You're welcome. I'm sorry, sir."

He ignored the apology. "Was anything else said? Perhaps how he plans to murder my patient?"

"No, sir. That was it. He just said that and then hung up

the phone. He looked in our direction again, but then turned around and walked out."

He opened the door and motioned her through it. "Don't mention this to anyone. Make sure your... uh... friend doesn't either."

She lowered her head and nodded again. "Yes, sir."

"And Selena, when this is over, we're going to discuss this again... I expect professionalism from all my nurses on staff. We're not filming a medical drama. This is a real facility, and we'll manage it properly."

"Yes, sir," she said without making eye contact. "It won't happen again."

As she walked out, Dr. Poole was already making a phone call. He paused and waited for the person on the other end to answer.

"Yes, Detective Mayes. This is Dr. Poole. I know you're in New York, but I need your help, and I need you here before evening tonight. It's concerning Hayden Smith."

33

The king was incredulous. "You can't be serious. You'd dare call your own king to the stand in your defense. What sort of ruse have you got up your sleeve, Mr. Shamash? I'm easily offended, and that could very well be your death sentence."

"I'm afraid I've no other choice, sir. You've purposely eliminated my other witnesses. I'll not have my grandson murdered in the street like some common criminal."

The king looked to his overweight assistant for advice. The larger man shrugged. "He has the right to invoke the Babylonian Voice. The leader involved must answer, unless you choose to rewrite policy."

The king turned back to Marcus. "Fine, I'll humor you, only because I know I have nothing to offer your case. As a Babylonian leader, I swear to allow my voice to offer only truth toward the resolution of this case."

Marcus smiled. "Thank you, sir. And since you've thus agreed, I must make you aware of the ramifications. The decision in this case has been moved to the panel of witnesses before us. As an acting witness, my king, you no longer have the power to decide the outcome of the case."

The king stared toward the obese man, who was rolling through a scroll on Babylonian Legal Proceedings. He obviously found the section, and then nodded in the king's direction, indicating that Marcus was telling the truth.

"He's right, sir. One can't be a witness and judge the final outcome of the same case, regardless of official rank."

The king was visibly shaken. "How'd you miss that? Why'd you allow me to agree to his terms?"

"I'm sorry. I-"

Marcus interrupted, "It doesn't matter, King Sharukkin… I only have a few questions for you."

The king nodded. "Make them quick, before I lose my patience."

Marcus respectfully bowed. "Of course, my king. First of all, are you aware that the High Babylonian Parliament held a case concerning Hayden Smith and a young, female thief a few short months ago?"

"Yes. I was aware of that case."

"Were you also aware that the Parliament found Captain

Dearth's actions unacceptable in regard to what occurred between him and the two suspects?"

"I know what happens under my rule. I was well aware of that too."

"Then you were also aware that the Parliament gave Captain Dearth and the others strict guidelines concerning interaction with the people who had been found innocent of all charges?"

"I was aware of that, yes."

"Did you inform Captain Dearth that he could disobey the explicit directives of the Babylonian Parliament in an attempt to recapture Mr. Hayden Smith and his companions? You do respect the decisions of your Parliament, do you not?"

The crowd subconsciously leaned forward, eagerly awaiting the reply.

"I gave Captain Dearth no such commission," the king bellowed.

"So you acknowledge that Captain Dearth was on an unsanctioned mission outside of the Babylonian Commonwealth, against direct orders of the Parliament, and without express permission of his king. Doesn't that speak to the irrational state of his mind?"

"I don't think-"

"I'm sorry Your Highness, but I would like for you to tell the court please, did you not discuss with me the morning after the trial that my family and I were to be insulated from his anger? Did you not give me your assurance that you had personally talked to Captain Dearth, and he understood that he was to back away from pursuing revenge on the Shamash household?"

The king paused, sternly looking from one member of the panel to the next. Finally, he looked back at Marcus Shamash.

"You are extremely clever indeed. You've strategically managed to use my words against me."

"Did you tell me such a thing, sir?"

"Yes, but-"

"So, Captain Dearth was pursuing my grandson and his companions against the direct orders of the Babylonian Parliament and the wishes of his king? Is this how we have determined our war heroes should behave? I thought the first step of a Babylonian soldier was learning to follow orders. A man who cannot follow can never learn to lead. Isn't that the warrior's code?"

"It is indeed."

"Then I must ask for my grandson to be cleared. He's innocent of the irrational charges brought against him. As a Babylonian citizen, he was fully within his rights in every action undertaken. As to Captain Dearth's untimely death, the argument is made that it is the fault of others because they fled to the Fortress. However, no one made Captain Dearth pursue. He did so against the orders of Parliament and the wishes of his king. Ultimately, a man who cannot follow orders is a man destined to die alone. That's in the warrior's creeds as well."

The king looked fiercely toward Amarsin and Marcus, and then moved toward his large assistant. The two men whispered together for several minutes. Finally, the king separated himself. His statesman mumbled, "Marcus can't allow his image to be tainted. He'll choose life to protect the Shamash name, no matter the cost. It's the Babylonian way."

The king smiled and looked at the members of the panel. "Clear the courtroom."

They remained seated, unsure of what to do. This was against more procedural ethics.

"Now," the king emphatically yelled. His men drew their swords, as the members of the panel stood and began moving outside.

"What are you doing?" Marcus nervously questioned. He looked at the members who were fleeing from the room.

"Our blood be on your hands. If we die today, our blood be on your hands and your children's," he yelled at them.

The last man exited, and the door was closed. Marcus's six men moved near him and Amarsin, each drawing a sword and forming a circle around their master.

The king's men had them outnumbered three to one. King Sharrukin moved closer to Marcus.

"Parliamentarian Shamash, I'm afraid I've taken the advantage."

"You've gone too far. Your father would be disheartened, should he be alive to see how you've learned to bend the rules to your benefit."

"On the contrary. I think he'd be quite proud of what I'm going to do today."

"King, your family name will be marred with the respected blood of the Shamash household. No greater family has ever served Babylon outside of the throne. My blood has been spilled on several fields over my years… And you'd so willingly desecrate those sacrifices, for pride?"

"Give me thine ear, Parliamentarian Shamash. It's only because of your esteemed historical contributions and your faithfulness to my father's house that I'm not consumed with vengeance for your daring move at making me testify. Never before has that been considered. I admire your audacity. So, I've a proposal."

"What do you propose, oh king?"

"One of you must die. A life for a life. Neither of you adequately rival the greatness of Captain Dearth, but because of your historical significance, I'll allow this. The survivor must serve me overseas."

"Overseas?"

"Yes. I'm afraid your escaped slave is the prince of Aksum, which has become a pivotal player in a quickly developing world crisis."

"I know not of what you speak. What crisis are you

referring to?"

"There've been whisperings for weeks now that a private conglomerate from around the world is plotting the overthrow of Jerusalem. From there, they plan to move together against all Babylonian strongholds. Their aim is to eradicate the Babylonian way of life, to rebuild the ancient tower, and establish it as a global governmental centerpiece, causing all commerce, commercialism, and communication to flow through its center. They long to develop a one world government with the framework of a new Babylon, led by influential men from all nations."

Marcus was curious. "And they intend to completely dismiss us?"

"As of now, they feel we're too into ourselves to become allies with those we deem uncivilized. However, one of you will travel to Jerusalem by special Babylonian envoy. You'll be there within a week. The other of you will die in exchange for Captain Dearth."

Marcus looked to Amarsin. Tears formed in his eyes. He slowly shook his head.

"I've never gone against family. Amarsin, I'm sorry."

The king smiled. "You've made a wise choice, old one. Parliamentarian Shamash, you're sacrifice shall be forever noted. You're country needs you now more than it ever has. You'll make a fine statesman, who'll be more than capable of getting us into the fray with the rest of the world. You'll be able to offer Aksum and Jerusalem as consolation prizes because of your connections there."

Marcus closed his eyes and nodded toward the king. Tears openly fell down his cheeks. He opened his eyes and swiftly borrowed a long blade from one of the men nearest him. He stepped toward Amarsin, whose eyes opened wide in instantaneous horror.

"I'm so sorry, Amarsin," he cried, "Without family, we are nothing."

The men gasped, as Marcus lunged forward, purposely falling on his own sword."

"No," Amarsin screamed. "Grandfather. No. No. No."

He fell down beside him and took Marcus in his arms, holding him near his chest. Marcus touched the left side of his face.

"Make your family proud, Amarsin. Babylon needs you now. Join with the world or Babylon will be destroyed. Find a way, Amarsin. I believe in you."

The famed parliamentarian's head dropped onto Amarsin's chest. Just like that, a historical icon was gone.

The king looked down at Amarsin with disdain. However, he shrugged and cleared his throat.

"A deal is a deal, Amarsin. You can accept the assignment or join your grandfather on his blade. The choice is yours."

Amarsin angrily glowered, something turning cold inside him. He'd been fighting it for days now, this selfish and repulsive nature from within. He'd cried himself to sleep several nights, hoping it would go away, but it wouldn't. Now, it this moment, it had conquered him. He knew what he had to do.

Irately looking at the king he grumbled, "Prepare the vessel. I'll sail for Jerusalem in the morning. What I do, I do for my grandfather... for family... for myself. This has nothing to do with you."

34

Hunzuu leapt from the hayloft they'd been sleeping in. He threw a small rock in Hayden's direction. It bounced off the wooden beam and rattled away. Hayden slightly stirred.

"Hurry, Hayden. Get up. Men are coming. Someone must have told them we've been sleeping here."

Hayden grabbed the belt beside him, strapped on the sword of Tiber and ran to meet Hunzuu by the back doorway leading away from the barn. He slowly slid the door open just enough for them to slip through and stepped outside into the coolness of the morning air.

He stopped abruptly, just outside the door. Hunzuu was following and ran into him from behind, almost knocking him over.

"What's wro-"

He didn't finish, looking up and seeing what had stopped Hayden in his tracks.

There were at least forty of them. Dressed in normal tunics. However, their faces were covered with bizarre masks. Some of them festive. Some frightening. Some decorative. All out of place.

Hunzuu stood shoulder to shoulder with Hayden. "I don't know, sir. This one's got me. I don't know if I should draw my sword, run, laugh, or find a mask of my own."

Hayden was about to reply, when they both heard movement from behind. The men Hunzuu had seen coming had entered the front door of the barn and made their way to the back. They swung the door open wide, revealing another twenty people inside, all wearing various masks as well.

One of them stepped from the group. "Welcome to Tyre. We've been expecting you. It's only been three weeks since you killed that Roman assassin. You've covered some ground since then. No wonder you're both so tired."

"How'd you-"

"Word travels. We know things in Tyre, or haven't you heard."

"How'd you hear about-"

"No concern of yours. Gentlemen, we've prayed for your safe passage since we were told you'd be coming. You've no need to worry while with us. We worship the one God of Israel and are compassionately indifferent to the plights of

Jerusalem. We're hoping you'll be able to turn the tide. No doubt, God is with you."

Hayden was confused. "There are one God believers in Tyre? I thought Tyre was-"

"Was what, Sir Hayden, ruled by a tyrannical madman?"

"Something like that. Only much more sinister."

The leader peered at him through the mask. "Much more, I'm afraid."

"What is he? No one can seem to tell us."

The man smiled, "Come... Commune with us. We'll feed you, clothe you, and allow you to rest... Come"

Hayden and Hunzuu followed, as the man lead them away from the barn and further into what appeared to be a great city.

A few hours later, Hayden and Hunzuu sat alone at a small table in the basement of a stone building. They'd been treated to a hot bath, great food, and fresh clothes. The people's hospitality had been as their leader had advertised.

Hayden scooted his small chair closer to Hunzuu. "Are you at all concerned about these people? You find anything strange?"

"I find this entire circumstance uneventfully awkward. Something is awry in Tyre. Things aren't as they appear; and the masks, they are awful."

"Why do you say that things aren't as they appear?"

"They never remove their masks, even among themselves. They always keep the façade going... We are staying in their leaders home, but even his interaction with his family seems strained by the disinclination of the members to show themselves to the others."

Hayden nodded an agreement. "Have you noticed the complete lack of emotion?"

"Have I? It's uncomfortably uncommon. The men and woman mingle together, but with no difference between them."

"There's-"

"What?" Someone interrupted them from the doorway. They hadn't seen the leader approach.

"Sorry, we meant no disrespect." Hayden worriedly apologized, unsure of how much the leader had overheard.

"None taken. We aren't easily offended here. We teach our children not to be... So, go ahead and finish your statement."

"It's okay, sir. I was pretty much done."

"Then I shall finish it for you. There's no compassion. No love. No intimacy. Is that what you wanted to convey?"

Hayden shrugged. "I don't know. I'm sorry."

"No need for apology, Sir Hayden. What you feel is partially true. Not totally accurate. We choose to love in our own way. We don't show it the way the rest of the world does, but that doesn't mean that it's not there."

Hayden paused, as if not wanting to press the issue further. Reluctantly, he continued.

"I'm puzzled... Earlier by the barn... You stated that you were compassionately indifferent toward the plight of Jerusalem. I'm afraid you have me at a loss. I don't understand your stance. How can you be indifferent and compassionate? The very nature of true compassion demands action and emotion, does it not?"

"We don't believe in emotion. It weakens a man, makes him vulnerable. We're better servants of God if we make it easier to give him everything."

"Really? You serve God by trying to remove your humanity? How does that benefit his kingdom?"

"We believe in formal love. That type of love breeds equality. There's no difference between classes. No difference between sexes. We're all the same in God's eyes. Therefore, we should all be treated as such in this life."

"I've got a problem with that description," Hayden gently argued. "Except for formal love. There's nothing special about that at all. Shouldn't love be fulfilling? Powerful? Life changing? Isn't love a two-way street, a nonverbal communication between two entities? How can you say you love someone and not have an emotional demonstration of what you're feeling?"

"Love isn't about feeling. It's about what is, and what still exists when the feeling has faded. Too much of the world wants to reduce God to an emotion. He's so much bigger than that."

"But doesn't he choose to commune with man on our level, instead of demanding we step up to His? I'd find moving to the level of this one God most impossible, and would thus feel hopeless trying to obtain him. Doesn't the rest of the world feel the same dejection when you present your gospel to them?"

"We don't care about that. We serve God the way we feel he'd be more satisfied. We aren't called to worry about offending the rest of the world."

"It's not about offending the rest of the world, but how can you introduce your God to them, when you make Him so hard to approach and so difficult to fathom?"

"We don't feel the emotion, so we aren't concerned with that. That's the beauty of our life. It brings such peace. Such contentment."

"Are you happy?" Hayden asked.

"What is happiness? It's but a fleeting feeling, here today and gone tomorrow. Who needs happiness when you have been born into faith."

"What is love then, if it's got no feeling?"

"It's merely the connection between us and the one God. The way we live it for Him. That is love. The sacrifices we make are for him. That is love. We wear the masks to separate ourselves from the rest of the world. That is love. Our masks keep us hidden, where only his truth can radiate. That is love. We embrace unselfishness and equality. That too is love."

"Don't you think perhaps your definitions are too broad? You live with priceless convictions, but if those convictions are erroneous, what have you accomplished? A man can be sincere, but sincerely wrong."

"What do you mean?" The man pondered.

"You live by the rules you've created, but you don't demonstrate the emotions of the God you serve. Others have told us the stories of a god who passed his feelings down to mankind, so man would feel the way that he does."

"So, you question our devotion?" The man asked, growing more concerned than angry.

"No. I don't question your devotion at all. I question the object of your obsession. If it's not the god you serve, it's pointless commitment. One cannot be in love with two things at once. You cannot serve only the law, and not the one who created the law. You mustn't embrace precepts and not the one who defines the precepts."

"That's absurd. We aren't that way. It would be impossible."

"It's far easier than you think, sir. It's easy for one to love the idea of worship, and not the god they claim to worship. People get lost in their service and devotion, until they're only doing chores, intoxicated with the idea of serving a higher power, until true love has exited the equation. They are in love with love. That's a far cry from being consumed with the God of the universe."

"To love to worship is to love this God. It's ever evident in the way we separate ourselves from others. We've chosen to make it known that we are his true disciples."

"One must be careful that the way of holiness hasn't desecrated one's relationship with the most Holy. Without intimately connecting to the One whose presence brings revolutionary change, true purity can't exist."

"So-"

"Furthermore, I don't understand how you could feel compassion toward people who are lost in their way, but be callously indifferent to them because they aren't like you. Shouldn't you be hungry to convert as many people to connecting with your god as possible? If he's as powerful as everyone proclaims, how can you know him and not want others to meet him in the same light as you?"

"Compassion truly demands action. That's what you believe?" The man asked, genuinely seeking illumination.

"I believe if there's no reaction once you've united with a god so pure and mighty, then either he's not real, or there's been no real connection. If he is real, a union between man and this sort of god would forever change the man."

The leader nodded. "And you propose that if we're truly changed, we'll take on his nature, and want others to share in this same experience."

Hayden smiled. "That's about the gist of it. That makes

sense to me. Self must die, and we must unite for God's purpose."

The leader looked troubled. "Perhaps we've been living this wrong. I have much to ponder, Sir Hayden. This discourse has been incredibly enlightening."

He paused, before looking directly into Hayden's eyes. "How do you propose getting others to believe in Him?"

Hayden firmly stared back. "I'd start by removing the mask... Expose yourself... Let them see who you really are... Let others see your humanity... Your struggles... Your failures and shortcomings... Let common people know that your god loves the average just as much as He loves the super spiritual... Give them hope... Let them see that it doesn't take perfection, that's just the mark we should strive toward."

Tears trickled from underneath the mask, as the man nodded in understanding, "If all they see is the mask, they feel they could never attain. I comprehend now."

He slowly took the mask from his head and stared at it for a few seconds. Then abruptly, as if the decision had finally been made, he tossed it to the ground,

"That's the first time I've been without that mask in ten years, and I've never felt more alive and free."

Hayden smiled, "You're doing the right thing."

The man weakly grinned back, "I can't wait to share this with the others. This is truly the reason you've come, to liberate us from the arrogance of our fictitious beliefs. Thank you, sir."

"Actually," Hayden stated, "I came for the one the King of Tyre has decided to marry. I've come for the girl named M'ya."

The man frowned. "I'm afraid you've missed her by a couple of days. King Apollyon is marching toward Jerusalem. She's fearlessly riding by his side. The two are to be wed before the great feast of the Jews. Their wedding is to be consummated the evening of the Sabbath of Sabbaths... The end is near, Sir Hayden... The end is near."

35

Overhead, fiery arrows illuminated the darkened sky. It wasn't normal. The darkness was multiplying more intensely than ever before. The moon and stars were being swallowed into a vortex of dense blackness.

The mother cradled the child intensely, searching for a way from the room. The child cried. Each tear that fell seemed to cause the earth to shake with surprising hunger.

There was something about the child's eyes as he looked into them. It moved him. A baby was causing him to feel naked and exposed. A baby's stare was making him feel wounded and incomplete. It was too much. He wanted to get away.

But he couldn't. The soldiers were coming too forcefully. They were in the streets, murdering, pillaging, and eliminating every person they encountered. Men, women, small children, and babies. It didn't matter. They were all being destroyed like lambs in the slaughterhouse.

Toddlers and babies were being systematically eradicated. He'd always known that infanticide was a cultural norm. He'd even argued with Hayden about its validity and importance to the propagation of the human race. However, he'd never witnessed it exercised with such fury. Bashed against trees. Feed to ravenous dogs. Thrown into the well in the midst of the city, not only ending lives, but also contaminating the water supply. The violence was horrific.

The Sin Cloud grew darker and darker. It erupted before them in the distance, slowly advancing, as if it were going to devour the city. Darius could also see its reflection in the eyes of the warriors murdering in the streets. It was as if the cloud was somehow controlling them. Its rage was consuming their thoughts. They were fighting its battle.

The men were coming. Hunzuu was killed at the entrance to the house. Hayden sat near the back door, his own blood covering almost ever portion of his body. M'ya was nowhere to be found. Leib's body was hanging on a cross by the street. He'd been crucified near the city's entrance. Darius was alone to fight the onslaught of advancing warriors.

He had to protect the baby. He didn't know why, but there was something refreshingly commanding about this child. No one told him, but instinctively, he knew. It had to be him. This had to be the Godchild. He was the one.

The door burst open and soldiers pushed into the room to seize the infant. His mother screamed and valiantly fought the assailants, but to no avail. They ripped the baby from her arms and tossed him to their captain, who laughed, as he held the child high in the air. They were amused at the lack of complexity of the one others had labeled as their Messiah. It was impossible. Killing him would prove too easy.

The captain lifted his dagger and raised it high, preparing to ram it through the baby's small chest, ending the pulsing, rhythmic beating of Heaven's heart.

The baby suddenly turned its tiny head toward Darius and spoke clearly. There was no mistaking the words. They were enunciated beautifully. It was not the expression of a toddler. The innocent eyes left an indelible impression on his heart.

Darius unbelievingly blinked for a moment, and when he opened his eyes again, the toddler had been replaced in the captain's arms by the whitest, most spotless lamb he'd ever seen. The baby's words echoed through his mind, slicing like a razor into the depths of his soul.

"You must protect the lamb. You must give all to protect the lamb."

. . .

Darius shot up in the makeshift bed, gasping for air, his own screams awakening him. It had been too real. The baby had spoken, and he'd suddenly known his purpose for coming to Jerusalem. He'd try to prevent the war. However, if he couldn't stop it from occurring, he was being sent there to find and protect the Lamb of God.

Bennett and Leib stood over him. Leib was worried.

THE SIN CLOUD

"You okay, King Darius?"

Darius shook his head, unable to control the flow of water falling from his eyes.

"It was just a dream. Only a dream."

36

The next morning, Darius, Leib, and Bennett sat around the diminutive table in a private stonewalled home. It had taken Darius a couple hours to fall back asleep. He hadn't been able to get the images out of his head.

The children dying.

The lamb in the soldier's arms.

The bloody dagger hanging overhead, ready to thrust into the lamb's flesh.

It had all been too much. He'd never had a dream that felt so real. He'd never received such divine instruction. Finding and protecting the child was an absolute necessity.

He tiredly wiped his eyes, just as the door swung open. Two armed men entered the room, followed by Hayden and

Hunzuu. The first man smiled at Darius.

"We found them near the entrance to the city. They fit your description perfectly. The blade on his side is larger than any I've seen. I knew it had to be the sword you told us about."

Hayden and Hunzuu walked more fully into the room. Darius stood to greet them, clasping Hunzuu's arm, and then embracing Hayden.

"Good to see you my brothers. I'm guessing by M'ya's absence, you had no luck finding her?"

Hayden despondently shook a negative reply. "They said she'd already been taken toward Jerusalem. We joined with a gypsy band and got here as quickly as we could. No one on the road had seen a group of Tyrinians marching this way. No one had seen their king either."

The Jewish man in the doorway shook his head. "They wouldn't have. The Tyrinians are experts at not being seen. It's almost like they're invisible."

Hayden muttered, "How are things looking here?"

The man interrupted before Darius could answer. "Scouts tell us that things aren't good. Our armies are spread thin around the three main routes into the county. Most of them have been sent here to Jerusalem, for it appears the other nations are focusing on our city first. They are two days march away, maybe three, depending on how eager they are for war. It's a waiting game now. However, tis not good, for much blood will be shed. Never a good thing."

Darius looked at Hayden. "I sent a dispatch four days ago, pleading with the other kings to allow logic to override their destructive advance. I got replies from them all over the past couple of days. The reply was the same. *Jerusalem must fall.*"

Leib stood. "There's nothing we can do here, King Darius. As your advisor, I'm suggesting we remove ourselves from the city. Your brother will certainly have us killed once they overrun this place. We must decide between self-preservation and suicide. Sir, your kingdom needs you."

Darius was pondering his thoughts when another man entered the room accompanied by a four-year-old boy at his side. He was a jovial fellow, late thirties to early forties, dressed nicely, and obviously a man of position. The respect the others demonstrated proved it to be true. He held a baby boy in his arms.

He walked to Darius and reverently bowed. "My name is Simon. We've much to discuss."

Darius guardedly looked at him. "Who are you?"

"Oh, please forgive my rudeness," the man laughed. "I'm Simon, respected leader of a group of rebels who have long since wanted to drive Rome and all other influences from the Jewish provinces. We must return to our holy roots if we're going to survive. What's happening now is no doubt the judgments of God."

Hayden and Darius exchanged concerned glances. Simon noticed and continued. "However, as in the days of Eden, even in judgment God has provided a way of escape, a ram in the bush."

"Okay, and what's that?" Darius inquired.

"His only son."

"You know where the Godchild is?" Darius excitedly asked.

"Certainly. At least, we think we do. I've narrowed down the search and at least know the proximity."

Simon held his son high into the air. "My pride and joy, gentlemen. We must keep him protected. He's destined to meet the Messiah one day. I feel it in my bones. Destiny."

Leib moved forward. "If what you're saying is true, you should go to this child's family at once and have them sail out of your ports. We're surrounded on every side. Perhaps they could slip through on the seas."

Simon sternly shook his head. "No. They thought of that. There's a naval blockade outside every major harbor. All vessels have been grounded. One trading ship tried to move past the blockade. They were boarded, every member murdered, and the vessel burned to sink at the bottom of the sea. They made an example out of them, and no one wants to try leaving since."

"Surely you must know a way out of this place. There must be secret paths whereby you could run for safety. Take your son and let him live. All who stay in Jerusalem are going to die. You must know that."

He shook his head again. "No. God will save us."

Hayden moved toward him. "Sir, tell us where to find this

baby and his family. I must speak with them."

Simon gave him the directions, even narrowing it down to a few houses he thought they'd been staying in.

"Good luck to you, sirs. If you're still here in the midst of the battle, the rally point will be this building. It's strong, well fortified, made of the finest stone, and there's only one entrance. We could make a fine defense here if need be."

Hayden looked at the others and then clasped hands with the man. "I shall meet you here then when the battle begins. We'll fight as brothers. Live or die, we shall do it together."

37

Hayden stepped onto the small wooden porch. The others waited below on the ground at the opposite end. The lone woman sat in a swinging chair that was hanging from a large beam on the top. She watched her toddler shuffle sand in the front yard. She warmly smiled, as Hayden approached.

"I dreamed you were coming," she said, with little emotion.

He was unsure how to respond. She warmly smiled again. "Excuse me," she said, as she stepped from the porch and picked up the toddler, returning with him to sit down near Hayden.

The toddler laughed, and gently nestled against his mother's chest, as she softly ran her fingers through his dirty sweat streaked hair.

"He's tired. It's just about time for his nap."

Hayden looked into the child's eyes. His heart fluttered. Something indescribable welled up within. He could hardly contain the emotion. He wanted to laugh, cry, scream, sing, love, give, hope, and live, all in the same moment. He'd never experienced emotions so deep and strong. He quickly turned away from the toddler.

The baby cheerfully cooed again, as if he hadn't felt anything different at all. The boy's mother smiled.

"He's different, you know? He'll change things. That's why they're coming."

Hayden's eyes narrowed. "You already know?"

"Yes. My husband and I have been miraculously warned. We're looking for a way out of the city. Don't worry. God has promised to keep us protected."

Hayden winced a little, "Sorry ma'am, I'm a struggling believer. I do what I can and then hope God covers the rest. I can't just sit back and wait, blindly believing he'll just magically make the amassing armies disappear."

She politely smiled, "When you've experienced what I have, you'll know that He's fully capable. You'll know not only that He can, but also that He will keep you... You too are a man of destiny. I see it now."

"I'm just trying to stay alive. I have no destiny-"

She interrupted, "Not here, Sir. Your future awaits in a land far away. You have a powerful future. You'll walk through perilous times. Times more deadly than these, but your God will walk with you. You have that assurance. That's why you're here, to gain insights and wisdom that will carry you through. However, you must leave this behind, take a leap of faith, and embrace the terrifying world ahead."

"How could you-"

She looked deep into his eyes. "I know."

Holding the child out toward him, she said "Hold him close for a moment."

Hayden shook his head. Just the thought of touching the child terrified him. "I can't."

She didn't pull the child back toward her. She kept him at arm's length toward Hayden. "Please, just hold him. You need this. Trust me. You need this."

Hayden reluctantly pulled the child near, and the toddler wrapped his small arms around Hayden's strong chest.

Something surged through him again. This time much more powerful than the first. He felt the intensity of pure love. He'd never felt it like this before, such extreme joy and peace. His body wanted to shake. He fought to control it.

The others joined him on the porch. Darius, Leib, Hunzuu, and Bennett beheld the child. Each feeling lost, but yet completely found. Although none could have adequately described it, all felt the power of eternity surrounding them, the surreal benefit of holding a fragment of Heaven.

Hayden cried, as he lifted the boy from his chest and handed him back to his mother. He bowed before the boy.

"I'm humbled to have held him in my arms. I shouldn't have. He's far too high for the likes of me."

Pausing, he then lifted his eyes to the mother. "I pledge my life to protect him. I'll give my all to make sure you and your family make it out of the city."

Hunzuu bowed as well. "I shall stand with him."

"As will I," the other three replied, all overwhelmed with the power of the moment.

Hayden stood. The others followed his example.

"What's the child's name?" he reluctantly asked.

His heart pounded, his mind wanted to explode, a sudden surge of power, as the mother meekly replied, "We've named him Jesus."

38

Amarsin stood before the dark leader and the others that were with him. He moved toward a chair that his envoy had designed just for him. It was larger and wasn't swallowed by his plump frame. The image of a baby-faced, hugely overweight, young leader sitting on a small stool hadn't been imposing enough. Some had even found the sight comical. Now, he sat in a chair constructed like a throne. Obviously, he was a powerful player in the nation of Babylon. As long as the other world leaders felt that way, Amarsin knew he controlled the floor.

He motioned for the dark man to approach him. As the man came near, Amarsin spoke in a low tone.

"Thank you all for agreeing to see me under the banner of peace today. I trust we can find an agreement that will be pleasing to both the royal family of Babylon and the respective countries you distinguished gentlemen represent."

Demsas held his stare. "Perhaps we can, if the price be right. If not, we're prepared to go to war. The days of your kingdom holding power over the opposite hemisphere are over."

Amarsin didn't appear rattled. "I'd not be so confident in sheer numbers, lest you forget that Babylon is still home to most industrial factories, military weapons experts, agricultural advancements, and technological breakthroughs. Without Babylon, the rest of the world will indeed suffer."

Demsas overconfidently grinned, "We don't intend to be without Babylon. That's where you're mistaken. We plan to renew Babylon, replace what is with something more powerful, to restore the significance of Babylon by building a new one, far greater than what you've even imagined."

Amarsin showed no emotion. "I would that were true. We could use a greater Babylon. The world needs one."

"So, you'd so willingly sacrifice what you have now? You'd so easily surrender your way of life?"

"To take what we've known and make it better; you must know I would. So would King Sharrukin. He longs for the day when the prominence of our nation will be restored. Perhaps we could find a way to make this day meaningful for all of us. We could all have major roles in the redefining of the greatest empire the world has ever known."

"We aren't only dreaming of restoring Babylon. We're talking about building a system whereby one corporate body controls the intricacies of the world. One government sets the standards and laws. The whole world is judged by a fair group of leaders from around the globe. Each empire and territory is represented. We refer to it as Babylon because we want to restore the dreams of our ancestors when we were all unified in our effort to build the ascending tower to Heaven. One governing body was powerful enough to get the gods' attention then, and what we need today more than anything, is to once again awaken the sleeping giants."

Amarsin smirked and shook his head in silent agreement. "King Sharrukin is ready to commit to such a plan. He has sanctioned me to aid in the formation of such a group. His only stipulation being that he have a prominent role in the headship of such a one world position. After all, he is the leader of the most powerful empire on the planet."

"We could negotiate."

"There is to be no negotiation. This is a one-time offer to help bring peace to your hemisphere forever. Should you decline my proposal, the wrath of Babylon will be shortly unleashed where you least expect it… We've recognized your threat for weeks now. Don't make the mistake of thinking we don't have spies in your camp. Babylon wasn't built by blindly trusting the rest of the world to exist outside the jealousy of human nature. You all want what we have. You're just not powerful enough to get it. So, you'll join together long enough to try for victory, and then you'll turn on each other like dogs. Save yourself the trouble. We aren't the kind to idly sit back and pray you'll leave us alone. After today, there'll be no other warning, and no other opportunity to save yourselves from Babylonian destruction."

Demsas was highly offended and livid that Amarsin wasn't intimidated by his power play. "You stand before us all and make empty threats. While I appreciate your audaciousness, I must tell you that I'm rather unimpressed with your understanding of what's taking place here. The world's finest nations have gathered with a common goal of Jewish eradication and Babylonian deprecation. That's what has united us. The other Emperors hold the common belief that we'd be better off establishing a new power instead of bowing down to yours. You've no position on which to stand. You've nothing to offer us."

Amarsin moved close enough to grab Demsas by the top of his garment. He placed his large hand around Demsas' neck and lifted him from the floor. Amarsin was surprisingly strong, and Demsas was helpless against his unexpected action.

Demsas' men immediately surged forward, but were expertly cut off by Babylonian soldiers. Amarsin held him in the air, pinned to a sidewall until his face turned a shade of purple, then let him crash to the floor gasping for air.

Emperor Cassius Augustus narrowed his eyes and intently stared toward the obese man before him, his gaze a mixture of amusement and bewilderment.

"You're the best specimen Babylon had to send? What a disgrace. It's an outrage you come to negotiate and bring nothing but filth and violence. This is the very Babylonian usurping of authority that we're trying to do away with. Rome will no longer be held hostage by your empty rhetoric."

Emperor Khu joined him, "Nor will Egypt."

Emperor Narcisso smiled. "Wait gentlemen, I knew this man's grandfather well. He was a respected and noble warrior. He lived and would have died honorably... Let's be honest, we've all wished we could have choked King Demsas at some point... I also know a fellow opportunist when I see one," Narcisso chuckled.

He looked at Amarsin, "What if we make you a counter offer?"

The others questioningly looked on, so Narcisso continued, "What would you give to be the new leader of Babylon? What would it be worth for you to carry on your great family tradition?"

Amarsin smiled. "I'll hand you Babylon on a platter, tell you everything you need to know to topple it to its knees. I've always wanted a seat at the table."

"And why would you do that? Why would you mar your grandfather's memory by turning on the nation he fought to build?"

Bitterness burned deeply in Amarsin's eyes, "Because, the old Babylon has died. I envision a greater one. One that unites the world, dominates all who would oppose it, and provides answers instead of creates more questions. It's foolish to preserve one's heritage if not willing to evolve into something far greater. Babylon will live. I'll make sure of that. Only, I will be its leader, and I'll work hand in hand with other world leaders to ensure a new success for all. Raise the Babylonian tower again. Even the gods would fear us."

"You'd oppose your king?" Emperor Khu asked.

"King Sharrukin is an old fool. There's no advantage for my people if we stay under his rule. He kills the old ones who have given their lives to build his empire. He's responsible for the death of my grandfather. I have no respect or loyalty to him and hope to see him crucified on our new streets."

Demsas stood up, having finally caught his breath. He was still angry, but he'd been listening with interest.

"You honestly think you could give us your nation so easily?"

"The people are ready for revolutionary change. They'll cave to the strongest players. As long as they feel they'll have adequate representation in a new, more dynamic government, they'd do anything. The Shamash name is revered in Babylonian circles. I'll tell them it was the desire of my grandfather, make him a martyr, vilify Sharrukin, and the people will follow."

Emperor Farooq laughed, "I must admit, this is not what I expected to come from the arrogance of Babylon. An opportunist. I like you. Too bad Emperor Sharrukin didn't recognize you for who you are. He'd have gained a most valuable ally had he tried."

He turned to the other Emperors. "I like his plan. It guarantees us Babylon without the losses we all expected. We'll still have war, but with his knowledge, it will be much easier."

Demsas looked uneasy, "But can we trust him to deliver, or

is he merely pulling us in to play us for fools?"

Emperor Narcisso turned back toward Amarsin, eyeing him suspiciously. "What do you have to offer besides your word? There must be something you can give us to prove your heart has turned."

Amarsin was conflicted for a moment, but then crookedly grinned. It had indeed conquered him now.

"I'll also give you my friends, and with them the heart of Aksum."

"Your friends? What good are friends to us?"

Demsas beamed. "He refers to my elder brother, one who has sworn allegiance to defend to the Jews. He also refers to Sir Hayden Smith, formerly of Babylon, one who currently incites the Jews to withstand our invasion."

He stared back at Amarsin. "You're certain you could hand them to us?"

"They'll be expecting me to be as they remember. There's a lot of water under that bridge, but I'm no longer the man they knew. I'll give them to you by this time tomorrow."

Amarsin turned to move away. That's when they saw it. Behind his gaze, peering through the windows of his soul, a dark cloud. It was there for a brief flash, and then it was gone.

39

Aizan silently moved through the shadows until he stood over the little man by the wall. Leib had motioned him closer when he'd appeared around the southern post. As Aizan approached, Leib had checked their surroundings. No one was there. Neither he nor Aizan seemed to have been followed.

"What have you found out?" Leib asked.

"It's not good, sir. The king will not be pleased."

"He needs to know the truth. That's why I agreed to start meeting you here. Tell me what you've learned."

"It's your friend from Babylon. Amarsin Shamash. He's come from over the sea."

"Good. Good. That'll be most pleasing. We've missed him

tremendously."

"No. I'm afraid you don't understand. He's sworn allegiance to the New World Order. They've agreed to eradicate the Jews and then destroy the old Babylon. Your friend has been overwhelmed by a thirst for power. Hatred for Sharrukin burns brightly against the darkness that surrounds him. I'm afraid your friend is gone."

"No. No one is ever gone, Sir Aizan. He's still there. He just needs someone to rekindle the fire, remind him what's important, and help him see the light."

"You are wrong... I wish it were not so, but you are terribly mistaken... You must return to Darius and let him know that his friend has agreed to betray him. Amarsin Shamash has agreed to willingly sacrifice Darius, King of Aksum, and Sir Hayden Smith of Babylon to prove his loyalty to the new regime."

"What? He said that? That's impossible." Leib was floored. "Amarsin is a good man... Honest... Loyal."

Aizen sullenly nodded, "He said it with his own words. He said he wasn't the man you remembered. There'd been too much water under the bridge. You'd left him alone to fend for himself at the Fortress, and he was almost killed because of it. He's bitter, and he's intoxicated with the idea of power. There's no deadlier combination."

Leib disgustedly shook his head. "I'll tell them at once. Thank you, Sir Aizan."

Leib turned to leave and heard someone from behind, a

sudden movement, as he turned to see Aizan sprinting away. A voice bellowed from the velvety haze beginning to blanket the darkened ground.

"Halt. Who goes there? I command you to stop by order of the New Kingdom. Stop immediately."

Leib turned back around to run, but three men blocked his path. One of them spit into the sand, stamping the spittle into the grains with his foot.

"What have we got here boys? A wee runt to practice on before the real battle. The gods must favor us to send such a plaything."

Leib laughed. "I'm just a miniscule problem, my wee runtness shall be best exhibited elsewhere. Excuse me gentlemen, but I'll be going now."

The lead man grabbed him. "I'm afraid not. Jerusalem is under siege. No one goes in or out without express consent of one of the Emperors, and I highly doubt they'll be giving it to you."

One of the other men eyed him, recognition coming to him, "Hey, aren' you tha dwarf tha' travels with King Demsas' brotha? Tha midget advisa, I believe. Tha rumas be true then."

"No. Tis not me. I wouldn't know the man if I saw him."

A rough tussle from behind turned their attention. Three guards came toward them with a prisoner. It was Aizan, and he'd been severely beaten. His left arm was limp at his side. His right eye was almost swollen shut, nose broken, and face bloodied. The first guard threw him on the ground.

"He came here carrying information to be passed behind enemy lines. Says he was meeting an informant. We had to beat that out of him."

"Imagine that," the leader of the group with Leib replied. "We've got a traitor to our king meeting his brother's advisor in the middle of the night. I wonder what Demsas would decree."

Leib nervously shuffled. "I'm not who you believe me to be. Please. I don't know what-"

The first guard picked Leib up and hurled him into the sand at Aizan's feet. Picking Leib's face up out of the sand, the guard turned his eyes toward Leib.

"You've one chance to answer correctly. Is this the man you came here to meet? Is he the one you gave your information to?"

Aizan looked into Leib's eyes. To tell the truth meant Leib would die. If Leib died, King Darius could not be warned. To tell the truth might also mean that he could possibly live long enough to make a plea to his former best friend and confidant, Demsas. Perhaps Demsas would spare him based on the old memories. It was a long shot, but sacrificing Leib could secure his safety, at least long enough to stand before the king.

Aizan continued to stare for a moment, squinting as if to see the short man more clearly.

Finally he spoke, "No. I'm afraid I don't know this man. While also little in stature, he isn't the elf of Darius."

The guard shook his head and exhaled deeply. "You never were a good liar, Aizan."

He moved so quickly no one saw it coming. His dagger was thrust through Aizan's midsection before anyone could respond. He pulled Aizan close, his blade still in Aizan's belly. As Aizan neared him, he whispered into his ear.

"It didn't have to be this way, my brother. You could have chosen to stay allied to the king. You never knew how to pick a winner."

Aizan cried. "It's not always about winning."

He looked into the guard's eyes, wishing he could change what had happened. "Don't tell our mother it was you," he whispered. "It'll kill her."

His voice slipped away, and he slumped against his brother's body. His brother held him close for a moment, and then shoved him harshly to the ground and turned to the other guards.

"Empire before family, right? You are my brothers."

He hastily turned back to Leib. "You're not worthy to die by the same blade bearing the blood of my brother."

Walking away, he called back over his shoulder, "Make it quick. Hang the little one at the eastern entrance. Let them see what happens to anyone who betrays our cause. Write an inscription on the top of his cross. *City under siege. Don't enter or leave. Death awaits."*

"Wait," Leib pleaded. "Please. You don't have to…"

The man had already moved on. The rustle of armor and the sounds of the night drowned Leib's cries, as the soldiers violently pulled him toward the eastern gate.

40

Hayden smiled when he saw him, running to greet him with a warm embrace.

"It's great to see you. It's been a long time. It seems you've done well. Things at the Fortress must have turned out nicely. You look good."

Amarsin was cold, standoffish, "It's a good thing, seeing as how you all left me there alone to face the onslaught of the Babylonian guard. Did you know the king himself came down to condemn me to death for murdering Abaddon Dearth?"

Hayden was stunned. "No. That's not what-"

Amarsin rudely interrupted, "Well, that's what occurred. I was ridiculed, mocked, and if not for my grandfather, I would have been tortured and killed. And what were you doing? Chasing Darius' dream of being king."

Hayden hurtfully ignored the suggestion. "Did your grandfather make the trip with you?"

A brief expression of grief flashed over his face, "Afraid not. He won't be making trips with anyone. He killed himself so I could go free. That was the great king's stipulation. One of us had to die. How do you think that makes me feel?"

Hayden lowered his head, "I'm sorry, Amarsin. I truly am. None of us knew what was happening there. We hadn't heard anything."

"Of course not. And you were too busy in your own little world to notice I was almost dying in mine. But it's okay. I've got a plan now, and you and Darius are the only things standing in the way of it."

"What do you mean, Amarsin? I'll not stand in your way."

"Afraid you will. You're right in the middle of what I'm going to do."

"What-"

Amarsin held his hand up for Hayden to be quiet. "Shh… I'm going to rend the kingdom from Sharrukin and claim it for the Shamash family. I'm going to help King Demsas, Emperor Khu, Emperor Farooq, Emperor Cassius Augustus, and Emperor Narcisso build a strong and better Babylon. Babylon once ruled the world, and it will rise again. We'll rebuild the tower and re-establish supremacy with a one world government that I shall be a founding member of."

Hayden's mouth dropped, "Amarsin, you know that's not

the way. That's not what your grandfather would have wanted."

"My grandfather is dead," he powerfully snapped the words. "His last request was for me to make him proud. I shall."

"Amarsin, your grandfather was a reputable man, a man of honor. You can't move forward and hope to please him without the same moral convictions he would've hoped had been passed down."

"Moral convictions? You talk to me of moral convictions. And what of you, dear friend? The rest of us can be ruled by the underworld. Gross darkness can slowly strangle the earth. The Sin Cloud grows larger everyday, suppressing and subduing the power of the gods. And what do you do? You chase your own selfish agenda, forgetting the souls hanging in eternal balance. And for what, because you're in love with M'ya?"

"I-"

Amarsin overrode him, "No. I don't want to hear your hypocrisy, Hayden. You can't judge me for making tough choices, when you continue to make your own. Selfishness has many faces, my friend. Man forever chooses his own temporary agendas over Heaven's eternal ones. That's what makes this world the evil place it is."

Hayden stammered. "But… But I've changed, Amarsin. So can you."

"Change isn't that easy. Not from this."

"Amarsin... I've seen him. I held him in my arms," Hayden pleaded, feeling the strange warmth overshadow him again, as he spoke of the child.

"Who?" Amarsin wondered aloud.

"The Godchild of the Jews. He changed me. He changes everything."

"You expect me to believe a child changed your heart?" Amarsin disbelievingly asked.

Hayden continued, "I looked into his eyes, and... there was..."

"What? What was there, Hayden?"

"Life... Joy... Peace... Eternity..."

Amarsin laughed, and then suddenly stopped, whipping his head around to stare into Hayden's eyes, his teeth were tightly clinched together.

"You chase the dreams of fools. I'll build an eternal superpower that will humble even the gods. The great tower will be rebuilt. It will once again unite mankind, and we shall live as gods ourselves."

"That was never meant to be. We weren't meant to reign without God. We were meant to reign through Him."

"Then he shouldn't have allowed Marcus to die. He shouldn't have positioned evil men in high places. He shouldn't have allowed the Sin Cloud to continue growing."

"But what you're doing will change none of that. It'll only

make it worse. You must know that."

Amarsin smiled, a dark fury rising in his expression. Hayden's head abruptly moved backward, as he thought, only for a moment, that he saw the cloud pillowing in Amarsin's gaze.

It seemed to clear, and Amarsin continued, "If you can't beat 'em…"

"Please, Amarsin. Don't do this," Hayden stammered.

"It's done. All that remains is you and Darius. My two tickets into the ultimate alliance."

"Why us?"

"Because Demsas influences the others, and he wants both of you brought to him. Darius, for obvious reasons, and you, because you create turmoil and rebellion everywhere you go."

Amarsin seemed deep in thought for a second, and then snapped out of it and continued, "However, I can see another way for you to survive."

Hayden shook his head. "Not interested. Neither should you be. You're one of us, Amarsin."

"Not anymore," he deflected Hayden's attempt to emotionally connect.

"Revenge toward King Sharrukin is the wedge that divides us? You're going to allow him to not only kill your grandfather, but to also kill the man you've become? Amarsin, I know that there is still good inside of you. You aren't this selfish person anymore. You are better than this… I believe in you."

Amarsin's eyes flickered with a soft emotion he'd been fighting to conceal. The good inside of him started to ebb forward, fighting to connect with Hayden's attempts to draw it from the hardened man before him. Hayden continued,

"Amarsin, we love you. You are better than this… Please."

The warmth faded, as Amarsin laughed, the feeling much more sinister than humorous, "It's not killing me, Hayden. It's recreating me. It's a new birth, a new day, a new dawn. The beginning of an era, and I'm sitting on the precipice."

"Please don't-"

"All you have to do is give me the Godchild. Where'd you see him? Deliver us the Godchild, allow me to speak with Darius just once, and you can rule by my side."

"What's happened to you?" Hayden pleaded. "You're not yourself, Amarsin."

"Life. It gets us all, I suppose."

"But how we respond to life's tragedies is what defines us. Our legacy will be the culmination of every choice along our journey. Each footstep, every decision matters."

"And when the end is written, Sir Hayden, the candle of my life will have outshined yours. My legacy will long be remembered."

"I'd rather be a brief flutter in the wind for good, then have a lifetime of illumination for evil."

Amarsin wouldn't buckle, "So, you won't give me the child?"

Hayden didn't respond for a few seconds, and then slowly answered. "I won't compromise his innocence to have him defiled by much lessor men."

Amarsin was dejected. The pain was clearly written on his face.

"I was hoping for the best, Sir Hayden. I truly love you, but I'm afraid you've left me no choice. Next time we meet, it shall not be as brothers."

"Then what?" Hayden asked, his eyes betraying the pain he was feeling.

Amarsin didn't hesitate. There was no emotion, just a blank stare. "As mortal combatants... Enemies."

41

Mrs. Andrews stood over him. Dr. Poole interrupted from behind.

"Ma'am. They're here."

She turned, ignoring them for the moment. "Dr. Poole... He's been stirring a lot on his own tonight. Quick hand jerks. Slight leg jolts. Eye flutters. He almost seems to be mumbling under his breath. Is that a good sign?"

Dr. Poole approached her and looked down at him. "I would say so. I'm not sure though. We'll have to monitor him more closely the next few days. Possibly run some tests. But remember, we have more pressing needs at the moment."

"Yes... Yes... Of course," she replied, turning back to them.

Dr. Poole introduced them, "Mrs. Vice-president. This is Detective Torben Mayes." He wasn't sure how to introduce the others.

Torben extended his hand and then motioned toward the others, "These are my friends, Ms. Jane… uh… and Mr. Gino Rovati."

She smiled, shook his hand, and then looked toward Gino. "Italiano?"

"As Italian as spaghetti," he replied, his smile filling the room.

She smiled too, before looking back at Torben. "Well, Dr. Poole says he filled you in a little earlier. Do you think you'll be able to keep my son-in-law safe? Doesn't seem like he's supposed to make it out of this."

"Of course. You're in my city now. No one… and I mean no one goes in or out of this room. I've called a couple of friends of mine. They're law enforcement, and they'll be manning the doors. I've already informed them that this has high governmental ramifications. They're not gonna let the secret service through that door, ma'am. Unless the president himself asks to come inside, the only people allowed in this room will be you, Dr. Poole, and us."

Mrs. Andrews looked relieved, "Thank you. Thank all of you."

"Before we leave, I was wondering if we could ask you a few questions about the case?"

"About Hayden?"

"Yes, I'm continuing to look into everything."

"You should probably stop, detective," she worriedly interjected.

"I can't, ma'am. I'm already in too deep."

Her concern was genuine, "If you aren't dead yet, it's not too late. You should all stop whatever you're doing and get out while you can."

"We're not interested in doing that, Mrs. Andrews. We're pursuers of truth."

"It can't be found, son. The truth is buried so deeply that no one even knows what it is anymore."

"Then we're going to unbury it, ma'am... Please, will you assist us?"

"Sure." She motioned for them to go sit on a small couch next to Hayden's bed.

After they were situated, Torben started, "Do you know anything about The Affair?"

She was stunned. "How do you-"

"I don't, Mrs. Andrews. I'm trying to figure it out, but I don't have much to go on."

"Where'd you hear about that? I wasn't even supposed to know. There are many things my husband doesn't tell me. Government secrets. You know?"

"And that's what this is, a government secret? Some sort of cover-up?"

She shrugged. "Something like that I suppose. I'm afraid I can't help you much. I really don't know."

She paused for a moment, obviously trying to decide if it was okay to go further.

He placed his hand over hers. "It's okay, Mrs. Andrews. We really need help. We're in trouble, and obviously so is Mr. Smith here. He found something he wasn't supposed to, and they're willing to kill him for it. Please, help us."

She nervously smiled. "All I know is that it reaches deep into the United States government and beyond. I heard my husband talking to someone from the Mossad one night-"

"Israeli intelligence?"

"Yes. A conference call. The Mossad and some other foreign dignitary. I'm not sure whom, but they were talking about The Affair. I couldn't hear all the words, but it sounded like it possessed a strong anti-Christian bias. They were pretty heated."

Gino thoughtfully shook his head. "One world government, man. I'm telling you. Mark of the beast. Six-six-six. We're heading there, man. They're gonna push us in that direction."

She was worried. "I can't say anything to the contrary. I'm sorry. I honestly don't know much. He kept me in the dark."

Torben tapped her hand. "It's okay, ma'am... Have you

ever heard of something called Iscariot?"

"Other than the traitor from the Bible, I'm afraid not. What is it?"

"We don't know. Something else we heard along the way. We'll keep you in the loop if we hear anything."

She weakly forced her lips into a half grin. "Thank you."

"Is there anything else you can tell me? Anything may help."

"Not really. No… I will tell you this, not that it matters. But whatever my husband has been into really scares me. It feels almost otherworldly sometimes…"

She stopped talking again, silently pondering what to say next. Finally, after the awkward silence had lingered, she looked at them.

"Mr. Torben, despite my husband's not so popular political decisions, I'm a devout Christian. If this is an anti-Christian agenda, which it very well could be, I want you to know where I stand. I'll not join my husband or anyone else in a war against God. I have private funds at my disposal. If you're going to persist in your pursuit of this, you'll probably need me. If you need anything, don't hesitate to ask."

42

The man entered Amarsin's chamber and handed him a small vial.

"He's almost here, my king. This will take care of him. Just pour it into a little wine, and he'll be dead within an hour of first exposure."

Amarsin shook his head. "Just a few weeks ago, we were friends. My how life has an unexpected way of changing things."

"Are you sure you want to do it here?" the man asked.

"Here is as good a place as any. Not public. No one will know until you've removed his head for me and bundled it in a basket to present before them. The other Emperors will be impressed and a little afraid that I've acted so swiftly."

"Indeed they will," the man said, placing an aged bottle of wine on the counter.

There was a sudden knock at the door. The man shook his head at Amarsin, moved toward the small door, and bumped into Darius as he exited. Darius graciously moved aside and allowed the man to fully pass. Entering the room, he quickly assessed the surroundings.

The ceilings were exceptionally tall and held together by large beams. On top of each beam were decorative bundles of straw and palm branches. The obscure undersurface of the ceiling created soft shadows from one end of the wall to the other.

"Have you spoken to Sir Hayden?" Amarsin asked, breaking Darius' evaluation of the room.

He cautiously entered further, unsure of how to take Amarsin. Something wasn't right. There was an unexpected dissonance.

"No. I haven't seen him since he told me he was meeting you. Did you get to see him?"

"Of course. We reached an understanding. That's part of the reason I sent for you. We need to all be on the same page."

Darius still felt uneasy, but moved closer anyway. "It's truly good to see you again, Amarsin. We've missed you since our days at the Fortress. I'm glad to see all is well with you."

Amarsin whipped his eyes in Darius' direction, coldly

staring him down. "All is not well, Darius. Babylonian forces killed my grandfather for crimes they say we committed. His death looms heavily over me."

Darius choked back tears. "I'm sorry. I truly am. Your grandfather was a good man. The whole earth weeps at the loss of him."

Amarsin reached the counter and removed the old bottle of wine. "Will you drink with me?"

Darius affirmatively shook his head. "Only a little. I'm afraid sobriety must be my lot these days."

"Of course. A little is all it takes... To knock the edge off."

He momentarily turned his back to Darius and emptied the contents of the vial into a chalice, and then poured the wine in as well. Darius was oblivious to the fact that Amarsin had just released a deadly toxin into his drink.

Amarsin turned and handed the cup to Darius with one hand, as he finished pouring his own drink with the other. Picking up his own cup, he held it into the air.

"For my grandfather. In his memory." After downing the drink, he slammed the bronze chalice down on the table. The force reverberated through the otherwise still room.

Darius paused, the loud echo further confirming that something wasn't right. The cup was a couple inches from his lips when he suddenly lowered it.

"Are you sure you're okay? You seem agitated."

Amarsin recovered quickly, appearing calmer. "Of course, it's just been a rough few days. Ocean travel. Hate everything about it."

Darius laughed, but was unable to control the anxious feeling in his stomach. Amarsin poured another round of wine into his own cup.

"Don't worry," he said, a little too bitterly. "I'm used to drinking alone."

Darius sat the glass down for a second and stepped closer to Amarsin. He was near enough to touch him now. Amarsin stepped backward, as Darius extended his hand toward his shoulder.

"This was a bad idea," Amarsin angrily stated. "I thought we could drink together as brothers. But just for a couple hours, and you can't even allow yourself the pleasure."

Darius stepped back two paces. "I'm sorry, Amarsin. I must remain alert. It's the only way I've remained alive thus far."

Amarsin grimaced, pretending to be hurt by Darius' lack of interest. "Of course. One drink to honor my grandfather would be too much... This wine isn't that strong."

Darius picked the cup up from the counter again. "To your grandfather, a wise and noble man if ere one did live."

Something whizzed by his head the moment his lips touched the cup. The breeze from the projectile startled him, causing him to stagger backward, dropping the cup. The contents spilled onto the floor, soaking into the dusty surface.

Amarsin and Darius saw the arrow protruding from the wall the same moment. They frantically searched for its origin. The room was sealed, so the arrow had been launched from inside Amarsin's chambers.

Darius had fired countless arrows before and immediately realized that the trajectory indicated that it had been released from above them. He looked among the rafters for movement. Nothing was there.

Amarsin cursed under his breath. The poison hadn't worked. It seemed this sort of thing could never be done easily. Grabbing a blade from his belt, he decided it would have to be completed a less honorable way.

Abrupt movement caught Darius' attention from behind. He whirled around to find Amarsin approaching, dagger in hand. He whipped an arrow from his quiver and quickly placed it on the slide of his bow, lifting it into position to pull the string back and let it fly. It was too late. Amarsin knocked it from his grasp and grabbed him with the hand not holding the blade, threw him onto the counter, and forced his forearm over Darius' throat. Darius futilely resisted, pulling at Amarsin's robe to try and break free. The dagger was lifted high in the air.

"It doesn't have to be like this," Darius grunted, trying to catch his breath.

"I'm afraid it does," Amarsin replied, and abruptly plunged the blade toward Darius' chest.

It harmlessly clanged to the floor a few feet away. Amarsin held his arm high into the air, screaming in pain, as an arrow protruded from both ends of his right hand. Half turned, he was struck by three more arrows in succession, each burying into his stomach and forcing him to his knees.

He was crying.

Fear of death.

Anger at failing.

Disappointment at being so close but not making it through.

Searing pain.

Trying to stand again, he winced and exhaled a weak breath, as another arrow pierced his heart. Darius ran to him, as his heavy body fell to the ground.

"Amarsin, why?" He cried. "Why'd you do this?"

Amarsin grasped Darius' hand but was too weak to speak. Darius leaned close to him, hot tears streaking his face and falling onto his garment.

"Amarsin. I forgive you. You can't die without knowing that I forgive you."

A half smile formed on his lips. His eyes cleared. The dark cloud that had encased them seemed to disappear. Darius could see it. Amarsin understood. He closed his eyes, and his soul was gone.

A soft thud from behind caused Darius to turn around.

She'd been hiding among the shadows of the rafters, probably for hours. Everything had obviously gone as she'd planned. Darius knew immediately whom she was, the bouda.

He cautiously and confusedly stared at her. She stepped toward him, an arrow still laced and pointed, ready to fly if needed. Narrowing his eyes, he studied her more intently. Something about her was familiar. Dressed differently, hair and face now covered, but there was no doubt he'd seen her before.

The arrow trained on him made it impossible to move. Trying to deduce why she'd been helping him was impossible. Unless…

"You wanted the money for yourself? You eliminated the competition so you could earn it all?" He boldly asked.

She didn't answer.

He slowly knelt down and inhaled deeply, trying to control the fear that was overtaking him. If the stories were true, and she'd proven their validity, then he wasn't walking away this time.

His voice held a slight quiver. "Do it quickly. Let me die with honor."

She calmly lowered her bow. "I've not come to kill you. The obese man was trying to do that. He was trying to poison you… Good thing you dropped the glass."

He was still puzzled, "Why would he do that? He had a lot of rough edges, but he's changed a lot since his days in

Babylon. I don't know why."

She remorsefully stared at Amarsin, understanding Darius' emotions at seeing his friend die. "Sometimes the hardest thing to save a man from is himself."

Darius nodded. "No truer words have been spoken…"

He hesitated again, before letting the question rush from his mouth. "If you're not here to kill me, then why are you here? Aizan, my informant, told me that you sought him out, requesting to go after me."

"Yes, but not to kill you. I want only to serve you, my king… Evil men killed my mother and father. A ship's captain took me in as a child and raised me, saving me from the lonely asylums reserved for orphans. He taught me how to fight, how to survive. I heard you were a good man, like your father…"

She paused, looking away from him. Finally, her voice sounded, holding back tears. "I could not allow another evil man to ruin our homelands. Your brother wasn't meant to rule."

It suddenly became clear to him. The clothes she wore couldn't conceal her beauty.

"You… The captain's daughter… The one who saved M'ya when the ship was sinking… We thought you drowned in the shipwreck off the coast of Dahlak."

A deep smile creased her lips. "Most find I don't die so easily."

"The Mamluk on the ship; the gladiators from the tents; the Roman in the water; it was you every time?"

She nodded.

Hesitation was replaced with a warm smile. "Thank you, bouda. I owe you my life, many times over."

She shook her head. "You owe me nothing. Rule the way your father did. Make Aksum what we both know it can be."

His fear was melting. "You can't truly be the bouda."

She stifled a grin. "That's what they've called me since childhood. I've gained toughness from the reputation. I know how to fight, survive, and kill. Some think that makes me evil… but there's no dark power here. I'm no different than you and the ones who travel at your side."

"Why didn't you just join us then? Why stay in the shadows?"

"Because if I joined you, they'd be looking for me, planning on killing you without me knowing. By remaining anonymous, I was a non-factor. They couldn't prepare for me if I didn't exist."

He was still unsure. "So what now?"

"Now, King Darius, we finish what's been started. War is coming to Jerusalem, and we both know you're right in the middle of it."

She knelt down before him. "I pledge allegiance to you… And solemnly swear an oath that I'll give my life for yours if that's what's required of me."

She choked on the words, "I've nothing left to live for, save this kingdom. Take this life, as I now offer you my eternal service."

"Stand," he whispered, fighting back the unexplained warmth he was feeling inside, "I have a plan to save him…"

He thoughtfully paused before continuing, "There's a child I think you should meet."

43

The other leaders sat around the round table in the small room they'd taken over as their temporary headquarters. Demsas was the only one standing. He shattered his glass against the brick wall, spraying wine over its porous surface. The other world leaders looked upon his lowered countenance with half disdain and half concern. Finally, Emperor Khu spoke up.

"King Demsas, why are you so disheartened? Should we be concerned?"

Demsas angrily snapped his head around. "What do you think?"

Emperor Khu didn't like being spoken to like a child, but he concealed his agitation, his curiosity keeping his emotions in check.

"I don't see the need for concern. Our navies have blocked an escape by sea, and our infantries have them outflanked to the west and south. We're currently closing in on the north."

Emperor Farooq spoke from his seat at the table. "Tomorrow, the entire city will be under siege. Jerusalem will fall within weeks, if we decide to wait it out."

Emperor Khu flashed an evil grin. "Or within days, if we decide to take them by force."

Cassius Augustus disgustedly shook his head. "Both are good plans. I like either, but we aren't addressing the elephant in the room."

Demsas was furious. "And what is that?"

Fear flushed Augustus' face, but he abruptly removed it.

"The king from the north is claiming part in this. He's moving his armies to march against Jerusalem as we speak."

Demsas almost screamed the words, "Then let him come. He has no place among us. Tyre isn't worthy of standing among the elite empires."

Uncertainty lined Cassius' brow. Demsas heatedly turned on him.

"Is Rome to run from a Tyrinian like a scolded dog, or will it wag its tail and pray the Tyrinian king pats him on the head?"

Demsas slammed his fist into the table so hard it split his knuckles. "As for Aksum, we will attack with the viciousness of a lion. After Jerusalem comes Babylon, and if Tyre gets in the way, it can fall as well."

Emperor Khu stood up. "King Demsas, I think I speak for all of us. You seem a bit unstable this morning. Are you certain you're up for the task before us?"

Demsas spoke so feverishly that spittle flew from his mouth with every word, drowning the table beneath him in its thick residue.

"This plan was born of my ingenuity. Don't forget that none of us would be here if not for me. Now, you dare ask if I'm capable of carrying out the very instructions I've so masterfully designed?"

Emperor Narcisso lightly spoke. "I think we should all calm down. We're a little anxious about the upcoming battle. No one likes war... King Demsas, we're all just wondering why you're in such a foul mood today?"

The rage returned in Demsas' eyes. "Amarsin Shamash, the one who was going to hand us Babylon and my brother, failed to return. No one has seen him. He played us for fools."

Emperor Narcisso laughed. "Then so be it. Why should that matter? We're well on our way to victory."

Emperor Augustus was still apprehensive. "The King of Tyre is no small matter. Have you not heard the stories? Rome will cower before no one, but neither will it blindly run into a devilish hailstorm because some arrogantly proclaim power we don't possess yet."

He looked contemptuously toward Demsas. "I'll not let your temper dictate our foreign policy. Pending the approval of this committee, I plan to send a dispatch to find the king of Tyre and offer him a place at our table."

The other leaders murmured among themselves. Finally, Emperor Narcisso spoke for the group. "We're willing to offer him a chair. However, he must promise to use his dark power to help us overthrow the great Babylon and rebuild the tower."

Emperor Augustus looked at Demsas, "And you, are you in agreement?"

He wasn't happy about the decision, but neither did he want to rock the boat. One can only win the war by choosing which battles to fight, and if the King of Tyre could really control the darkness, he was a most powerful ally.

"I've a feeling we shouldn't play with fire… I'm not intimidated by him, as you all seem to be… But if he offers powers that'll aid against the superiority of Babylon, so be it… Send your precious envoy."

44

Hayden banged on the door, looking over his shoulder. People were panicked, running wildly through the streets. A woman stumbled in the fray, dropping a small toddler onto the sandy ground. The child immediately wailed, his high-pitched cries echoing through the stone crafted streets.

The deafening echo of horses' hooves could be heard in the valley surrounding the city. Jerusalem was surrounded. The enemy had been hanging back, keeping anyone from entering or leaving the boundaries. However, thirty minutes ago, the Roman infantry to the south had started marching forward. Within minutes, the Tyrinian infantry to the north had begun a slow march forward as well. To the east, the armies had fortified but were not advancing. They were amassed just over an arrows shot from the walls, making sure no one could escape. Within hours, Jerusalem would have either fallen or been miraculously saved.

Hunzuu ran to the door and banged on it with Hayden. Out of breath, he yelled, "Are you certain they're here? They could have left in the confusion."

Hayden shook his head. "No. Simon said they'd be here when the battle started, and they will. He wouldn't leave his family exposed in this madness."

The door swung open, and Simon stood in the entrance, fifteen to twenty armed men behind him.

He worriedly smiled, "Good to see you gentlemen again. I would that it were under better circumstances."

Suddenly, a loud swooshing sound was heard overhead. They looked upward in time to see the morning sky interrupted by the brightness of hundreds of fiery arrows. The group dove inside the door, as the arrows thudded into the streets, burying people underneath. Loud moans and painful screams filled the air, as another swoosh was heard overhead.

Simon closed the door behind them. Hayden entered the room followed by Hunzuu, Darius, Bennett, and the Bouda. Simon curiously tilted his head and narrowed his brow toward her.

"What's she doing here? Her reputation precedes her."

Darius shook his head, as another round of arrows thudded on the buildings outside.

"Don't worry about her. She's with us."

Hayden intervened, interrupting them. "Simon, did you do as I asked?"

Simon smiled, "Yes. Your plan was set in motion two days ago. No one knows but you and me."

"Thank you," Hayden quickly replied.

Darius animatedly turned to Simon. "I noticed the tall tower extending above us from the center of this building. How fortified is it?"

Simon shrugged, "Yes... The watchtower... It's never had to stand up to this sort of assault before, but I'd imagine it would hold its own. The only way to access it is from inside. If they wanted to get up there, they'd have to climb over the walls of this building first, and then run on the roof to get you... What are you thinking?"

He pointed to the Bouda. "Her... Me... Any archers you've got. Send them up with us. Once they close in, we'll keep them at bay as long as we can."

Simon nervously nodded. "I'll have them sent to you immediately, as well as the arrows we've stockpiled. We've been preparing for this."

Hunzuu stood near the entrance to the door. "Give me your best soldiers. We'll hold them off here until the last man stands. No one will get through this entrance."

"Done," Simon yelled, turning to go toward the men he'd amassed. Soon, several of them joined Hunzuu near the door and a few had taken bow and arrows up the tower to join Darius and the bouda.

Hayden looked around the room. People stood shoulder to

shoulder, nervously anticipating their demise. Being a city under siege isn't a promising position, especially when surrounded by four of most powerful militaries in the world.

Glancing around, Hayden's eyes rested on the inner room he'd had Simon seal off as part of his plan. The inner sanctum. The last resort. The safest place in the building. It had been reserved for the child. Everyone who had joined them knew that the main objective was to keep the enemy from unsealing that entrance. That one room needed protection at all cost...

. . .

A few hundred yards from the northernmost wall, Apollyon sat atop his royal steed. The horse was pure as the winter snow. Taking it all in, he smiled at the striking woman seated on the horse next to him. Smiling, he gently took her by the hand.

The young woman returned his gaze, her long hair flowing gently, like dancing tendrils in the breeze. Colorful flowers lined her hair, adding contrast to the beautiful melancholy surrounding her. A dazzling, jeweled crown completed her, sparkling in the sunlight, casting rainbows.

"My men are getting over the wall... Soon we shall wed," he whispered, as darkness clouded her pupils...

. . .

Darius held his position; his back planted against one of the posts. He watched in horror as the innocents were slain in the street by ungodly soldiers. Noncombatants were treated with the same hostility as those wielding swords. The chaos below was indescribable and sickening.

As of yet, no one was within range of his arrows. The infantry from the south had just reached the wall, battling their way through the streets.

The bouda removed a small looking glass from a pouch at her side and extended the metallic instrument. It expanded to almost a foot. She looked through it toward the south.

She tensely turned to Darius. "Jewish soldiers are holding their own at the southern gates, but they won't be able to withstand long. The numbers are too much for them. They're being overrun…"

She looked again. "Oh… So many have fallen. There are no more than three hundred of them left. Thousands are still scaling the wall. They need to fall back."

"And the north?" Darius hurriedly asked.

She whirled around, peering through the instrument in the opposite direction than before. She tilted it down and deeply exhaled.

"You need to see this."

Darius moved near her, so close he could feel her breathing. Intently staring, he realized again how incredibly beautiful she was. Reminding himself that this wasn't the time, he shook off his thoughts.

Taking the oblong instrument from her hand, he peered through it. Men were pouring over the wall like ants.

However, that wasn't what concerned him most. About two hundred yards from the wall, was an obscurity he hadn't seen since the islands. He almost dropped the looking glass, shuttering as he glanced at her.

"The Sin Cloud…"

A loud trumpet blast suddenly shook the atmosphere. It was more piercing than anything Hayden could remember. From above, he heard Darius calling him.

"Hayden, get up here. Hayden…"

He hurriedly climbed several curved flights of stairs and burst into the doorway once reaching the top. Finding Darius leaning against a post, he jogged the short distance to him.

"What's wrong?" He asked, concern over his face.

The blaring reverberation resounded again across the valley. Darius covered his ears, and then removed them once the last note was played.

"That's the Horn of Aksum. Demsas and his armies have arrived. They said he was stationed to the east."

Fear was evident in the trembling intonation of his voice. "We can't see past the hills to the east to know how we're faring, but we're getting destroyed to the north and south," he said, hurriedly shoving the looking glass in Hayden's direction.

Hayden gazed to the south first. What he saw brought tears to his eyes. The last of the Jewish soldiers were being slain in the streets. Others were fleeing for their lives, hotly pursued by legions of advancing warriors. The wall had almost completely crumbled from the barrage of battering rams relentlessly pelting its weakest segments.

From where he watched, hundreds of yards away, the loud clank of metal on metal reverberated clearly. The smell of blood was thick in his nostrils. Death was clinging to the fragile atmosphere. The screams of the wounded and dying were being drowned out by the shouts of those doing the killing. War is hell, and no one escapes without it affecting his soul.

Hayden turned his attention to the north. The Sin Cloud hovered over the advancing army like a storm, set to unleash its wrath. The line was visibly drawn, clearly creating a separation between the darkness and the light. As the army advanced, the light of the sun's rays disappeared above the thick darkness that encased the land, seemingly devouring everything in its path. The cloud seemingly pushed them forward, urging them to continue killing every man, woman, and child in sight. They were taking no prisoners.

The protective battalions had fallen. The walls had collapsed. Pandemonium had settled in. Utter chaos ensued. There was nowhere to go. Every exit was blocked. Families fled for their lives, left defenseless to an advancing madness. Everywhere they turned, they encountered the enemy. The only line of Israeli defense had been buried under a deluge of cloud-enshrouded combatants.

There was no answer. Surrender was impossible, for even when the people freely gave themselves up, throwing their hands into the air, they were murdered in the street. There was no hesitation. Not even to take spoil of the women. These men had been given specific orders, and they were carrying them out with a vengeance.

Suddenly, he saw her, gallantly riding next to the tall man on the white horse. The way he carried himself left little doubt. The feared king of Tyre had made it to the northern gate, his posture erect, and his sword in his hand. His henchmen plodded ahead, slaying everything that moved. As the king gallantly rode, death preceded him.

Hayden couldn't hold back the tears. Looking again to be sure, he held the looking glass out to Darius once he'd confirmed his first glance.

"Behold the King of Tyre near the gates, and look who rides beside him."

Darius couldn't contain the smile, although instinctively he wasn't sure how to feel.

"M'ya," he laughed. "She's alive…"

. . .

Twenty to thirty Jewish soldiers ran around the corner of a building down the street, hustling toward the building selected as the refuge of last resort. The doors opened, as Hunzuu and the others shuffled them through, preparing for an enemy advance on their heels. It didn't come.

Darius looked again. It had been twenty minutes since they'd seen M'ya. Suddenly, he frantically looked at one of the men next to him, grabbed his arm, and urgently yelled.

"Get down there and inform them that we're being closed in on all sides. The last remaining occupants of the city are funneling this way. They're leading them right toward us."

The soldier ran down the stairs, almost tripping over himself to get the message to Simon as quickly as possible.

Back upstairs; the bouda notched an arrow, as a line of Roman infantrymen appeared from behind a building. Their armor was thick and their shields tall. They were almost completely protected.

A second line formed behind them, and then a third. The first line slowly advanced. After notching the arrow and carefully taking aim, she released the string, letting the arrow fly.

It made a gentle whisper, as it zipped through the wind toward its target. It found the only area in the faceplate that was open. Falling to the ground, he never knew what had hit him. She notched another arrow and let it go. A second man fell.

Darius turned to see what she was shooting at. He excitedly yelled to the men around them.

"Follow her lead. Aim for the gap in their helmets. Aim true. Release smooth. Kill them all..."

. . .

The King of Tyre converged on the isolated area from the north. A scout came riding to him with a report. Leaping from his horse, the scout ran toward him with purpose.

"King Apollyon, the Romans have converged on their stronghold from the south. We've arrived from the north. The last survivors are holed up in a private safe house. It will take a while, but our people are working to find a way in."

The King flashed a victorious smile. "Don't come back until you do. Once inside, come and get me. I want to personally destroy the hope of the earth," he smugly stated. "By taking the Godchild…"

. . .

The bodies were piling up in the street outside. They'd opened the door two more times, allowing the final refuges into the last temporary safety. It wasn't clear how long they could survive the onslaught, but even a few extra minutes when facing death can seem like an eternity. At times, even temporary reprieve from the hell of war is a blessing.

The room was now completely full of terrified men, women, and children. They were completely surrounded.

The King of Tyre spurred his horse forward, carrying a white flag with him. Darius motioned for the archers to hold their fire. Hayden watched him come closer.

"I'm guessing he's not going to offer a complete surrender," he whispered toward Darius and the bouda.

Darius laughed. "I would we could be so lucky."

The bouda inhaled and restlessly shook her head. "How can you two joke at a time like this? The Sin Cloud comes. Death is imminent."

The noonday light began to disappear as she spoke. It turned from midday to midnight in a matter of seconds. Hayden looked into the sky, but there was no sign of impending storm. The Sin Cloud had blotted the sun from the earth. They were emptily alone to face the cold reality of eternal night…

. . .

There was a sudden silence, as all eyes fell on the King of Tyre. Demsas watched from a nearby hillside, as the Aksumite, Persian, Orient, and Egyptian armies closed in from the east.

He agitatedly turned to Emperor Farooq. "What does he think he's doing? He's in no position to negotiate peace without us."

Emperor Narcisso stood on Demsas' opposite side. "I don't think peace is in his plans. He wants to kill them all."

"No," Demsas yelled, the sudden concern ebbing through his exterior. "He wants the Godchild for himself. Combining the power of the Godchild with his own delusions, there'd be no stopping him… We must get down there at once."

. . .

Emperor Cassius Augustus pulled his horse alongside the King of Tyre, his legions from the south meeting Apollyon's armies in the middle.

"What's your plan?" He curiously inquired.

"I guess we shall see. You can kill them all, but I want the child alive."

Augustus was appalled, "Alive? Our agreement was to kill him. That's the only way to completely neutralize the threat forever."

His eyes made Augustus hesitate before saying anything else. He quickly looked away, praying his soul hadn't been compromised.

Apollyon continued to stare in his direction. "Feel free to try and stop me anytime you please."

Augustus shook his head, trying not to show his fear. "You know what you're doing. You're one of us now. The others will back you."

Apollyon pulled his horse forward, separating himself from the rest of the group. He yelled toward the tower above them.

"All remaining citizens of Jerusalem, hear me once, and hear me well. You all shall live. Your families, your sons, your daughters, your wives. All remaining civilians will be allowed to leave of your own accord. Flee toward the south. The southernmost province of the Jewish lands will be rewarded to you. You'll be protected under the banner of the New World Alliance."

His words lingered, registering with each man and woman in the building. One man hollered back from the tower before anyone else could answer.

"What are your terms? Nothing in war is free. You have us

at a disadvantage, why would you suddenly negotiate our freedom?"

Apollyon smirked. "At least one of you is thinking clearly."

He paused, allowing his next words to build. "All we want is the Godchild, his mother, King Darius, and his Babylonian traitor. Send them out to us, and the rest of you will be allowed to leave."

"What guarantee do we have?"

"You have my word…"

The man turned to Hayden and Darius. His apprehension precluding him from realizing the lie he was being fed. Fear was paralyzing his ability to reason.

"We should take the offer. Many lives in exchange for a few, even the prophets wouldn't scoff at such a suggestion."

Darius was angry. "You can't be serious?"

The man was genuinely offended. "Are you suggesting we all die for a child? For you? I'm supposed to sacrifice my wife and six month old baby to save the life of a child and mother I don't even know, or for men who've already lived their lives foolishly enough to turn the whole of the world against them? You've gone mad."

He took a step toward the staircase. Hayden quickly moved, standing between him and being able to walk downstairs.

The man shoved him. "Get out of my way. The others

need to be allowed this choice."

Hayden shoved him back. "There is no choice," he yelled. "We've sworn to protect the child, and there's no going back on that."

"Maybe not for you," the man said, as he drew his weapon and took a step toward Hayden. He abruptly rocked forward, two arrows protruding from his back, as he fell onto his stomach. The bouda and Darius had both simultaneously released an arrow.

Hayden nodded a quick thanks in their direction, "He'd have killed me. I wasn't ready for that."

He then moved toward Darius, the concern evident in his expression.

"Perhaps he was right, Darius. Maybe-"

Darius passionately interrupted, "We aren't giving up the child. I'll offer myself if that's what it takes, but the child must live."

"I agree," Hayden replied, "But perhaps the others deserve a choice."

He yelled over the side. "King of Tyre… There are those of us sworn to protect the Godchild. We'll not be laying down our swords. However, there are others not so inclined to give their lives to protect him. Are you offering them safe passage from the city?"

Apollyon looked quizzically toward Emperor Augustus. "What say you, Augustus? Letting them go dwindles the numbers in the building. It would be easier to get the Godchild."

"Why not just wait them out? They can't survive more than a few days in there. The wait will cause them to turn on themselves."

"Do you know how long they've prepared for this? Any idea how many supplies they've stored? Besides, exciting mutiny could lead to unwanted deaths, collateral damage, and I want to make sure I get the boy alive."

Augustus shook his head. "Then, why not just charge the door and kill them all?"

Apollyon was agitated, "That's your suggestion? The more who are killed, the greater chance the Godchild has of escaping in the confusion... I'd say reduce the numbers. Then, we'd be certain that neither he nor any of his followers escape."

The Roman emperor nodded a silent agreement. "You're plan has no flaws, seems to be the most sensible."

"Agreed," Apollyon stated, as he looked toward the tower again. He cleared his throat and yelled.

"Anyone who wishes to leave may do so, save the aforementioned wanted few. Any male child under the age of two will be required to stay. We can't have anyone sneaking out with the boy in question."

Hayden turned toward Darius, and then peered over the sidewall. He hung his head, but hollered back.

"Give us a few minutes to make decisions. There are those who'll be coming out the door... Thank you for your consideration..."

. . .

Inside the house, Hayden watched as a large group formed near the exit. Simon stood right next to it, ready to leave. Hayden approached him, sadly frowning.

"You've decided to go too?"

Simon hung his head. "I'm sorry. I must. I have no choice. He held his baby into the air. They'll take a look at him and know he's not the one. I know I can get him through. My wife and I can start over south of here. Land's not the best, but it's better than having to watch them die. Besides, starting over, the people will need a good man to lead. The opportunity is great for my family and me."

Hayden clasped his hand over Simon's shoulder. "I'm saddened my brother, but I don't fault you."

"Thank you," Simon softly replied, choking back tears. He turned and embraced Hayden fully, his tears dripping onto Hayden's shoulder.

"Go... Tell the King of Tyre we're coming out. Good luck to you, Sir Hayden. I wish you all the best. History will be written today. You brave men and women will never be forgotten. I'll make sure that it's so."

45

Demsas and the other emperors came riding hard into the streets surrounding the last remaining stronghold. Demsas was wroth, as he approached the King of Tyre.

"What do you think you're doing? You can't just override our well-laid plans. We voted and decided what we felt was the best course of action. You can't make decisions autonomous of our council."

He paused, waiting for a response that never came. The King of Tyre ignored him. Demsas' anger overshadowed his judgment. He stepped forward and grabbed Apollyon by the arm. Apollyon whirled around, his eyes locking with Demsas'. He almost vomited the words.

"Don't let a good mind fail you. You don't have to die today."

Demsas forcefully turned Apollyon around to face him. A dark cloud flashed through Apollyon's eyes.

"Well, perhaps you do," he said, as his dagger quickly sliced through Demsas' throat. Demsas fell, grabbing at the open gash, desperately trying to stop the torrent rushing from his body. He couldn't even plead for mercy, as his life slipped through his fingers.

The King of Tyre displayed no compassion, as he turned to the other emperors. "Does anyone else have a problem with the way I exercise our policies?"

Thunder ominously rumbled from the Sin Cloud, silencing any thought of insurrection. Emperor Augustus stepped before the others.

"I'm impressed with King Apollyon's wisdom. He's everything Demsas wasn't. I'd be honored to have him serve as head of our fellowship."

Emperor Farooq silently and thoughtfully nodded. "I'll second that motion. The Orient has long since recognized the power of his kingship."

The other emperors failed to speak, their silence completing the vote. Apollyon was the new leader of the One World Alliance.

He dismounted his horse and nestled next to M'ya who'd been watching from the corner steps of an abandoned building. His eyes flashed an emotion others had assumed he wasn't capable of.

"One more thing until our purpose is complete, dear M'ya. As soon as I have the child in my possession, we'll be united."

46

It had been hours since Simon and the others had left the stronghold. Those who remained had hunkered down, trying to mentally prepare for the inevitable. There were fifteen archers still in the tower and thirty-three men guarding the door with Hunzuu.

The Sin Cloud had blotted out the sun so entirely that all sense of time had been lost. They were unsure if it was even day or night beyond the cloud's dense covering.

Hayden watched Darius standing next to the beam, fighting against the tiredness to keep his eyes open. The bouda stood a few feet away from him. She demonstrated no emotion.

No fear.

No nervousness.

No tiredness.

She was an ultimate warrior. However, despite her hardened demeanor, there was an uncommon softness. He doubted many had ever seen it, but it lurked beneath the surface, waiting to be discovered and embraced.

Hayden smiled. If they were lucky enough to escape this, and if Darius played his cards right, he could have an extremely beautiful and intelligent wife to help him restore the intrigue of Aksum. The murder of his wife and children was nearly impossible to recover from, but every man deserved another chance. Perhaps he could marry for purpose and eventually love would follow. Aksum could use her strength and nobility.

His thoughts were interrupted. He knew they were coming even before he heard them. The instinctive flinch, the sudden tenseness in her muscles alerted him. The rushed rattle of armor as men ran toward the stronghold gave away their intentions. They were coming. Not just a few, most of them.

Darius, the bouda, and the archers rained down a flurry of arrows into the advancing horde. However, there were simply too many of them. For every soldier an arrow dropped, five more took the place of their fallen comrade.

The first wave hit the door with a thunderous echo that literally shook the tower itself. A repetitive, pulsating roar echoed through the shadowy sky, as men used an oversized battering ram to try and cave the door in. Each hit weakened the door's hold on the walls to either side of it.

Hunzuu stood slightly behind it, drawing both swords, as

the door began to splinter. He quickly turned to the men who had stayed with him.

"Here they come," he screamed with every ounce of strength he possessed. "To the last man... To the last man..."

. . .

Upstairs, Hayden heard the door completely give. He knew the onslaught of soldiers would be coming inside. He motioned to Darius, the undeniable shade of dread overcoming him.

"We're needed downstairs. We can't let them get in the room."

Darius touched the bouda on the arm and looked at Hayden. "Take the rest of them. We're staying here. Our best chance is to get a shot at Apollyon. If he dies, maybe the others will retreat."

Hayden nodded, as he motioned for the others to get down the stairs. "Hurry, before it's too late."

He turned back toward Darius and held his fist high over his head in Darius' direction. He searched for words that wouldn't come. "My brother... My brother," was all he could tearfully manage...

. . .

A few seconds later, Hayden followed the last of the men down the stairs. The room was a flurry of movement, as Roman and Tyrinian soldiers battled the few remaining infantrymen.

Hunzuu's blades whirled through a mass of men with brutal intent. He was covered in the blood of countless warriors whose life he'd just taken. Slowly, he was being backed into the center of the stronghold. Most of his accompanying swordsmen had already fallen. Fifty of the enemy was already in the room, and more continued pouring inside.

The archer's arrows found countless targets, knocking them to the ground. Bodies were stacking up, making it difficult for most to move across the floor.

Bennett stood near Hunzuu, tiredly swinging a battle-axe he'd found among the weapons the Jews had stored in the stronghold armory. The axe sank into the chest of a Roman centurion. Three of his men were on Bennett before he could swing it again.

He strongly grabbed one of the men and flipped him over his head, slamming the man against the blunt end of the axe still protruding from the centurion he'd just killed.

He felt a searing pain in his abdomen and turned to see blood flowing from a spear roughly imbedded in his stomach. He swiped at the spear, breaking it in the center, taking the piece he'd just snapped, and ramming it through another one of the men grasping him.

He turned toward an advancing number of them, but was a moment too late. Three more spears pinned him against the wall. He loudly moaned and fell to his knees. Once on the floor, he swiped at the last man still holding him, knocking him to the ground. He grabbed the man's head and forcefully twisted, a loud snapping was the last sound he heard, before a final spear pierced his chest, ending his life.

Hayden moved beside Hunzuu, both of them penned against the wall. The archers were still releasing arrows, but they were being eliminated, their numbers dwindling down to six. In a few seconds, those six bows had also been silenced.

Hayden and Hunzuu stood back-to-back, against too many warriors to count. The first wave was rushing them when the King of Tyre entered the room, followed by Cassius Augustus and Emperor Khu. He forcefully yelled for the advancing soldiers to stop. They immediately heeded his command.

Hunzuu held his voice low. "When I tell you to, dart quickly to the right. There's an opening to the left. I'll have Apollyon's head before I die."

"No. Wait." Hayden pleaded. "You won't get close."

"It must be done. We're going to die today, but he goes to hell first."

"No... Hunzuu... Stop."

It was no use. Hunzuu wasn't listening. "Now," he yelled, and Hayden had no choice but to move quickly to the right. Most of the men instinctively shifted that direction, as Hunzuu shot toward the opening he'd found and swiftly moved toward Apollyon. He swung his first sword, and it opened a shallow cut along Apollyon's chin. His second sword swiped downward a step closer, but the motion was never completed. Augustus forced his blade through Hunzuu's side, causing Hunzuu to fall hard against the entrance to the building. Augustus followed his initial thrust by quickly removing the blade and swinging it down toward Hunzuu's head.

Hunzuu weakly deflected it with the sword in his left hand and thrust his other one through Augustus' midsection. He twisted the blade upward. Augustus was one foot from him, and Hunzuu watched the life fade from his eyes, followed by a brief flash of darkness.

Hayden's scream registered a moment too late. "Hunzuu, behind you."

He was half turned, when Apollyon's own weapon knocked him to the floor again, opening a massive wound across his chest. He struggled to get up, but it was no use.

"No," Hayden screamed. "Hunzuu. No."

The King of Tyre marched toward him and grabbed him by the throat, knocking the Sword of Tiber harmlessly to his feet. Apollyon picked him up and held him against the wall, high into the air.

He screamed into Hayden's face. "Enough of this. Where is he? Where is the Godchild?"

Reluctantly, Hayden's eyes turned toward the safe room in the house.

Apollyon dropped him. "You'll get to watch his mother and father die before I take your life."

He tried to open the door before irritatedly turning to the

men behind him. "Bring in the battering ram. You've got three minutes to beat this door down before I have you all killed and replaced by another group who'll get the job done… Do it… Now," he shrieked.

The first hit shattered the hinges the door had been holding to. The lock turned sideways in the door jam, slightly creating a crack.

"Please," Hayden pleaded. "Don't open the door…"

. . .

Darius and the bouda watched, as the darkness gathered in one spot outside the refuge, allowing the sun to momentarily peek from behind the areas the Sin Cloud had just vacated to culminate in front of the door.

It was as if the Sin Cloud had come alive and was awaiting the arrival of the Godchild. Apollyon's excitement at being near the family of the Jewish Redeemer had awakened it. It drifted a few feet before the soldiers outside, who backed up, afraid of what it would do to them.

The cloud pulsated, as if it were a beating heart, fueled by Apollyon's hatred of the child. No doubt, Apollyon was being driven by it as well, receiving strength from its magnetic pull.

Darius opened the door and cautiously moved down the spiral staircase. At the last flight, he peered down and immediately caught Hayden's eye. Hayden nonchalantly motioned his head, subtly telling Darius to stay away.

Darius caught his signal and gently retreated back to the

tower. He stepped in, barricaded the door, and turned to the bouda. She was halfway over the wall, about to drop onto the rooftop well below the tower...

. . .

Apollyon momentarily stared into Hayden's eyes. He contemptuously mocked him by his tone.

"This is it, Sir Hayden, The end is near."

He was taken back by Hayden's smile. "This is only the beginning of your sorrows, oh king of darkness."

Apollyon entered the panic room, as the last ram shattered the door. Emerging moments later, his voice penetrated the delicate ambiance with a high-pitch whine.

"It's empty. What have you done?" He dejectedly wailed.

M'ya moved by him and peered inside. She turned and blankly stared at Hayden, confusion on her face... The child was supposed to be there. How else would she be able to marry the great King of Tyre?

. . .

"Wait. What are you doing?" Darius yelled to her. "Don't leave me. We can get out of this together."

She removed a gold chain from inside her shirt. At the end was the red stone the woman had given them to defeat the Sin Cloud. It fervently emanated a brilliant glow. He could almost feel the heat radiating from the orb.

"I'd have liked to know you better," she mouthed the words, as she gracefully flipped herself completely over the side.

He barely heard her, as she softly landed and rolled a couple of times before coming to her feet. She never missed a step, immediately rising to a full sprint.

Darius reached the side of the tower in time to see her take the necklace in her hand and plunge over the side, toward the sickening darkness directly below…

. . .

M'ya appeared to be struggling against conflicting emotions. Apollyon looked at her inner turmoil with disdain. Picking up the Sword of Tiber, he handed it to her.

"You… Kill him… Prove your love to me," he shouted, pointing toward Hayden.

She gazed into Hayden's eyes. He shook his head, as she slowly moved the blade toward him.

"M'ya, please…"

He lifted a bow from the floor and notched an arrow. Tears filled his eyes, as he lifted the bow toward her advance.

"M'ya, please stop… Don't make me… M'ya, please."

. . .

The dark cloud erupted, as the bouda landed in the midst of it. The glowing ruby was buried inside the shadowy haze.

The beating heart exploded, spewing darkness in every direction. The earth was rocked with violence, as an intense shadow resonated through the land. Then, as suddenly as it began, it ended. The Sin Cloud was silenced, disappearing into the warmth of the sun.

. . .

M'ya's eyes intensely fluttered. When they cleared, Hayden saw a clarity that hadn't been there moments earlier. She emptily looked toward the King of Tyre, who suddenly appeared weak and sick, and unexpectedly thrust the sword of Tiber through his heart. Staggering backward and unbelievingly clutching the sword, Apollyon fell into the empty room he'd moments ago found no Savior hiding behind. He died that way.

Empty.

Dark.

Alone.

47

Darius opened the door and briskly moved down the stairs. The soldiers in the room moved aside. Bending over, he lifted the injured Hayden from the ground, with M'ya helping from the other side. She threw Hayden's arm around her neck, and they both moved him toward the door.

Emperor Khu stood right outside the doorway, as they exited into the sunlight. He intentionally blocked their way, looking toward Hayden with respect. Sizing Hayden up, he blinked a few times, not willing to believe that the weakened man before him was the one to cause so much turmoil. Finally, he muttered under his breath and walked away.

Darius and M'ya led Hayden across the street to an empty porch and sat him down there. Hayden surveyed the unfolding scene. The enemy warriors weren't concerned with the battle anymore. Emperor Khu had formally ended the league of empires declaration of war.

The world was officially in shambles. Three of the world's leaders had been killed in battle, leaving Aksum, Tyre, and Rome with no leader. The plans to overthrow Babylon had been significantly derailed. The remaining rulers had decided to end the hunt for the Godchild. No one knew his whereabouts.

. . .

Darius looked back toward the entrance where the Sin Cloud had mercilessly hovered, anxious to devour the Godchild.

There she was, buried under a mountain of sand, clothing torn from the explosion. The bouda lay among the trash littering the street. He ran to her and kneeling down, lifted her head into his lap. She was limp and lifeless.

He tried to find a pulse but detected nothing. Sadly glancing to the ground, he noticed the ruby amulet she'd been wearing. It lightly brushed across her face, as he lifted it to hold tightly against his heart. The orb majestically illuminated one last time, sending a reddish glow across the walkway.

She inhaled deeply; her breath coming hollow and ragged. Opening her eyes, Darius' warm smile was the first thing she saw. He pulled her close to his chest and whispered, "I believe the blood is not only responsible for salvation from sin, but it also brings miraculous healing."

She seemed to understand too, as she tugged on his shirt and pulled him closer.

He clutched her tightly and suddenly remembered his pledge. He looked her in the eyes and laughed,

"Do you remember the promise I made your father on the ship? I told him that I'd take care of his family if we made it out of this."

She nodded and he continued, "Not exactly what I had in mind at the time, but it works…"

They both chuckled, as she leaned in and nervously whispered, "That first day on the boat… I… I picked the wrong man."

Darius remembered the attention she'd shown Hayden that had made M'ya jealous. He sheepishly grinned, "Not to worry, we've got a lifetime to sort that out… Fate has made it so."

48

Four hours had passed since the Sin Cloud had disappeared. The invading armies had pulled out, leaving behind a wake of destruction that would take years to recover from. More of the Jews had survived than originally supposed. They came from basements, hidden rooms, storehouses, haystacks in barns, and other places they'd hidden once they'd been overrun.

Hayden sadly viewed the devastation. M'ya silently walked beside him, both unsure of what to say. Pulling up next to a small building overlooking a town square, they both stared into the ruins below.

Men and women searched for family members. Mothers held their deceased children and cried to the heavens for their loss. Husbands ineffectively tried to console wives, masking their own pain in attempts to be the needed strength of the moment. Others looked into what used to be their homes, businesses, and property, only to now be reduced to rubble.

M'ya finally spoke, holding back tears. "It's tragic... Pointless... For so many, this is the end."

Hayden took her hand in his and turned her toward him. "No, M'ya, it's only the beginning."

Her eyes flashed confusion, but Hayden seemed freshly alive with revelation. "He makes all things new, M'ya. The Godchild, I held him in my arms. He survived. He'll help us all begin again. It's far from over."

"But... they've lost so much," she stated, the sadness causing her voice to tremble.

Hayden choked back his own tears now, the fullness of what was taking place mingling with the unknown pain of his past. It all flooded together, his understanding suddenly opened.

"It's true they've lost much, but they've gained greatly as well. They move forward with experience and wisdom, with a better understanding of what truly matters."

He paused, considering his words. "Rebuilding comes with a price, M'ya, but it also comes with a recommitment to the principles and people who are truly valued. A man doesn't lose everything and rise from the rubble the same way he fell. He grows... He changes... He rises a more complete person than he'd been before. Failure isn't final. Disappointment isn't the completion of the matter. They are both blessings that move a man forward, into a destiny he could never achieve without knowing the misery of defeat."

He stopped again, clinching his teeth to stop from crying. A single tear escaped his eye.

"Without the loss, the fallen man would've never gained the strength to build better things. Without having everything stripped away, he'd never have discovered a reason to advance... Sometimes loss is the greatest catalyst of change."

She moved closer to him and placed her head on his chest. Slowly tilting her gaze upward, she spoke through the emotional pain.

"I knew what was right, Hayden. I could feel it, but I don't know... I couldn't change what I was doing. When he handed me the sword, I didn't want to... I hesitated, but I don't know if I could have stopped myself. I felt helpless against it on my own. If she hadn't destroyed the cloud..."

She burst into tears, as he gently ran his fingers through her hair, pressing the back of her head more firmly into him.

"It's okay, M'ya. It's okay."

He allowed her to cry for a few moments, and then tilted her head to look into his eyes again.

"In a sense, that's why He came, M'ya. We're powerless to combat sin on our own. We're defenseless against it. The woman at the tree told Leib that the crystal was symbolic of the blood of innocence."

He paused again, the full revelation flooding through his mind. "That's why He's come to the world. The blood of innocence must be spilled in order for sin to be defeated. There's unmistakable power in the blood. It covers the past, shields the present, and directs the future."

She looked at him. "So, we don't have to be powerless to its grasp anymore."

"Not for long, M'ya… The child, Jesus, has come to save us all."

M'ya smiled, her eyebrows inquisitively narrowing. "We all thought the child was in the room, the last line of defense. Everything centered on you all being there to protect him. Apollyon thought he was there."

Hayden lightly chuckled. "That was the plan. In reality, I had his family escorted across enemy lines by shepherds from a far away land. They were able to slip through the checkpoints. The child is safe."

"So you drew us in to buy him time…"

He covered her lips with his finger. "Shh." He whispered, as he leaned forward to kiss her.

She slowly turned away from him. He was puzzled, "M'ya, you okay?"

She looked toward him again. "Aren't you going to try and find the child now? Make sure he's protected."

Hayden earnestly shook his head. "No, we don't need to. This wasn't about His protection at all. Never was… This was for us."

Now, she was baffled. "But, they were coming for him. They wanted to destroy him."

"He won't die until He's ready. No man can take his life. He'll one day willingly lay it down."

"But... you defended him."

"I thought we needed to, but realistically, He was protecting us. He doesn't need us to defend him. He merely needs us to continue living His purpose, to let his light penetrate the darkness."

He choked up, remembering his friends who'd fallen along the way. He weakly smiled at her.

"He's called us to give ourselves, the way the others did, to make the same sacrifices as those who've gone before us, to continue living the story he's already written. He desires that we give ourselves for the eternal kingdom."

She was still a little confused. "So, he wants us to live in defense of him?"

Hayden shook his head. "No, therein is our mistake. We're not called to merely defend Him. We're supposed to actively reflect Him... To reconnect Him to the world... To demonstrate Him to those who are lost..."

He openly cried now, swept away in the emotion of the moment. Finally, he composed himself enough to speak,

"What I felt as I held Him... M'ya, it's inexpressible. There was a warmth, a love, a power that goes beyond words. We're part of that now. It's completely His; we must merely learn to be its conduit."

She nodded, her head still against his chest. "I understand now," she quietly whispered.

They stood like that for several minutes, both secure in the tenderness of each other's embrace.

49

Darius and the bouda walked up to them. Hayden released M'ya and embraced Darius. The two men hugged for a few moments and cried.

Separating, Hayden spoke softly, "Sorry about your brother."

Darius put his head down, "Me too... I truly wish things had turned out differently. He had so much potential, had he chosen to apply it in the positive direction... I'm having him buried in Aksum, in the royal tombs of our fathers... I know he lost it, but he's still my brother."

Darius nodded, "We've lost much. Guards from Amarsin's political entourage took Hunzuu's body to be buried at the warrior's cemetery in Babylon. I had Leib and Bennett buried on a beautiful hillside on the outskirts of Jerusalem. Amarsin will also be returning back to Babylon to be buried next to his grandfather. I sent the letter you wrote to the Parliament on his behalf... Because of you, he'll not be remembered for his betrayal. His prior acts of heroism are what he'll be remembered for."

Hayden smiled. "Good... He was a friend who was overwhelmed by sin; the darkness had overtaken him. He deserves nothing less than to be remembered in good standing."

Darius placed his hand firmly on Hayden's shoulder. "And what of you, my brother, will you be returning to stand at my side in Aksum? There will always be a place for you."

Hayden slowly shook his head, his smile fading. "I'm afraid not Darius... You will rule well..."

He turned toward the stunning woman at Darius' side. "And you've got the right companion to lead the people of Aksum back to the state of your fathers."

She graciously bowed and slyly grinned. "I'll take good care of him."

Darius embraced Hayden again, speaking low, trying not to show emotion.

"I'll never see you again, will I?"

Hayden wasn't sure where it came from, but it spilled out before he realized what he was saying. "Not in this life, my brother. Not in this life."

Darius tapped him lightly on the back. "Then I wish you the best. May the God of Jerusalem guide and keep you along whatever path you forge."

"And what of you, Darius? Are you returning to the gods of Aksum?"

He laughed. "I've seen and felt enough. I've no need for the gods of my forefathers. As soon as I've established my kingship, the God of Jerusalem will be heavily introduced to our people. My nation shall be cleansed, and we'll offer support to their country forever."

Hayden nodded. "Then go your way, my brother. You've much work to do. My prayers shall forever be with you."

As Darius and his future bride departed, Hayden pulled M'ya close again. She resisted him again, pulling slightly away.

She sadly looked up at him. "We both feel it, don't we?"

He reluctantly nodded. "I've tried to fight it. I want to deny it, pretend it isn't real."

"But it is Hayden, and we both know it. We're only delaying the inevitable."

"I love you, M'ya." He said it matter-a-factly, like it was natural. He unwaveringly looked into her eyes, unafraid to peer into them.

Her lower lip quivered. "I love you too, Hayden. More than life."

He tried to pull her near again, but she once more held him at arm's length, looking away.

"That's why I must do the most painful thing I've ever

done."

His eyes flooded. "M'ya... No."

She didn't stop. "Hayden, we both know what must be. As strong as this is, as much as we love, as good as it could be, neither of us are done yet. Eternity is at stake."

She stopped, stifling her own tears. "Please understand. I want the happily ever after. I love sappy stories that end with a prince on the white horse, but it's not our time, and this isn't our story. It's His."

He shook his head in understanding. "I know. I know you're right, but it hurts so badly."

"Hayden, your destiny is bigger than this. Your legacy grows from here. I see it, feel it, believe it with everything inside me."

He interrupted, swallowing deeply before starting. "And you could go with me. You could be part of that."

She sadly smiled, "We're pursuing a dream, and we both know it. I'm called for different things. I feel my eternal purpose as strongly as you long to move into yours... I'm staying here in Jerusalem to help them rebuild... There are many orphans now because of this. They'll need a place to live and people to care for them... This is my place now."

He smiled, "And you'll do well, M'ya. You will."

She weakly smiled back. "Please understand, Hayden. Your destiny can't be fully obtained if you stay here. I can't be the reason you don't accomplish His plans for you. If I love you, I must let you go."

He couldn't move, so she continued. "You've offered him yourself even unto death. Now, you must place your life in his hands. Completely."

The tears were there, but just wouldn't come. He looked at her again. "I know... I know."

She took his hand in hers. "Some become martyrs through death, Sir Hayden, but some are martyrs through life. Both are just as needed in order for the Kingdom to flourish, and both sacrifices are equally important."

He gently squeezed her hand. "I'll never forget you, M'ya. You hold my heart."

"And you mine, Sir Hayden. But the eternal struggle continues, and you'll change many lives out there. The world awaits your future. The kingdom must go on."

He pulled her close, and this time she melted into him. They both unleashed the tears they'd been battling to control.

Finally, he pulled away from her, wiping the tears from her eyes.

"I must go for now, M'ya, but no one knows what the future holds... Wherever I go, you go with me. If Jerusalem is your home, I know where you'll be. If one day-"

She stopped him with a slender finger to his lips. "Let's leave things as they are. No promises. No plans. Only hopes and dreams."

She leaned forward and lightly kissed his cheek. "Good luck," she stifled tears. "Until we meet again."

She turned and left him there, quickly walking away into the gathering crowd. Tears streaming down his face, he fought against the urge to call out to her, chase her down, and bring her back. Every fiber of his being screamed against the image of her that grew smaller with each step. She kept moving and didn't look back, becoming part of the crowd, merging into the fray of their movement. Finally, he could see her no more.

EPILOGUE

Two weeks had passed since he'd seen anyone. He'd gone alone to the mountains outside of Jerusalem for solitude. He mourned the death of his friends, and the fact that the others were all moving in different directions.

He reached into the familiar pouch he'd been carrying since his journey began and removed an old reliable tool. Unrolling the parchment, he began to write.

Life has a funny way of separating people. They're here today, influencing, strengthening, and even battling the darkness beside you. But then, they're gone, moving on to influence and strengthen others the way they did you.

I can only hope I've impacted them in the same ways. I can only pray that the influence is a two-way street. My world is a better place having known each of them. Their paths intersected mine but for a season, but that season taught valuable insights that will enable me to rise to higher levels of kingdom service. Each memory hurts. Every moment is acutely remembered. The tears still fall, and I'm not sure they'll ever stop. But,

I'd change nothing. This journey has defined me, made me who I am, and is fashioning me through the fire into the man God wills me to become.

I've learned that I'm not big enough to walk alone. I need help. I no longer carry bitterness in my heart toward God or man. Time is too short and uncertain. Each day is a blessing from the heavens, for every moment is truly a gift from above. Both good and bad times are of infinite worth, both working together to yield the most victorious outcome for those who allow the process to continue. Pain is but a precursor to providence. Struggle is but a prerequisite to victory. Loss is but the bitterness strengthening the sweetness of fulfillment. Without the one, I'd not fully understand the completion of the other.

As for M'ya, I miss her dearly and will always love her completely. I pray there comes a day when our paths will again cross in His service. But, if that's not what the Master intends, I wish her the best as we both plod forward.

I shall not forget the past, for it's been my strength and a sure foundation on which to stand. I embrace the future on the stable ground of all those who have delivered a bit of themselves to encourage and empower me thus far. I'm merely the culmination of ancient prayers and present encouragers who've stood with me, battling darkness, and preparing me for whatever future the God of Israel has in store.

. . .

It was growing dark, as the westernmost point of the mountain eclipsed the sun. A sudden movement in the brush drew his attention. He rolled the scroll and thrust it and the writing utensil into the pouch. Quickly removing the sword of Tiber, he turned to where the sound had originated.

"Come out and stand before me. I only want peace. I've no quarrel with you."

Someone began to emerge from the shadowy confines of mountainous terrain. "I come in peace. Please. We're in search of food."

Hayden narrowed his eyes, as the man approached from the shadows. "Simon?"

The man weakly smiled, instantly recognizing him. "You made it? I thought for sure you'd all be killed."

Hayden removed a satchel and handed him some bread. He looked at the small child in Simon's arms.

"I'm afraid that's all I've got. Hopefully the lad will be able to eat some when he wakes up."

Simon held his head low. "He'll have to. Food has been scarce, and his mother was killed by a band of rebels a couple weeks ago. We've been trying to survive alone. God has taken care of us thus far."

Hayden apologetically frowned, "I know it has been tough, but He will continue to keep you, Simon... He will continue."

Hayden motioned to the small fire he'd recently started to fend off the cool night of the higher altitude.

"Please, join me for the evening."

Simon sat down beside the fire. As he sat, the baby stirred in his hands. He tapped the child's back a few times, trying to console him to continue sleeping. The baby turned its head toward Hayden and gently cooed. The soft, almost purring sound made Hayden smile. Perhaps one day, he too would have a son.

"What's his name?" Hayden peacefully asked.

The father proudly beamed. "His name is Judas, surname Iscariot."

Suddenly, the coos turned to cries. The baby's face briefly contorted. His eyes opened wide, and Hayden recognized the cloudy flash of darkness swirling inside…

He yelled, "No… No… No…

. . .

"No… No… No…" He screamed, frantically sitting straight up in bed, grabbing at the wires connecting him to the beeping machines at his side. Torben opened the doorway and screamed down the hall.

"Nurse. Nurse. He's awake."

Hayden sat wide-eyed, staring at the woman beside him. He knew her. His mother-in-law. The memories came flooding in, drowning those of a strange, faraway world. His wife and children's death. The accident. The letter. The gun to his head. It all came back.

He turned, as he heard footsteps quickly approaching. He didn't recognize the man who grabbed him, as he started to fall back toward the cot.

Dr. Poole held him up, trying to gently lay him back down

on the pillow. Torben leaned over the bed railing to assist Dr. Poole. Jane shuffled the pillows underneath him.

Hayden rapidly blinked a few times, as frightening images of the toddler near the firelight flashed through his mind, the child's eyes blanketed by a black tornado.

He pulled himself back up using Dr. Poole as leverage. His eyes wildly blinked a few times, as he fought to understand the conflicting images of another world.

His eyes frantically locked on Torben's. "I've got to get out of here... Must stop Iscariot... Stop Iscariot," he said, and then passed out in Dr. Poole's arms

www.ingramcontent.com/pod-product-compliance
Lightning Source LLC
Chambersburg PA
CBHW032023290426
44110CB00012B/639